Lecture Notes in Computer Science

Edited by G. Goos, J. Hartmanis and J. van Leeuwe

T0237796

Springer

Berlin
Heidelberg
New York
Barcelona
Hong Kong
London
Milan
Paris
Singapore
Tokyo

Peter Kropf   Gilbert Babin
John Plaice   Herwig Unger (Eds.)

Distributed Communities on the Web

Third International Workshop, DCW 2000
Quebec City, Canada, June 19-21, 2000
Proceedings

Springer

Series Editors

Gerhard Goos, Karlsruhe University, Germany
Juris Hartmanis, Cornell University, NY, USA
Jan van Leeuwen, Utrecht University, The Netherlands

Volume Editors

Peter G. Kropf
University of Montreal
Department of Computer Science and Operations Research
C.P. 6128, succ. Centre-ville, Montreal QC, H3C 3J7 Canada
E-mail: kropf@iro.umontreal.ca

Gilbert Babin
Laval University, Department of Computer Science
3908 Adrien-Pouliot, Sainte-Foy QC, G1K 7P4 Canada
E-mail: babin@babs.ift.ulaval.ca

John Plaice
The University of New South Wales, School of Computer Science and Engineering
Sydney, NSW 2052, Australia
E-mail: plaice@cse.unsw.edu.au

Herwig Unger
University of Rostock, Department of Computer Science
18051 Rostock, Germany
E-mail: hunger@informatik.uni-rostock.de

Cataloging-in-Publication Data applied for

Die Deutsche Bibliothek - CIP-Einheitsaufnahme

Distributed Communities on the Web : third international workshop ;
proceedings / DCW 2000, Quebec City, Canada, June 19 - 21, 2000. Peter
Kropf ... (ed.). - Berlin ; Heidelberg ; New York ; Barcelona ; Hong
Kong ; London ; Milan ; Paris ; Singapore ; Tokyo : Springer, 2000
    (Lecture notes in computer science ; Vol. 1830)
    ISBN 3-540-67647-3

CR Subject Classification (1998): C.2, D.1.3, D.4, H.4, I.2.11, K.4.3, K.4.4, J.1

ISSN 0302-9743
ISBN 3-540-67647-3 Springer-Verlag Berlin Heidelberg New York

Typesetting: Camera-ready by author, data conversion by Steingraeber Satztechnik GmbH, Heidelberg
Printed on acid-free paper   SPIN: 10721195   06/3142   5 4 3 2 1 0

Preface

Communities are groupings of distributed objects that are capable of communicating, directly or indirectly, through the medium of a shared context. To support communities on a wide scale will require developments at all levels of computing, from low-level communication protocols supporting transparent access to mobile objects, through to distributed operating systems, through to high-level programming models allowing complex interaction between objects. This workshop brought together researchers interested in the technical issues of supporting communities.

This workshop was the third in the *DCW* series. The first two, entitled *Distributed Computing on the Web*, took place in 1998 and 1999 at the University of Rostock, with proceedings published by the University of Rostock Press. This year, the workshop also incorporated the *ISLIP* (*International Symposium on Languages for Intensional Programming*) symposium. The *ISLIP* symposia have taken place every year since 1988, and have led to two volumes published by World-Scientific (*Intensional Programming I*, 1995, and *Intensional Programming II*, 2000). While the two conferences emerged from different needs, their focus merged to such an extent that it became clear that a joint conference promised to offer great opportunities.

The 19 papers presented in these proceedings were selected from 30 submissions from around the world. Each submission was fully refereed by at least three members of the program committee or by other external referees. The reviewers of each paper were carefully selected to ensure they showed the required expertise for the papers' topics. If a reviewer felt that a paper was not in her/his field of expertise she/he was encouraged to inform the program chair. In this case another program committee member or additional referee was asked to review the paper. Special care was taken to avoid conflicts of interest by ensuring that if a program committee member was co-author of one of the submissions, then the paper would be reviewed by program committee members or additional reviewers who were not close collaborators of the submitters.

This year, we were pleased to welcome two invited speakers who are at the forefront of academic research and of industrial development. Jacob Slonim of Dalhousie University (Canada) presented his work on the *KALI project* about *Creating an electronic commerce device which promotes universal access*. Peter Beckman from TurboLinux' TurboLabs (USA) exposed the most recent developments of emerging on-line communities on the Internet that thrive on instant response and privacy in his talk *Clusters, servers, thin clients, and on-line communities*.

In addition to the papers, the workshop includes a tutorial presentation about the Web Operating System (WOS^{TM}), a working decentralized operating system where the different nodes are *versioned*. This system has been jointly developed by researchers in Canada, Germany, Australia, and the USA.

Along with the official presentations published in these proceedings, a number of poster presentations and system demonstrations of networked systems were given. Summaries of these presentations and demonstrations can be found at the Web site www.wos-community.org/dcw2000.

We would especially like to thank all the members of the program committee and the additional reviewers for their work in preparing the thorough reviews of the submitted papers. A special thanks also to Rachel Lapierre for the administrative support before and during the workshop.

We would also like to thank all the sponsors for their support and especially Laval University for hosting us. Finally, we would like to thank all authors for submitting their contributions and the authors of accepted papers for their collaboration in preparing these proceedings.

We are convinced that this workshop series is very timely, and answers the needs of a great many researchers who want to focus on building networked communities. We hope that you find the contributions of this workshop interesting and stimulating.

June 2000   Peter Kropf
                                                                          Gilbert Babin
                                                                            John Plaice
                                                                          Herwig Unger

Organization

Program and Organization Committee

Peter Kropf   University of Montreal (Canada)   Program Chair
Gilbert Babin   Laval University (Canada)   Organization Chair

David Abramson   Monash University (Australia)
Ioana Banicescu   Mississippi State University (USA)
Arndt Bode   Technical University Munich (Germany)
Thomas Böhme   Technical University Ilmenau (Germany)
Marc Bui   Paris 8 University (France)
Weichang Du   University of New Brunswick (Canada)
Wolfgang Fengler   Technical University Ilmenau (Germany)
Michael Franz   University of California, Irvine (USA)
Thierry Gauthier   IRISA (France)
Beat Hirsbrunner   University of Fribourg (Switzerland)
David Hutchison   University of Lancaster (United Kingdom)
Rudolf Keller   University of Montreal (Canada)
Oliver Krone   Swisscom (Switzerland)
Pierre Kuonen   Valais Engineering School (Switzerland)
Armin Mikler   University of North Texas (USA)
Wolf-Dieter Oberhoff   IBM Heidelberg (Germany)
Joey Paquet   Concordia University (Canada)
John Plaice   University of New South Wales (Australia)
Bernhard Plattner   ETH Zurich (Switzerland)
Panos Rondogiannis   University of Ioannina (Greece)
Peter Schulthess   University of Ulm (Germany)
William Wadge   University of Victoria (Canada)

Reviewers

Morad Benyoucef   Detlef Fliegl   Martin Schulz
Brahim Chaib-draa   Mehmet Orgun
Alessandro Fabbri   Athanassios S. Poulakidas

Sponsoring Institutions

SGI – GI – CIRANO – rcm_2 – APIIQ – Laval University – WOS-Project Group
DCW 2000 is organized in cooperation with ACM SIGPLAN/SIGSIM/SIGCHI

Table of Contents

Distributed Communities on the Web (DCW 2000)

Tutorial

Keynote Speaker I

Session I: Collaboration in Communities

Session II: Business Communities

Session III: Managing Communities

Session IV: Multidimensional Information Management

Session V: Communications and Communities

Keynote Speaker II

Session VI: Intensionality

Session VII: Mobile Agents for Community Support

The Web Operating System – WOS

John Plaice[1] and Herwig Unger[2]

[1] School of Computer Science and Engineering
University of New South Wales
UNSW SYDNEY NSW 2052, Australia
plaice@cse.unsw.edu.au
[2] Fachbereich Informatik
Universität Rostock
D-18051 Rostock, Germany
hunger@informatik.uni-rostock.de

The rapid development and the heterogeneous nature of the Web ensure that it is impossible to develop a complete catalog of all of the resources and services available on the Web. As a result, no single operating system can be used for Web computation, since it will necessarily be incomplete. Furthermore, it is unclear that such an operating system would even be useful, considering the different levels of granularity of service that need to be provided.

The Web Operating System (WOS[TM]) approach to Web computation envisages a series of versioned servers, possibly offering different services, themselves versioned, that use the same basic protocol for communication amongst themselves, and that are capable of passing on requests for service when appropriate. The WOS allows remote invocation of tasks from anywhere in the Web, without the use of any centralized servers. It is not defined by the actions of any single server but, rather, by the combined actions of the different servers.

To support the WOS, significant conceptual and theoretical work has been undertaken. This work is the natural development of intensional programming, where computations are assumed to take place in a multidimensional context. In particular, focus has been placed recently on the manipulation of multiple contexts that can be shared by the different objects that may be found in the Net.

This tutorial starts with an introduction to intensional programming and its application using the ISE (Intensional Sequential Evaluator) language. It then presents the status of the WOS, as currently implemented.

The tutorial also includes demonstrations of working networked software, and should be accessible to people new to the field, while still offering interesting insights to those who are currently developing networked systems.

P. Kropf et al. (Eds.): DCW 2000, LNCS 1830, p. 1, 2000.
© Springer-Verlag Berlin Heidelberg 2000

Creating an Electronic Commerce Device Which Promotes Universal Access: The KALI Project

Jacob Slonim, Theodore Chiasson, and Carrie Gates

Faculty of Computer Science, Dalhousie University, Halifax, Nova Scotia, Canada
{slonim, theo, gates}@cs.dal.ca

Abstract. As information technology continues to evolve, it is becoming apparent that technological advancement is creating an ever-widening gap in society between those who are able to quickly grasp and adapt to this new knowledge and those who cannot. Much of the research and development occurring in the field of electronic commerce continues to focus on facilitating users who are technologically savvy, as opposed to catering to the needs of those who cannot adapt to change as easily. The aim of the Knowledge-Acquiring Layered Infrastructure (KALI) project is to create a universal access electronic commerce device which can be used by the broadest possible segment of the population, including individuals who are functionally illiterate. This paper provides a high-level description of the research in progress towards this design goal.

1 Introduction

While technological advancement has the potential to be a great equalizer, to date this has not been realized. Instead, technology is creating an ever-widening gap in society, and those less technologically inclined stand to be left behind. Much of the current research and development in electronic commerce assumes that the end user is highly computer-literate. Our research is different, in that it focuses on using technology as an enabler for persons who have a low literacy level. The goal of the Knowledge-Acquiring Layered Infrastructure (KALI) project is to create an infrastructure in support of a universal access electronic commerce device that allows users who are functionally illiterate to participate in the new knowledge-based economy.

The KALI project is still in the initial stages, and so this paper concentrates on defining the problem and identifying areas of the problem that require further research. Section 2 provides background information concerning the target population. Section 3 discusses the ongoing paradigm shift from client-server computing to device-oriented peer-to-peer computing. In Section 4, the need for a human-oriented approach to computing is described. Sections 5 and 6 describe our approach to mediation through user profiling. In Section 7, authentication techniques are discussed. Finally, Section 8 provides some brief conclusions.

P. Kropf et al. (Eds.): DCW 2000, LNCS 1830, pp. 2–12, 2000.

2   Background

2.1   The Growth of the Internet

Internet usage has been growing at an exponential rate. In Canada, for example, the proportion of all households using computer communications from the home increased from 16.0% in 1997 to 22.6% in 1998. During this same time frame, the number of households in Canada that purchased goods and services at home via the Internet increased by 71.4%.[2] This growth of online purchases is predicted to continue.[14] With this growth, more and more goods and services are becoming available online. Furthermore, many government services are already available via the web. Businesses are offering goods and services online, often at reduced pricing as compared to their regular distribution channels.

Concurrent with the explosive growth of the Internet is a similar growth in wireless products, including PDAs (personal digital assistants), Palm Organizers, smart cards and cell phones. Many users now gain access to the Internet via remote, wireless connectivity for services such as news, stock trades, and e-mail. The area of wireless access is forecast to grow exponentially over the next few years and become the next generation of computing.

Given these factors, it is not unreasonable to anticipate most interactions occurring over the Internet via mobile, hand-held devices within the next decade. Demand for online goods and services is increasing, as is demand for easy, remote access to these services. As wireless technologies evolve, more transactions will occur over the web and fewer will occur in traditional venues.

2.2   The Target Audience

As more emphasis is being placed on accessing online services, a gap is growing between those with Internet access and those without. This phenomenon has been described in the media as the "digital divide" and represents the differences between the "information have's and have-not's". It is believed that this gap will continue to widen, where the information have-not's will increasingly become excluded from partaking in society as more and more services migrate to an online format. The National Telecommunications and Information Administration (NTIA) in the United States has released three reports on the growing digital divide[8,9,10]. The Digital Divide Summit[3], hosted by the United States Department of Commerce on 9 December 1999, is another example of government initiatives in this area. Studies have shown that blacks and Hispanics have less access to the Internet than their white counterparts, pointing to a digital divide along racial and ethnic lines. Furthermore, this gap is widening even when economic factors such as income levels are taken into account[9].

In Canada, education is shown to be a factor in Internet access. According to statistics from 1998[14], only 12.6% of individuals with less than high school education had access versus 68.1% of individuals with a university degree. Other relevant factors include income level, geographic location (urban versus rural), and household type (e.g., married couples with children versus single parent households).

While much emphasis has been placed on decreasing the digital divide with respect to race, geography, and income level, very little research has been done on the role that literacy levels play in this problem. Most interactions with the Internet result in the display of textual information. Unless alternative interfacing mechanisms are developed, the Internet will continue to be inaccessible to individuals who are functionally illiterate.

3   Paradigm Shift

Advances in technology during the eighties and nineties enabled a paradigm shift from centralized computing to the client-server model. The driving force behind this shift involved the increased computing capacity of client machines and the increasingly distributed nature of networks as they evolved from local area networks to the global Internet. Centralized systems typically housed large applications written by expert programmers for a specific system and architecture. In contrast, distributed client-server systems partition the world into complex servers and relatively simple clients, with less expertise required to develop client applications than was needed for the large centralized applications.

With the advances of wireless technology, another paradigm shift is likely to occur, this time from the client-server model to a device-oriented peer-to-peer model. In a peer-to-peer model, each participant in an interaction is equal. Each process or component is independent and able to dynamically assume the role of a client or server based on the context of the interactions. Numerous specialized multi-applications can be written by applications programmers or even by the end user. The architecture is dynamically reconfigurable by the end user and applications are portable across languages, systems, and architectures[1]. While the evolution from dumb terminals to personal computers enabled the client-server model to proliferate, the advent of permanently connected home computers, broadband to the home, and wireless technologies will drive the next paradigm shift to device-oriented peer-to-peer computing.

The peer-to-peer model is already emerging on the Internet, especially in the business to business domain.[11] In the business to consumer domain, the consumer is typically viewed as a client, which restricts the models of interaction that are available. In the absence of a peer-to-peer model, content can be delivered to a client on a periodic basis by having the client poll the server for updates. This model has been adopted in products such as PointCast (www.pointcast.com) and Castanet (www.marimba.com). Further, some interesting new business models have arisen which communicate back to the client via e-mail. Examples include services such as Priceline.com, where consumers can name the price they want to pay for a product or service. Since the user is interacting in a client-server architecture, the response from the server must take the form of e-mail. In a peer-to-peer environment, the user's device would act as a server that Priceline.com could contact and interact with directly. Another example is the offering at Mercata.com, where buyers are aggregated to lower the purchase price of goods. In this case, a user can agree to the current price of a product and be guaranteed that the price will either stay the same or go down until the deadline for the sale. This forces the user to commit to the current price in order to participate. In a peer-to-peer environment, the user could potentially request notification when a product of interest dropped below a certain threshold and hold off on the commitment of funds until the desired price was reached.

4   Human-Oriented Computing

Technology is typically developed in consultation with end users, but the solutions which are implemented are often restricted by complexity issues to a subset of the users' needs. This "technology push" approach generates good solutions when the tasks which are pushed onto the end user are easy for the end user to perform but difficult for the system to encompass. As Internet connectivity and technology penetration continue to expand into the general population, this approach is starting to break down, and a more human-centric approach to computing is required. Assuming a certain capability set in the end user greatly simplifies the constraints on a project, but with a global user base this approach fails to address a large number of users who have neither the desire nor in some cases the capability to become technologically inclined.

A shift is required from computer-oriented design to human-oriented design. This can be accomplished in part by personalizing the user interface for each individual user. Thus, each user's profile will have information on the user which customizes the interface to their preferences. In this manner, sophisticated users can create shortcuts through menuing systems, for example, while more novice users can be guided through them. This interface should be able to take on the simplicity of other commonly used devices, such as the telephone or automated teller machines (ATMs).

Current trends in computing indicate a shift away from general purpose desktop computers towards mobile, hand-held devices. Advances in wireless technology may, therefore, encourage a shift to human-oriented computing. These devices are smaller, more mobile, and easier to use than traditional desktop computers. For example, users of specialized devices are not typically required to learn about operating system versions, software installation, or hardware upgrades, in contrast to users of multi-purpose desktop computers.

What is envisaged, therefore, is a wireless hand-held electronic commerce device that is easily accessed by the authorized owner and is designed for use by persons who are functionally illiterate. A framework for mediating transactions and hiding much of the complexity inherent in technological systems is proposed, which should help to ease or eradicate the learning curve associated with end-user adaptation.

5   Mediation Approaches

Examples of business-to-consumer systems which mediate transactions on the user's behalf include PersonaLogic, Firefly, Bargain Finder, Jango, Kasbah, and Tete-a-tete [5]. While these systems facilitate parts of the purchasing and negotiation process on behalf of the end users, the interface mechanisms are all beyond the reach of our target population. Furthermore, the interactions required in dealing with these systems require a relatively high degree of computer-literacy, which implies there is no easy way to simplify the interface mechanisms sufficiently for individuals who are functionally illiterate. Our approach to mediation resembles more closely the approach taken in business-to-business negotiation models[11].

In our approach, a peer-to-peer environment is assumed. This allows inclusion of the end user at any stage of the mediation process. A layered architecture is defined, with the following components:

End user device layer: This layer consists of the end user's hardware device, as well as the software applications, user profile and user interface modes available on the device. Information regarding the device's functionality is registered with directory services to allow connections from the mediation layer.

Mediation layer: The mediation layer offers services to the end user layer, including mediation services, profile storage, and dynamic profile updating services. These service offerings are registered with directory services. The mediation layer uses the services offered by the products and services layer to negotiate transactions on the end user's behalf. Alternatively, the mediation layer can use services from the community layer, which acts as an intermediary.

Community layer: This layer acts as an intermediary between the mediation layer and the products and services layer. This layer acts as a consolidator of similar requests from individual end users where amalgamation of purchasing leads to better negotiation on price, quality, delivery options, or other criteria. The community layer can itself make use mediation services.

Product and service offerings layer: This is the lowest layer of the architecture. This layer represents the offerings available for product and service purchasing. These offerings are registered with directory services. The directory services registration typically includes interface specifications, as well as information concerning the type of transactional model the service can support.

Directory services: The directory services provide a mechanism for entities to register their interface specifications and service offerings. All layers use the directory services.

When a user request is presented, the mediation process will attempt to fulfill the request based on the user's stored profile and the available product and service offerings. Information must be gathered from remote sources during this process. While it is possible to gather this information in a read-only manner, the information is not guaranteed to remain accurate unless a lock is held on it. Information is gathered from many sources, and it is not known in advance which of these sources will be chosen for purchasing during the mediation process. Furthermore, the end user is consulted during the mediation process to confirm the final chosen execution plan. If approached from a database perspective, the mediation process consists of a number of long-lived distributed transactions. In fact, the transactions will be several orders of magnitude longer than in traditional database processing due to the involvement of the end user in the commitment process. Holding the locks in the individual databases over this long a time frame would lead to unacceptable performance. This leads to a problem which is common in distributed processing - existing database transaction processing models do not adequately support distributed application environments.

In contrast to transactional models, workflow systems offer a great degree of flexibility in dealing with heterogeneous distributed environments. Workflow systems, however, lack the robustness of databases in terms of failure handling and concurrency control. In [1], Alonso et al discuss the problems with using a database approach when developing distributed applications, and show how workflows provide a flexible superset of the functionalities offered in transactional models. In our research, we plan to investigate a hybrid approach which is workflow-centric, but extends the workflow model in order to incorporate facilities for dealing efficiently with the underlying database system components of our overall architecture.

6   User Profiling and Mediation

Interaction with the device must be intuitive to the target population. To accommodate persons with literacy problems, it is anticipated that interaction will be accomplished through graphically presented cues for user input, while output from the device could take several forms including graphic display, simulated speech, and others. Negotiation of transactions can be accomplished through intelligent mediation, hiding the complexities of the transaction from the user while still affording the user control over the negotiation decisions. Information stored over time in the user's profile can be used to facilitate mediating decisions. Collection, access, and storage of profile information must be performed in a secure fashion. Further, the process of mediation must itself be protected from compromise.

The intelligence of the infrastructure mainly resides in the mediation of activities between the user and the remote servers from which goods and services are to be purchased. Factors that could come into play vary depending on the domain space in question. For example, in the domain of grocery shopping, a list of preferred foods is requested. A purchasing decision is required that takes into consideration all of the following criteria, and potentially many others:

- Budgetary constraints (both short-term and projected for the long term)
- Dietary constraints (from medical profile consultation)
- Nutritional constraints (based on publicly available sources, i.e., food guide)
- Family style (based on how many family members for which one is shopping and what their constraints are)
- Location constraints (shipping charges/convenience of pickup locations)
- Timing constraints (known long term needs for taking advantage of sale items, as well as seasonal constraints such as certain items not being available at certain times of the year)

Over a period of time, a personal profile is built up that helps to facilitate mediation over this range of constraints. The more information available to the mediation process, the more effective the transaction is for the end user.

The process of mediating transactions can be performed at various locations in the architecture, including on the device itself, on a dedicated server on the Internet, or on a shared Internet server. To ensure that privacy is not compromised, profile information is never shared with the vendor sites without authorization from the end user. Instances may arise where it is in the user's best interest to share their profile with vendors – one example being the purchase of prescription medication from various different pharmacies. While individual pharmacy chains track your prescriptions to ensure there are no known conflicts in the drugs prescribed, the user has to volunteer information if prescriptions are filled at different chains.

A catalog or directory structure is maintained by the device for use in contacting the appropriate mediation services for a given task. The mediation services themselves also make use of directory services for use in collecting information relevant to assigned tasks. During the mediation process, the user profile information is matched with the device request and the available sources of products and services on the Internet. Negotiation occurs on the user's behalf to enact transactions. These negotiations may cover areas such as price, quality, quantity, timing of deliveries, and payment mechanisms.

The device can also be used without the aid of the mediation layer. The end user can choose to bypass the mediation process and negotiate directly with communities or with product and service vendors. User preference information stored by the mediation layer can also be accessed and updated by the end user. This allows the user to override the mediation process at any time.

7 Authentication

Security involves policies and policy implementations that keep a user's data from being accessed by unauthorized individuals, and protect a user's transactions from being altered or imitated. Security mechanisms are used to enforce the privacy policies chosen by the user. Privacy here refers to what data a user will let other entities view, and under what conditions. Regardless of the strength of the security and privacy policies, this device will not be useful if its users do not trust it, or the transactions it performs. Thus, trust needs to be established so that users will feel as comfortable using this device to perform online transactions as they feel when using an automated teller machine at a bank.

Security and privacy policies play a large part in gaining a user's trust. As such, not only should the policies be complete, but they should also be customizable to each individual. Thus, a user should be able customize their security policy in order to accommodate exceptions to the general rules. For example, a user might state that their prescription drug history can be released only to a pharmacy with whom a transaction is being negotiated.

Additionally, the security and authentication mechanisms for this device need to take into consideration that the target population is functionally illiterate. As such, the end user should not be expected to perform complicated interactions. Thus the system must be simple, yet protect the user against exploitation by others.

In order to access the device, the user must authenticate themselves. Authentication can be broken down into four components:

− what you have (e.g. tokens such as smart cards),
− what you know (e.g. passwords),
− what you are (e.g. biometrics such as fingerprints), and
− where you are.

Given the target population, it is not reasonable to expect passwords to be used. Location can be used in some circumstances, but is not always a unique identifier. While the device can itself be used as a token, this is not secure in that it can easily be stolen. This leaves biometric techniques as the preferred method of authentication.

Multiple biometric techniques are available, such as fingerprinting, retinal scans, speaker recognition, iris scans, facial recognition, and signatures, where each of these techniques has its own advantages and disadvantages. Fingerprinting, for example, involves matching a user's fingerprint to one stored in a database for authentication. However, they have been found to produce variable results as they are subject to noisy or useless data. The image quality for the fingerprint plays an important role, with poor quality increasing error rates.[13] Additionally, some fingerprints have ridges which are too fine to be captured well by a photograph, while others are obscured by cuts or scars.[4] The advantage of fingerprints is that they are a non-invasive technique with which most people are comfortable.

Another non-invasive authentication method is facial recognition. The most commonly employed technique for this is eigenfaces, which are a derivation of eigenvectors applied to images of faces. An advantage to this method is that it mimics our own recognition processes, thus people are already accustomed to this procedure. Yet, this method is not very robust and can encounter problems based on spatial orientation and illumination properties.[12]

A final non-invasive technique involves voice pattern recognition. Similar to the previous techniques, this method is not entirely secure. There are two possible approaches to this method: (1) having a user say a predetermined phrase, or

(2) using a text-independent method such as conversational speech. While the second option is more difficult to implement it is clearly the preferred method. However, voice recognition suffers from many variables such as changes with age, health or even mood.[13]

The more invasive techniques include retinal scans and iris recognition. Both of these methods require that an image be taken of a user's eye. The patterns in the iris or retina are then matched against a database to authenticate the user. While these methods are potentially the most invasive, they are also the most secure.[7] It is anticipated that as biometric measurement techniques are perfected, and as we learn more about the biometrics themselves, that ultimately a user's DNA will be used for authentication.

Given the variability inherent in the non-invasive biometric techniques, methods need to be employed which decrease the number of false-rejects and false-alarms. One such method which has proven successful is that of combining biometrics.[4] This idea can be further expanded into creating a layered infrastructure for biometric identification. That is, different types of transactions can be associated with different levels of security. For example, a user may choose a fingerprint to be the minimum security required, and decide that all transactions of less than fifty dollars require only this minimal level. For a transaction requiring a larger sum of money, a combination of techniques, such as fingerprint and voice recognition, may be required. Additionally, a user's private information, such as income tax or medical data, can be protected in a similar fashion. Each individual user should be able to define their own security levels as well as the biometrics required to access their private information. In addition, the user should be able to specify another security mechanism, or some combination of security mechanisms, to increase their security requirements. For example, biometrics could be combined with a token such as a smart card or even the device itself to create an increased level of security.

One problem inherent in the use of biometrics stems from always having the "keys to the safe". Methods must therefore be developed to determine if a user is performing a transaction while under duress. One method for making such a determination is based on changes in the biometric due to increased stress levels. Examples of this include changes in voice tone, increases in heart rate, and galvanic skin responses caused by stressful situations. The device can monitor for symptoms such as these and either not complete the requested transactions, or flag them as suspicious. Another method for determining if the user is being coerced into making a transaction can be programmed into the device. A user can specify that the fingerprint to be used for all transactions matches that of their middle finger, and that if they use their index finger the transaction should be flagged as being fraudulent and should not be completed.

A further method for tracking fraudulent transactions involves the use of data mining techniques, where usage profiles are developed for each user. If a requested transaction is unusual for that user, it is flagged as being suspicious. Companies such as Visa already employ similar techniques such as neural networks to flag if transactions are suspicious in nature, alerting the owner of a credit card if such a transaction is detected.

Finally, security can further be increased by adding location to the transaction requirements. For example, security levels can be defined such that transactions over a certain amount require that the user be present at their bank branch. Another possible restriction is that access to a user's medical data can only be achieved when in the presence of a registered physician. Obviously, for these techniques to be applicable, a large deployment of the proposed devices must be realized.

8   Conclusions

Traditionally, computer programs have been designed with the assumption that the user will be technologically capable of dealing with complexities which the program was unable to conceal. As more businesses and consumers move to online transactions, the assumptions regarding user capabilities is challenged. Software needs to be developed which does not make assumptions regarding the user's abilities.

The KALI project defines a layered infrastructure for an electronic commerce device geared towards those who are functionally illiterate. Development of this device introduces new challenges in the areas of mediation, user profiling, user interface design, transaction modeling and security. The goal of the KALI project is to provide a device which allows universal access to electronic commerce.

Acknowledgements

This research is supported in part by grants from the IBM Canada Center for Advanced Studies, the Izaak Walton Killiam Fund for Advanced Studies at Dalhousie University, and the National Sciences and Engineering Research Council of Canada.

References

1. Alonso, G., Agrawal, D., El Abbadi, A., Kamath, M., Gunthor, R., Mohan, C.: Advanced transaction models in workflow contexts. Proceedings of the Twelfth International Conference on Data Engineering, (1996), 574–581.
2. Dickenson, P., Ellison, J.: Getting connected or staying unplugged: The growing use of computer communications services. Services Indicators, 1st Quarter (1999)
3. Digital Divide Summit. http://www.ntia.doc.gov/ntiahome/digitaldivide/summit/. (1999).
4. Frischholz, R.W., Dieckmann, U.: BioID: A Multimodal Biometric Identification System. IEEE Computer, Vol. 33, No. 2. (2000) 64–68
5. Guttman, R., Moukas, A., and Maes, P.: Agents as Mediators in Electronic Commerce. Intelligent Information Agents. Springer-Verlag, Berlin Heidelberg, 1999
6. Katz, J., Aspden, P.: Motives, Hurdles, and Dropouts. Communications of the ACM, Vol. 40, No. 4. (1997) 97–102

7. Negin, M., Chmielewski, T.A., Salganicoff, M., Camus, T.A., von Seelen, U.M.C., Venetianer, P.L., Zhang, G.G.: An Iris Biometric System for Public and Personal Use. IEEE Computer, Vol. 33, No. 2. (2000) 56–63

8. National Telecommunications and Information Administration: Falling through the Net I: A Survey of the 'Have Nots' in Rural and Urban America. http://www.ntia.doc.gov/ntiahome/fallingthru.html. (1995).

9. National Telecommunications and Information Administration: Falling through the Net II: New Data on the Digital Divide. http://www.ntia.doc.gov/ntiahome/net2/falling.html. (1998).

10. National Telecommunications and Information Administration: Falling through the Net: Defining the Digital Divide. http://www.ntia.doc.gov/ntiahome/digitaldivide. (1999).

11. Papazoglou, M.P., Jeusfeld, M.A., Weigand, H., Jarke, M.: Distributed, Interoperable, Workflow Support for Electronic Commerce. Lecture Notes in Computer Science, Vol. 1402. Springer-Verlag, Berlin Heidelberg New York (1999) 192–204

12. Pentland, A., Choudhury, T.: Face Recognition for Smart Environments. IEEE Computer, Vol. 33, No. 2. (2000) 50–55

13. Phillips, P.J., Martin, A., Wilson, C.L., Przybocki, M.: An Introduction to Evaluating Biometric Systems. IEEE Computer, Vol. 33, No. 2. (2000) 56–63

14. Spectrum Information Technologies and Telecommunications Sector, Industry Canada: Information and Communication Technologies: Economic and Statistical Information. http://strategis.ic.gc.ca/sc

_indps/sectors/engdoc/itt_hpg.html.
(1999).

AntWorld: A Collaborative Web Search Tool

Vladimir Meñkov, David J. Neu, and Qin Shi

SCILS, Rutgers University
4 Huntington St, New Brunswick, NJ 08903
vmenkov@cs.indiana.edu, djneu@acm.org
http://aplab.rutgers.edu/ant/

Abstract. We describe our experiences designing and using AntWorld, a tool developed to make it easier for the members of a common-interest user group to collaborate in searching the web. It is hoped that this report may be of interest to designers of similar systems, as well as to potential users.

1 Introduction

The amount of information currently available on the World Wide Web or in specialized full-text databases (e.g., patents, legal documents) often makes it difficult to find useful documents using only purely automatic techniques, such as the keyword search. Finding information on a particular specialized topic— e.g., "How does the Canadian tax law treat a Roth IRA?" or "How to use unsigned JavaScript in a layer within a signed HTML document?" may require the human user to apply his or her intelligence in various ways: trying several different queries with various search engines, reading a number of documents found by a search engine to determine if they are relevant, following sequences of links, learning new terms to refine one's queries, etc. Thus, if a number of people with common interests and needs often perform web searches on related topics, much effort could be saved with a system that makes use of the intelligence of all its previous users to guide the current user to documents that are likely to be useful for his goals.

AntWorld [1,7], developed at Rutgers University and publicly available at our web site http://aplab.rutgers.edu/ant/, is the result of our attempt to design a tool which harnesses the expertise of the members of a common-interest group, as displayed by their evaluation of documents encountered while searching. It stores users' judgments about the documents they find, and uses this information to guide other users to pages they may find useful.

Our design criteria included the following:

1. **Fine context granularity:** We need to capture not simply a "user's opinion" about pages, but his opinion about usefulness of a page *for a particular goal* he has in mind. The system should allow the user to specify his goal (*quest*) as precisely as he desires.

P. Kropf et al. (Eds.): DCW 2000, LNCS 1830, pp. 13–22, 2000.
© Springer-Verlag Berlin Heidelberg 2000

2. **Dynamic quest matching:** The system should continuously provide guidance for each user based on his current quest, as well as all quests (of this and other users) which are similar to the current quest. This selection of similar quests should be refined as the user keeps browsing and the increasing number of judged pages allows the system to "learn" more about his goals.
3. **Transparency:** A user's browsing experience with AntWorld should be maximally similar to that in a normal browsing session with his favorite browser. Ideally, we want the user to be able to use all the browser features he is accustomed to and to see all viewed documents in the same way he normally would.
4. **Easy entry:** The system should allow a new user to start using AntWorld without installing special software, reconfiguring their computer, or going through complex sign-up procedures.

In accordance with Criterion 1, the main concept behind AntWorld is that of an *information quest*: a persistent information-searching process [6], identified by a numerical ID. Each quest is owned by a user, and a user can switch between his quests at will. When the user starts a quest, he provides AntWorld with an explicit description of his goals. This description can be as short as a typical search engine query (just a few words), or it can contain several sentences. As the user keeps browsing the web, he is encouraged to tell AntWorld how well the documents he finds answer his question.

Since the user has to explicitly judge a page in order for his opinion to be recorded, our technique cannot collect as much data as systems that infer the user's opinion based on indirect parameters, such as the time spent viewing a document (e.g. [4]). Motivating users to make judgments, and not merely to use judgments made by other people, may be an important issue [8]. On the other hand, we hope that the data collected via explicit judgments are more reliable.

2   AntWorld Architecture

AntWorld uses a client-server architecture (Fig. 1). On the client side, as described in Sec. 3, each participating user's web browser collects the user's judgments and provides a variety of user aids: ranked lists of suggested web pages, marked links to suggested pages from the the page the user is currently viewing, etc. Each client talks to the Organizational AntWorld Server (OAWS), which is shared by the members of the user community ("organization") the user belongs to. The OAWS stores in its database profiles of all AntWorld quests ever run by the members of the community. Every time a new page judgment arrives from a client, the OAWS updates the quest profile, performs quest matching and link scoring (Sec. 5), and finally sends the updated suggestion list back to the client. The OAWS is implemented using Java servlets and a Sybase SQL server database; relevant technical details and installation instructions can be found at the project web site [1].

Although as of Spring 2000 there is just one Organizational AntWorld Server in active use, we expect that an organization or user group whose members desire

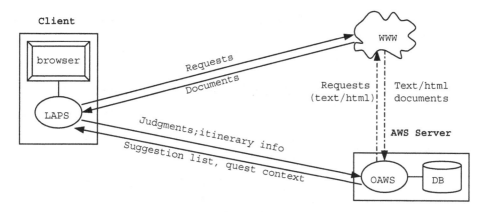

Fig. 1. Data flow in AntWorld. LAPS is an optional module (Sec. 4) inserting "ant marks" into the document and sending the itinerary to the OAWS. Solid arrows represent real-time communication; dashed arrows represent retrieval of judged pages for indexing purposes, done in a low-priority background thread.

to share their web searches will usually want to set up an OAWS of its own, to run on a computer within the organization's computer network (and within the organization's firewall, when applicable).

In a world with multiple organizations using AntWorld, we envisage three-level architecture for the entire system. The administrators of the participating Organizational AntWorld Servers may choose to periodically exchange their quest profile data via one specially designated OAWS: the AntWorld Central, using tools included into the AntWorld server distribution. For privacy reasons, exported quest data will normally be anonymized, so that they won't be identifiable with a particular person or e-mail address.

3   User Interface

To satisfy Criterion 3, AntWorld's user interface is designed as a "browser assistant". The user can navigate as usual in one browser window (the *document window*, seen in the lower part of the screen shot in Fig. 2), while another, smaller, window (the *console window*, in the upper part of Fig. 2) opens when the user starts (or resumes) a quest, and stays on the screen as the user works, providing two-way communication with the Organizational AntWorld Server. On the one hand, the console allows the user to access the suggestion list, generated by the OAWS based on the information AntWorld has about the user's current quest and all other quests. On the other hand, it lets the user judge (and, optionally, annotate) the page he is viewing in the document window. The user can also use the console to submit the quest description to a search engine as a query, switch to a different quest, start a new quest, view the quest summary (the complete list of judgments and annotations made during the quest), view the list of similar quests known to AntWorld, edit the description of the current quest, or tune the method AntWorld uses for finding similar quests. The front-end console functionality has been implemented using HTML and JavaScript, while most of the actual computation is done on the server side.

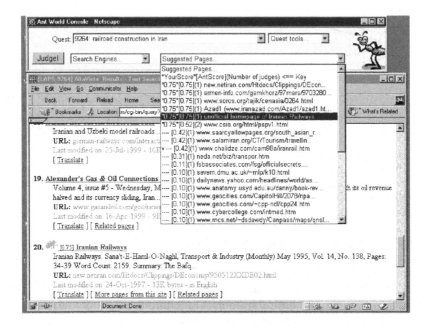

Fig. 2. AntWorld session screen shot. The console window is above, the document window below. The ant icon next to Alta Vista result No. 20 indicates that the page is on the AntWorld suggestion list for this quest.

Similar "browser assistant" programs have been developed for other purposes elsewhere, for example by Chakrabarti et al [3], where the console is implemented as an applet rather than a JavaScript program.

Security. For security reasons, web browsers normally don't allow JavaScript to perform the kind of operations that our architecture requires. Specifically, the code in the console window normally would not be allowed either to monitor or to control the content of the document window, since the documents in the two windows come from different hosts. Special techniques to override these restriction are, unfortunately, browser-specific. Our implementation utilizes the Netscape security model [5, Chapter21], which involves digitally signing our JavaScript code, and requesting the necessary access privileges from the user.

Implementation options: JavaScript vs. servlets vs. applets. In earlier versions of the system we experimented with implementing the console as JavaScript-less HTML code generated by a servlet, or as an applet. The main advantage of the first approach is its greater portability: the user does not need a browser that supports JavaScript, and is not troubled by the incompatibilities between different browsers' JavaScript interpreters. The main disadvantage of this approach is that in order for the console window to "know" what URL the document window contains, the AntWorld server would need to take complete control of everything the user sees. In order to capture all user's requests, the server in that implementation filtered each document and replaced each link <A HREF="α"> with a link back to the AntWorld server: <A HREF="AntWorldServerURL?url=α">. Besides the cost and delays involved, this approach was not particularly robust, breaking on documents that contained HTML syntax errors or that dynamically generated URLs using JavaScript.

Implementing the client as a Java applet would have offered us the advantage of a more powerful, compilable language. However, we did not pursue the applet approach beyond our 1998 version, primarily because at the time no mechanism for putting a standard Java Virtual Machine in a user's browser was available.

4   "Ant Marking" of Links

Web browser designers have long recognized that it is useful to mark (usually, by a changed color) links pointing to documents that the user have already accessed. AntWorld goes one step further, and allows an option for *"ant marking"*: marking all links to "relevant" documents (i.e., those that appear on the current quest's suggestion list), by inserting a small ant-shaped icon next to them. One such icon is seen in Fig. 2, near Alta Vista search result No. 20. In our experience this feature helps a user not only to collaborate with other people but also to "collaborate with oneself", because it lets him quickly identify those of the previously useful links that he actually found useful for this quest or a related one.

To mark links, the system must parse all HTML files requested by the user, and modify them when needed. Doing this at the OAWS is not scalable, and intervening network delays can negatively impact system usability.

Our solution is to supply each user who wants the ant marking functionality with a small client-side application ("Antscape"), whose main component is the Local Ant Proxy Server (LAPS). Antscape works like a wrapper around Netscape. It can be used to modify the Netscape preference file, for the duration of the session, so that the browser will forward all HTTP and FTP request to the LAPS, as shown in Fig. 1. The LAPS analyzes the content type of each document received, and if it is an HTML document, parses it for links.

Since all pages requested by the browser pass through LAPS, using LAPS also allows us log on the organizational server each page the user views, and not only those he explicitly judges. Although these "user itinerary" data are not as important for AntWorld as page judgments, they are used in some quest matching methods (See "Using LAD" in Sec. 5) and in usability studies.

LAPS needs to have a significant amount of knowledge about the general AntWorld setup (where the OAWS is) and the current quest (the quest ID to log the pages under; the suggested URL list). It receives this information from the OAWS. Fixed-length data are transmitted via additional headers that the OAWS includes in HTTP responses it sends to the browser when the user starts a quest, switches to another quest, or judges a page. Putting the suggestion list into HTTP headers would be impractical because of its size; instead, when the OAWS sends the suggestion list to the browser (as a JavaScript array in an HTML document), it simply indicates that fact in an HTTP header, and the LAPS parses the document body to extract the suggestion list.

Although Antscape is written in Java, which is a highly portable language, it needs to have some idea of how Netscape is installed on particular platform in order to be able to interact with it. The currently available version of Antscape works with UNIX and Microsoft operating systems. It needs no special configuring on systems where Netscape is installed in the most standard fashion, but on other machines some amount of configuring is required, depending on how the local Netscape browser has been installed and configured. In certain cases (e.g., where a local site administrator uses Netscape Mission Control to "prohibit" browsers from ever using a proxy server), LAPS cannot be used at all.

In accordance with Criterion 4, using the Antscape client is optional: we want most web users to be able to "test-drive" AntWorld without installing additional software on their desktop.

5   Quest Matching

If AntWorld is to be a useful tool for *collaboration* among members of a common-interest group, it needs an effective mechanism for making the user aware of the quests most similar to his current quest and guiding him to the pages that the owners of those quests found useful. To accomplish these goals, AntWorld uses a framework that consists of two stages: *quest matching* (QM) and *link scoring.*

Quest matching means finding quests in the AntWorld database which are "similar" to a given quest, and ranking them according to this similarity. This operation requires some quest similarity measure, $\mathrm{Sim}(Q_1, Q_2)$, which reflects how relevant quest Q_2 may be for a person whose goals and judgment history are encapsulated in quest Q_1. Most quest matching methods employed in AntWorld are *dynamic*: they update the list of similar quests list each time the owner of Q_1 makes a judgment, thereby providing AntWorld with additional information about his goals and preferences in this quest.

Although an AntWorld user has direct access to the lists of similar quests, it is also important to provide him with a list of suggested URLs ("links"). This ranked list is available to the user both directly in his AntWorld console and, if the Antscape client is being used, as ant marks (Sec. 4). The suggestion list consists of URLs that were judged as useful in some of the quests that AntWorld believes relevant to the user's current quest. We refer to the process of compiling this ranked list as *link scoring*. A link scoring method similar to the one currently used by AntWorld has been presented in our earlier report [6].

Vector space framework. AntWorld implements a variety of quest matching methods. The quest similarity measures $\text{Sim}(Q_1, Q_2)$ used in most currently supported methods can be described in the traditional vector space model framework with a cosine similarity measure (see e.g. [10, Chapter 4.4]). Since the vector space models have been developed as a framework for ranking documents (texts stored in the database, which may be quite long) with respect to their relevance to queries (short sequences of terms typed by the user), such models usually distinguish between queries and documents.

For the purposes of a vector model, any query q or documents d can be represented as a vector of term frequencies $\boldsymbol{f}(q)$ or $\boldsymbol{f}(d) = \{f(d, t_1), f(d, t_2), \ldots, f(d, t_n)\}$, where n is the number of distinct terms in the document collection, and f_i is the term frequency, i.e. the number of occurrences, of term t_i in the document or query in question. These vectors are usually very sparse, since every single document contains only a fraction of all n terms from the collection. In a document-ranking method using a vector model with a cosine similarity measure, the relevance of document d for query q is computed as

$$\text{Sim}(q, d) = \frac{\boldsymbol{u}(q) \cdot \boldsymbol{v}(d)}{||\boldsymbol{u}(q)|| \, ||\boldsymbol{v}(d)||}, \tag{1}$$

where $\boldsymbol{a} \cdot \boldsymbol{b} = \sum_t a(t)b(t)g(t)$ signifies a $g(t)$-*weighted dot product* of two vectors $\boldsymbol{a}$ and $\boldsymbol{b}$, and the norm is based on the dot product: $||\boldsymbol{a}|| = \sqrt{\boldsymbol{a} \cdot \boldsymbol{a}}$. The design of the actual document-ranking method defines how vectors $\boldsymbol{u}(q)$ and $\boldsymbol{v}(d)$ are computed from the raw frequency vectors $\boldsymbol{f}(q)$ and $\boldsymbol{f}(d)$, and what term weighting function $g(t)$ is used. Usually, vectors $\boldsymbol{u}$ and $\boldsymbol{v}$ are designed to take the document size into account (e.g., by dividing the term frequency in a document by the document length), while function g ensures that less common (and, thus, more significant) terms appear in the dot product with a greater weight than the more common ones.

AntWorld quest matching does not distinguish between "queries" and "documents", since it measures the similarity between entities of the same nature: the current quest Q_1 and some other quest Q_2. Thus a symmetric similarity measure $\text{Sim}(Q_1, Q_2) = \text{Sim}(Q_2, Q_1)$ seems more intuitive. Such a symmetric measure can be obtained if the vectors $\boldsymbol{u}$ and $\boldsymbol{v}$ in (1) are computed by the same formula, resulting in

$$\text{Sim}(Q_1, Q_2) = \frac{\boldsymbol{u}(Q_1) \cdot \boldsymbol{u}(Q_2)}{||\boldsymbol{u}(Q_1)|| \, ||\boldsymbol{u}(Q_2)||}. \tag{2}$$

A rather natural property of such a symmetric dot product is that the quest most similar to any quest Q_1 is Q_1 itself:

$$\text{Sim}(Q_1, Q_1) = 1 \geq \text{Sim}(Q_1, Q_2) \tag{3}$$

Quest profiles and vectors. Each AntWorld quest is represented by a *quest profile*: a set of pairs (λ, d), where d is a document (either a user-supplied explicit description of quest goals, or a Web document already judged in this quest), and the weight $\lambda = \lambda(d, Q)$ represents the importance of the document d in the quest Q [6]. AntWorld's quest matching methods use various algorithms to generate the vector $\boldsymbol{u}$ (or vectors $\boldsymbol{u}$ and $\boldsymbol{v}$) for this quest from the quest profile data.

An important vector for several AntWorld's quest matching methods is $\boldsymbol{\Psi}(Q)$. This vector has a non-zero component for every term t that appears in any of the documents in the profile of Q (the set of terms we will refer to as $\mathcal{Q}$). The value of the component $\Psi(t, Q)$ component is based on the frequencies of t in the underlying documents and the importance of those documents for the quest. All quest matching methods use the same term weighting function $g(t)$. Both Ψ and g are fully described in our earlier report [6], where we presented a quest matching methods extending the document matching method proposed by Singhal [9].

Some of AntWorld's quest matching methods, identified by their internal names, will be briefly described below.

Using full quest profile vectors. The quest matching method `Relevance02` computes $\mathrm{Sim}(Q_1, Q_2)$ as a symmetric dot product (2), where the vector $\boldsymbol{u}(Q)$ is the entire $\boldsymbol{\Psi}(Q)$. Thus the summation in the dot product is performed over $\mathcal{Q}_1 \cap \mathcal{Q}_2$.

The only difference between this method and the one in [6] is the denominator, which was absent in the earlier report. As one might expect, introducing this normalization did improve the quality of quest matching.

This quest matching method is *dynamic*: $\boldsymbol{\Psi}(Q_1)$ and the list of quests similar to Q_1 are updated every time the owner of Q_1 makes a judgment.

Using LAD. Some of AntWorld's more interesting quest matching method are loosely based on Logical Analysis of Data (LAD) [2]. LAD computes, for two given sets of documents (the positive and negative training sets), the *cut set* $\mathcal{S}$: a short set of terms that best discriminate between the documents from the two sets. In the AntWorld context, the positive training set for a quest Q consists of the quest's explicit description and the documents that have been judged useful, while the negative set includes those that have been judged useless, or visited but not judged at all. Our current use of LAD is rather simple: we use the quest's cut set $\mathcal{S}(Q)$, which is typically much smaller than the quest profile term set $\mathcal{Q}$ (10–30 terms vs. 10^2–10^3), to reduce the cost of computing dot products (1) or (2).

For example, the method `Relevance13` uses a symmetric dot product quest similarity measure (2) with $\boldsymbol{u}(Q_i) = \boldsymbol{\Psi}_{\mathrm{cut}}(Q_i)$: the vector $\boldsymbol{\Psi}(Q_i)$ restricted to the terms that are in the cut set $\mathcal{S}(Q_i)$. While this greatly reduces the scope of the summation (2)—from $\mathcal{Q}_1 \cap \mathcal{Q}_2$ to $\mathcal{S}(Q_1) \cap \mathcal{S}(Q_2)$, it also reduces the quest matching recall, i.e. it results in some relevant quests not being selected. Another disadvantage of this approach is that making this quest matching method dynamic would require recomputing $\mathcal{S}(Q_1)$ after every judgment—a rather expensive proposition.

A compromise approach, implemented as the method `Relevance07`, restricts only $\boldsymbol{\Psi}(Q_2)$ to the cut set $\mathcal{S}(Q_2)$, resulting in

$$\mathrm{Sim}(Q_1, Q_2) = \frac{\boldsymbol{\Psi}(Q_1) \cdot \boldsymbol{\Psi}_{\mathrm{cut}}(Q_2)}{||\boldsymbol{\Psi}(Q_1)|| \, ||\boldsymbol{\Psi}_{\mathrm{cut}}(Q_2)||}.$$

Thus, the summation is done over $\mathcal{Q}_1 \cap \mathcal{S}(Q_2)$. This solution facilitates computation as compared to the full-vector `Relevance02`, without unduly compromising the quality of similar quest selection. The quest matching is dynamic with respect to the current quest, because the cut set of Q_1 does not need to be updated after every judgment. Admittedly, the activity of other users (owners of other quests, such as Q_2) will not be reflected in the similar quest list produced by this list until the cut sets in question are recomputed. This is currently done only once every 24 hours.

Although the similarity measure used in this method is not truly symmetric, we make it obey (3) by the expedient of always computing $\text{Sim}(Q_1, Q_1)$ using full $\boldsymbol{\Psi}(Q_1)$ instead of $\boldsymbol{\Psi}_{\text{cut}}(Q_1)$.

Currently we are also experimenting with quest matching methods which use the LAD-produced cut sets in more complex ways, e.g. by taking into account the ranks of terms in the cut sets.

6   Usage Prospects

As already mentioned in Sec. 1, the main goal of AntWorld is to provide a finding-sharing tool for members of common-interest user communities. We hope it to be particularly useful for group of several people whose search tasks are both complex and overlapping, and who have a real need to find answers to their questions. We are interested in collaboration with academic or industrial groups who feel that the system may be of interest to them. So far, the main users of the system have been the AntWorld project staff and the students using AntWorld as paid testers or as an assignment for a class [8]. These two categories of users accounted for 4,200 judgments and 1,500 judgments, respectively, out of the 6,000 judgment recorded in AntWorld database from June 1998 to February 2000.

While current AntWorld users do benefit from discovering one another's quests, we have also observed the system's suitability for a number of other uses:

- **Bookmark and/or search management.** Although modern versions of web browsers allow more sophisticated bookmarking systems than simple flat bookmark lists, AntWorld's quest-based approach makes it more convenient for managing a large number of topical searching and/or browsing sessions, to each of which the user can return at any time, from any Netscape-equipped computer. A tool like this serves as a powerful aid for one's memory: on more than one occasions some of us were pleasantly surprised, after starting a new quest, to see AntWorld remind them of similar searches they performed many months previous.
- **Directory creation.** By judging and annotating pages and then viewing, saving, or linking to the AntWorld quest summary, one can easily generate updatable lists of links on a desired topic.
- **Query refinement or generation.** Using the cut sets generated by LAD (Sec. 5) to produce well-discriminating queries—sometimes, much better

queries than what the user originally came up with—is an intriguing possibility. If we are able to implement this feature, AntWorld will be able to offer you not only pages that other AntWorld users have already seen (in quests similar to yours), but also most relevant pages from anywhere on the Web (or, rather, the part of the Web that is indexed by the underlying search engine).

Acknowledgments

This work is supported by the Defense Advanced Research Projects Agency (DARPA) Contract Number N66001-97-C-8537.

Most of the ideas behind AntWorld were developed by the project's Principal Investigators: Paul B. Kantor, Endre Boros, and Benjamin Melamed. Bracha Shapira and Insuk Oh conducted user studies.

References

1. The AntWorld web site, http://aplab.rutgers.edu/ant/, 1998-2000.
2. Endre Boros, Paul B. Kantor, and David J. Neu. Pheromonic representation of user quests by digital structures. In *Proceedings of the ASIS Annual Meeting*, volume 36, 1999. Available at http://aplab.rutgers.edu/ant/papers/.
3. Soumen Chakrabarti, David A. Gibson, and Kevin S. McCurley. Surfing the web backwards. In *The Eighth International World Wide Web Conference*, May 1999. Available at http://www8.org/w8-papers/5b-hypertext-media-/surfing/surfing.html.
4. The Direct Hit web site, http://www.directhit.com, 1999.
5. David Flanagan. *JavaScript: the Definitive Guide*. O'Reilly, Sebastopol, CA, 3rd edition, 1998.
6. Paul B. Kantor, Endre Boros, Benjamin Melamed, and Vladimir Meñkov. The information quest: A dynamic model of user's information needs. In *Proceedings of the ASIS Annual Meeting*, volume 36, 1999. Available at http://aplab.rutgers.edu/ant/papers/.
7. Paul B. Kantor, Benjamin Melamed, Endre Boros, Vladimir Meñkov, Dave J. Neu, Myung-Ho Kim, and Qin Shi. Ant World. In *SIGIR'99: 22nd Annual International ACM SIGIR Conference*, 1999. Available at http://aplab.rutgers.edu-/ant/papers/.
8. Bracha Shapira, Paul B. Kantor, and Benjamin Melamed. Preliminary study of the effect of motivation on user behavior in a collaborative information finding system. In *SIGIR'2000: 23nd Annual International ACM SIGIR Conference*, 2000. (Submitted for publication).
9. Amit Singhal. AT&T at TREC-6. In *NIST Special Publication 500-240: The Sixth Text REtrieval Conference (TREC 6)*, pages 215–226. NIST, 1997. Available at http://trec.nist.gov/pubs/trec6/papers/att.ps.
10. Ian H. Witten, Alistair Moffat, and Timothy C. Bell. *Managing Gigabytes: Compressing and Indexing Documents and Images*. Morgan Kaufmann Publishers, Inc., San Francisco, CA, 2nd edition, 1999.

A Multimedia Session Manager Service for the Collaborative Browsing System

Sandro Rafaeli and David Hutchison

Computing Department
Lancaster University
{rafaeli,dh}@comp.lancs.ac.uk

Abstract. Browsing the Web is usually a lonely task. People visit sites, collect information and are not aware of other people looking at the same material, people with whom they could exchange experiences and ideas about the subject they are looking at. A Collaborative Browsing System (CoBrow) has been developed to bring awareness to the World Wide Web. CoBrow users can see other people looking at the same Web pages they are browsing. The Multimedia Session Manager (MSM) is one of the components that currently form CoBrow. It is responsible for initiating and managing multimedia sessions required by CoBrow users. This paper aims to describe the work performed by MSM in managing those users and their sessions.

1 Introduction

The World Wide Web (WWW) is growing quickly and attracting more and more people everyday. Although many users browsing the WWW may share common interests, the WWW lacks a mechanism for detecting this or establishing communication between these users.

CoBrow[15] is a project with a goal of enabling these users browsing the same web page at the same time to be aware of each other. In addition to such awareness another goal of CoBrow is to provide synchronous communication via Internet based communication facilities like the MBone tools [11] to enable collaborative working.

Figure 1 shows the CoBrow architecture. The server side is composed of a vicinity server (developed at the University of Ulm) and/or a CoMas server (developed at ETH in Zurich) and a MSM server. The vicinity server is basically responsible for matching users' information, creating virtual neighbourhood lists that are presented to the users on the CoBrow user interface. The CoMas server manages conferences in a high level, enabling users to create and control them. Both servers, working together or separately, depending of the configuration, make use of the MSM features. The CoBrow user interface also depends on the configuration being used on the server since the use of CoMas offers more functionalities for the user than one where only the vicinity server is present.

The Multimedia Session Manager (MSM) is the component responsible for managing the multimedia sessions used by those tools within CoBrow. Unlike

P. Kropf et al. (Eds.): DCW 2000, LNCS 1830, pp. 23–33, 2000.

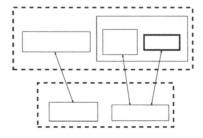

Fig. 1. CoBrow Architecture

the Session Directory tool [5], which only adverts the multicast sessions going on and enables users to create their own sessions, MSM creates multicast sessions on demand. Whenever two or more people want to communicate, they can pick the tool that is commonly available for those interested, and MSM will provide the means for the tool to be launched on each participating machine.

This paper is organised as follows: section 2 gives an overview of the MSM; section 3 presents the MSM internal framework; section 4 illustrates the use of the CoBrow user interface; section 5 describes how the external tools are launched from the user interface; section 6 discusses other applications which have similarities with MSM; finally, the future work planned for MSM is described in section 7, and the paper is concluded in section 8.

2   Multimedia Session Manager

MSM is a CoBrow component that gives the users of the system the ability to communicate with each other. MSM provides the necessary support within the CoBrow environment for users to join sessions and automatically open the appropriate external tool set. The MSM software has been designed to allow different communication tools to be easily integrated within the CoBrow system.

As different people use different operating systems and software, support for different conferencing tools is required. MSM is specifically designed to be extensible by allowing additional tools and services to be defined. Modules known as drivers are implemented as self-contained code blocks, using standard library routines and following a defined structure, for each new session type.

Implemented in Java, MSM provides an ideal topology for installing a driver on the fly without the need to alter any existing code or drivers. Java's ability to load custom classes is exploited for services offered by the server and by drivers handling the various session types. In order to support a new conferencing tool within CoBrow, the only alteration required is to include a new driver on MSM that copes with the tool's requisites. Placing the driver within the defined driver directory, and configuring the server to include the class, immediately allows the server to handle the new session type.

Freely available conferencing tools are currently used in conjunction with the standard Web browsers to provide an integrated platform for collaborative browsing and conferencing. Conferencing is performed by means of a selection of utilities that use the MBone as the transport medium. Conferencing over MBone allows us to deploy Internet Multicast capabilities and hence to support variable sized and dynamic groups. At present, tools currently supported by the CoBrow server are: rat [8] and vat [9] for audio; vic [12] for video; and wb (whiteboard) [10] and nte [6] (network text editor) for other forms of collaborative discussion or work. These allow video, audio and other shared facilities. Nevertheless, MSM is not restricted to those tools since to add other tools the only alteration needed on MSM is to include a new driver to cope with the new tool requisites.

3   MSM Basic Framework

The MSM central core consists primarily of a listener for connections which spawns handlers, which in their turn communicate with known services (components). This approach enables the handling of system defined components, by means of dynamically configuring the system to install those new components when required.[1] The components are known (internally) as services and/or drivers (see figure 2), and these components are specified in the configuration file, although an option to specify the association while the server is in execution, via a system console, is also available.

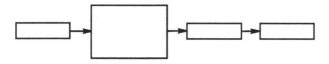

Fig. 2. MSM Topology

The *services* are those components which perform some sort of work for users or other components. They can be accessed by requests sent by users or other components. Two examples of this kind of component are the *streams service*, which is responsible for creating and managing the sessions, interfacing with the drivers (see below), and the *multicast service*, which is used by the *streams service* to allocate and advert multicast addresses. The general structure for *services* and the currently available set are described in the following subsections.

The so called *drivers* are those components that handle requests for specific multimedia sessions. The *drivers* components can not be accessed directly by

---

[1] The Java programming language, being modular and object oriented itself, proves fruitful in the way that service classes can be installed on-the-fly without need to restart the server, and without modifying any code (no recompilation required).

users, because they are encapsulated in the *streams service*. Any request to a specific session will reach the appropriate *driver* through the *streams service*. An example of this kind of component is a *driver* to handle requests for the MBone tool *vat*. A user sends a request to the *streams service* to create a new *vat* session and the *streams service* starts a *vat driver* that allocates a multicast address through the *multicast service* and returns the identification for the new session created.

The next sections give a brief description of the services and drivers available in the system. For a fuller description of the protocols and best practice see the MSM user manual [14].

3.1   Subscribe/Select Command

The *subscribe-select* [18] mechanism enables asynchronous notifications of events from server to client through client initiated request-response transactions. The events are changes in objects kept by the server. The client registers with the server to receive those notifications through *subscribe* methods. The *select* request blocks the connection until an event occurs or a timeout is reached. When the set or a sub-set of events occurs, the server responds with the set of notifications to events or an empty set (when a timeout has occurred). The client may then request the contents of these objects using the *get* method.

Typically, a client sends a number of *subscribe* requests followed by a *select* request. The client then waits for the *select* response to come back. The server responds with a set of events or an empty set. The client may then request the contents of these objects using the *get* method.

A possible optimisation for this mechanism is where the *select* response carries the new object content straight away. This is usually used if the event is urgent and/or the property-data is small. Furthermore, this saves a *get* request from the client.

3.2   Services

Services may be added when required. This is accomplished by placing the service class(es) in the service directory. Furthermore, it is also required to add a line in the configuration file, which specifies the service and class to use. This takes the form:

$$msm.service.myService = cobrow.msm.service.MyClass.class$$

where *myService* is the name of the service, which will be used in requests for that service and *MyClass.class* is replaced by the name of the class required to handle requests for that particular service.

MSM has some standard services which provide basic functionalities to the users. These services are briefly described as follows:

streams : Responsible for managing the multimedia sessions. It handles the requests for creating and deleting a session. It also relays to the drivers the requests for joining and leaving sessions, getting information, and subscribing and unsubscribing to events.

multicast : Allocate multicast addresses on behalf of the multimedia session tools that make use of the MBone. Besides allocating addresses, this service also announces the multicast addresses allocated by MSM in order to avoid collision with other tools or applications using multicast. The announcements are made using the Session Announcement Protocol (SAP)[7] and the Session Description Protocol (SDP) [3]. The allocation of multicast addresses does not use any of the recent protocols under development by the IETF Multicast-Address Allocation (malloc) group. It simply listens to the announcements at the specific SAP global scope port and allocates addresses that are not being currently used.

docs : Handles the requests for retrieving files. It returns the file content-type and file data to the requestor(s). All files are located in the specified file directory from the configuration file. The request may contain the parameter *type = on-the-fly*, in this case, rather than reading the file from the hard disk, it gets the stream file generated on the fly by a session driver.

msmusers : Holds some user properties regarding their status in the sessions.

sys : Responsible for managing the *select* operations at the MSM server. On receiving the request, the sys service starts a timer for $<time\_in\_secs>$ seconds. If before this time expires, any event (object change) occurs at the same requesting client, this service will respond to the request with the objects changed. If the timeout is reached before any event, then the response is empty. Moreover, the client will issue *get* requests for those objects.

3.3 Drivers

Conference drivers are of similar structure to the service classes. Conference drivers may also be added when required. This is accomplished by placing the driver class(es) in the driver directory and also adding a line in the configuration file, which specifies the driver and class to use. This takes the form of

$$msm.driver.myType=cobrow.msm.driver.MyClass.class$$

where *myType* is replaced by the type of conference session to be supported and *MyClass.class* is replaced by the name of the class required to handle requests for a particular session type requirements.

3.4 Properties

Each multimedia session created by MSM has some basic properties that can be retrieved by users. These properties are used to show the current status of the session or to know how to open a specific multimedia tool. The properties are named *users, control, html, type* and *color*.

The *users* property contains a list of session participants. Each time a user joins or leaves the session the *driver* corresponding to the session updates the list.

The *control* property holds the URL to the text file containing the description of the session. The URL points to this file which is stored in the MSM server. The user's browser uses this URL to retrieve the file. The *control* property is accessed when the user is making use of the remote control instead of the signed applet (see section 5 for details).

The *html* property is used to retrieve the text file. This property contains the information needed to open the external multimedia tool. The data is stored following the Session Description Protocol (SDP) [3].

More information about how the properties *control* and *html* are used can be found in section 5.

The property called *type* stores the type of the session (ex. vat, rat, etc). Finally, the property *color* maintain the color allocated for this session. The color is used to show in the CoBrow user interface in which session the users are participating.

4   User Interface

This section illustrates the use of the CoBrow user interface (UI). Therefore, the description will highlight the functionalities provided by the MSM. Using the messages described in the previous sections, the UI can retrieve information about other users and present it in a clear way on the screen. As it was seen previously, the MSM keeps information about the session each user is in and the communication tools available to them.

The UI that is shown here is one used in the CoBrow project. There are some elements in it that are not relevant for the MSM and thus will not be explained.

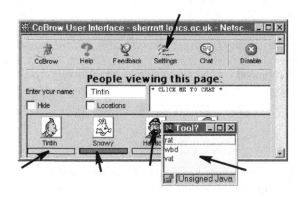

Fig. 3. Start talking.

In figure 3, the small pictures (A) are icons representing users. The small square located under the users' icons (B) shows the session in which each user is participating. Users in the same session have the square filled with the same color[2]. For example, (C) shows that users *Snowy* and *Calculus* are in the same session. The settings button (D), when pressed, opens a configuration window.

In the UI, the available tools are not directly shown. They are used to find out the common tools between two users willing to communicate. Whenever a CoBrow user wants to communicate with another one, (s)he locates the other user's icon in the UI and, by clicking the right mouse button on the chosen icon, causes a menu to pop up containing the conferencing tools common for both. If no tool is matched then the menu is empty. Furthermore, if one of the users is already in a session, only his/her conferencing tool is used in the matching.

Figure 3 (E) shows an example of the pop up menu presenting the tools that can be used between the users Tintin and Haddock. In this case, the tools are rat, wbd (whiteboard) and vat.

In order to use the communication tools, they have to be identified within the system. Thus, there is a panel in the UI Configuration window where the available communication tools can be configured. That panel presents the communication tools supported by the system and one has to select the tools he/she has available. The tools selected here will be used for the matching referred to above.

5   Starting the External Tools

Browsers enforce a security policy of giving no permission for server side applications to perform unauthorised actions on a client machine. This policy restricts server applications from starting applications on client machines without previous permission from the users. The user has to trust the server to allow it to install applications locally or to start local ones.

For CoBrow it is no different. Thus we provide two distinct ways to launch the multimedia tools on the client machine. One, which requires more trust from the client and more work, uses a small remote control application that must be installed on the client machine. Besides installing the remote control, locally the client needs also to configure a MIME-type telling the browser where to find the remote control.

The second way to launch the multimedia tools is an installation-free option where an electronically signed Java applet is employed. A signed Java applet is allowed to request to the user permission to perform risky operations. Executing an external application is one of them. When the user gives permission, the user interface itself can launch external applications and does not need to rely upon a remote control to do so. Everything can be done within the applet.

For both cases there is a need to identify and properly configure the tool to be launched. In order to provide that, the MSM generates a file that can be

---

[2] The color shown here is the session property *color* (see section 3.4)

retrieved by the user via the CoBrow protocol (as seen in section 3.4) . The file contains the information to open the tool chosen for the session. Despite both methods to use the file, each one retrieves the file in a different way.

Because the browser launches the remote control application, the user interface needs to pass to the browser a URL pointing to the configuration file. The URL is stored in the *control* property and can be fetched using the respective request (as described in section 3.4). After retrieving the URL, the user interface passes it on to the browser. The browser fetches the file using the URL that comes with a MIME-type header that tells the browser what to do with the file. The browser launches the remote control application and passes to it the configuration file received.

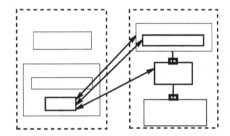

Fig. 4. MSM connections using the remote control.

Figure 4 illustrates the operation between the MSM, the user interface, the remote control and an external tool. The CoBrow client (UI) uses a connection to MSM (1) to retrieve the URL, which is passed on to the browser. The browser requests the file via connection 2 and MSM returns the configuration file and the MIME-type header (via 2) which is used by the Web browser to launch the remote control (3). The remote control launches the external conferencing tool (for example, vic) (4) and then contacts MSM using connection 5 to confirm that the external tool was launched successfully. Connection 5 is also used to keep track of the liveness of the conferencing tool. On one hand, if the conferencing tool is closed the remote control closes connection 5. Hence, the MSM will know that the user has left the session and will clean up the user's session information. On the other hand, if the user closes the UI, MSM will close connection 5. In this case, the remote control will then know that the user has left the system and will close the conferencing tool.

Differently from the remote control, the signed applet does not need a URL to pass on to the browser because the applet does not need the browser to launch the multimedia application. In this case, the user interface needs to retrieve the *html* property, which contains the configuration file itself. Using the configuration file information, the user interface can open the appropriate tool.

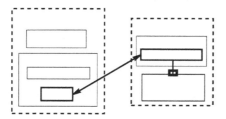

Fig. 5. MSM connections using a signed applet.

Figure 5 illustrates the inter-operation of MSM, the UI and an external tool. The CoBrow client UI uses the connection to MSM (A) to fetch the configuration file (*html* property) and launches the external conferencing tool (for example, vic) (B). If the conferencing tool is closed, the UI is acknowledged and sends a leave message to MSM to clean up the user's session information. On the other hand, if the user closes the UI, it closes the conferencing tool before shutting down.

6   Related Work

The Session Directory (SDR) [5] is a tool to allow the advertisement and joining of multicast sessions on the MBone. A user using SDR can find out sessions being announced by other users and can choose which conference to join. A user can also create a multicast session and them invite other users to join it. The invitation is done using the Session Initiation Protocol (SIP) [4].

The multicast Session Directory - mSD [13] is a tool similar to SDR. It has the same functionalities but instead of being a stand-alone application it uses a HTML[1] user interface. The advantage is that there is only one copy of the server running on behalf of all users.

CU-SeeMe Web [17] enables live, interactive communication over the Internet using a standard Web browser. The CU-SeeMe Web developer toolkit is used to embed audio, video, text chat, and conference control features in a Web page. These components are based on CU-SeeMe [16] core technology, Thus, any Web browser can be used to access those multimedia components. The system has a Java applet that allows end-users to create and schedule their own conferences. Other users can see the conferences created and choose which one to join.

The difference between MSM and three applications is that these applications do not provide multimedia sessions on demand. Using these applications, a user must create the session and then afterwards find other users to join in. With MSM this works in the opposite way; the user can find somebody else to communicate and then ask MSM to create the session required. Actually, the session creation can be completely transparent for the user, as happens in the CoBrow user interface.

7 Future Work

The present CoBrow protocol is based on point-to-point connections between each client and the MSM. Each time a property which can be subscribed by many clients changes, the server has to respond to all *select* requests, and afterwards will be flooded by *get* requests from those clients. This solution is not scalable and we intend researching a more scalable solution. Multicast may be the answer for that. Using a single message to update all clients would be very efficient.

At present, MSM does not have security features. Any client knowing the protocol can send messages to MSM, receive the information and join any session going on. There is no possibility for blocking intrusion from misbehaving clients. It is also not possible for a group of clients to have a private conference. The CoBrow project produced a deliverable[2] where it is proposed an extension to the CoBrow protocol in order to support user authentication and secure channels establishment. Based on this extensions we could use a simple solution for the conference key distribution using the subscribe/select mechanism. This issue is open for further analyses.

MSM has not left the lab so far and we do not have feedback from worldwide users. It is our intention to make available a demo version of our system in the near future.

8 Conclusion

In this paper, we described the Multimedia Session Manager, an application that manages multimedia sessions for Web based users. We presented the protocols involved and best practices. We also have shown the integration between the MSM and the user interface, which is the component that makes use of the facilities provided by MSM.

MSM, as part of the CoBrow project, allows collaborative browsing on the Web, which may enable innovative applications in the future.

Finally, despite the fact that MSM has been developed to work within the CoBrow project, MSM was implemented as a standalone application, has a very simple mechanism and employs well known protocols, therefore it can be used for other systems which need a manager for multimedia sessions.

Acknowledgements

The work presented here was done within CoBrow (RE4003) - a research project funded in part by the European Community under the Telematics for Research Program and by the Swiss Federal Office of Science and Education. We are particularly grateful to the excellent collaboration of our CoBrow colleagues at the University of Ulm and at ETH in Zurich.

References

1. T. Berners-Lee, R. Fielding, and H. Frystyk. (RFC1945): Hypertext Transfer Protocol – HTTP/1.0, May 1996.
2. Marcel Dasen. Security Aspects in a Collaborative Browsing Environment. Deliverable D4.8, CoBrow Project - RE 1003, May 1997.
3. M. Handley and V. Jacobson. (RFC2327): SDP: Session Description Protocol.
4. M. Handley, H. Schulzrinne, E. Schooler, and J. Rosenberg. (RFC2543): SIP: Session Initiation Protocol, March 1999.
5. Mark Handley. The sdr Session Directory: An Mbone Conference Scheduling and Booking System. http://www.vcas.video.ja.net/mice/archive/sdr.html.
6. Mark Handley and Jon Crowcroft. Network Text Editor (NTE) a Scalable Shared Text Editor for the Mbone. In *ACM SIGCOMM*, pages 197–208, 1997.
7. Mark Handley and Edmund Whelan. Session Announcement Protocol. draft-ietf-mmusic-sap-v2-06.txt, expires September 2000.
8. V. Hardman. Robust Audio Tool (RAT) Project: http://www-mice.cs.ucl.ac.uk/multimedia/software.
9. Van Jacobson and Steven McCanne. User Guide to vat. http://irb.cs.uni-magdeburg.de/ elkner/Mbone/.
10. Van Jacobson and Steven McCanne. User Guide to wb. http://irb.cs.uni-magdeburg.de/ elkner/Mbone/.
11. M. R. Macedonia and D. P. Brutzman. MBone Provides Audio and Video Across the Internet. *IEEE Computer*, 27(4):30–36, April 1994.
12. S. McCanne and V. Jacobson. VIC: A flexible framework for packet video. In *Proc. ACM Multimedia'95*, November 1995.
13. P. Parnes. The multicast Session Directory - mSD. http://www.cdt.luth.se/ peppar/progs/mSD/.
14. Sandro Rafaeli and David Hutchison. The Multimedia Session Manager User Manual. Technical Report MPG-99-28, Lancaster University, January 2000.
15. Gabriel Sidler, Andrew Scott, and Heiner Wolf. Collaborative Browsing in the World Wide Web. In *Proceedings of the 8th Joint European Networking Conference*, Edinburgh, May 1997.
16. White Pine Software. CU-SeeMe. http://www.wpine.com/Products/CU-SeeMe/index.html.
17. White Pine Software. CU-SeeMe Web. http://www.wpine.com/products/ VideochatYourSite/cusmweb10-readme.htm.
18. K. H. Wolf. Experiences with HTTP-SELECT and Asynchronous Updates. draft-wolf-http-select-00.txt, expires December 1999. http://www.ietf.org/internet-drafts/draft-wolf-http-select-00.txt.

Adaptive Portals with Wireless Components

Carolyn Watters and David Comeau

Faculty of Computer Science
Dalhousie University
Halifax, Nova Scotia. B3H 1W5
watters@cs.dal.ca

Abstract. In this paper we describe a class of portals, called adaptive portals. Adaptive portals support environments characterized by real tasks, collaboration, and integration of appliances, from desktop to wireless. Such portals provide support for communities of users to access shared content within domains, defined by corporate, community or private interests. The content must reflect the context of the current state of the task and, at the same time, the reality of the display characteristics of the particular device in use.

1. Introduction

Data access on the web is moving quickly past concerns with reliability and speed to concerns of usefulness and timeliness of information. Public portals, such as web search engines and corporate portals that facilitate access to enterprise information within a company, normally through the web, have been available for the last few years. Such portals are made up of "channels" of information and the purpose of these portals is to provide an interface that presents an organized view of the data to which the user has access, i.e., a straight forward means of access to this data.

The next evolutionary step in internet information management is to provide support for tasks, which may be collaborative and may include multiple target devices, from desktop to handheld. This means that the software supports the processes of the task, recognizes group interaction, and lets users migrate seamlessly among internet-compatible devices without losing the thread of the session. This extends the notion of portal from an organized view of web data to a managed view of task data.

The requirements of the software to support this level of task-dependent device-independent, internet/intranet services are significant. Such software must be generic enough to support a wide range of complex tasks in a variety of application areas. Group interaction and concurrent transaction support are needed for "real time" group support. Additionally, the state of both group and task must persist as members join and leave a task session. If users are free to migrate amongst devices during the course of a session then intelligent transformation of data is required to exploit the display and input characteristics of the appliance with minimal loss of content and

P. Kropf et al. (Eds.): DCW 2000, LNCS 1830, pp. 34-44, 2000
© Springer-Verlag Berlin Heidelberg 2000

context. Finally, such software must be standards based, rather than language or operating system based.

In this paper we describe an agent architecture that supports a class of portals, which we are calling adaptive portals, in the broad sense. That is, adaptive portals support environments characterized by real tasks, collaboration in completion of such tasks, and a wide variety of appliances, from desktop to wireless. As an example, a physician portal may be defined for managing information related to patient rounds. Members of the group may include the primary physician, attending nurses, physiotherapists, pharmacists, and other specialists. Individuals may join in the session from a desktop at the nursing station or office or from a wireless device while on rounds or in transit.

The emergence and domination of the web as the common information provider encourages the development of portals that support tasks and collaboration because of its deployment and acceptance in all sectors: education, home, entertainment, business, and government.

Portals provide much needed support for communities of users to access *content* within domains, defined by corporate, community, or private interests. Although the content of given web sites and databases may change, the "portal" provides a constant view for the users. Portals provide most of their value currently by organizing a domain of sites and data access for the user community. To be useful in more dynamic situations, the content must reflect the context of the current state of the task and the reality of the display characteristics of the particular device. This represents a convergence of task and device.

2. Adaptive Portals for Communities
Including Wireless Components

The power of adaptive portals comes from a convergence of *dependence on task* and *independence of device*. By dependence on task we mean that the portal encapsulates processes or procedures that work *proactively* to satisfy some enterprise or individual task. For example, a portal for physician rounds would co-ordinate patient records, lab test requests and notifications, as well as information resources, including database updates. Clearly many tasks require the co-operation of individuals, who may be part of a team or who may selectively join sessions in progress. In the medical example, shown in Figure 1, a specialist, nurse, or student may join in on-going rounds of a physician or for certain patients [WatS99].

By independence of device we mean that the user is free to migrate between devices within the same session. The device and communication particulars of a given session determine the amount and type of data displayed and operations available at any given point in time. From the user's perspective it is just bigger or smaller chunks of data related to the same task. It looks very much the same, and works very much the same whichever client device is in use. This means that the user has access to the same task related functions whether at the desktop or on the road, including, push operations, data input and update, and active agents.

From the user's perspective, the state of the current task session remains paramount while the device is less of a concern. In contrast, most of the current portals are designed to present information in a task neutral manner that is very device specific.

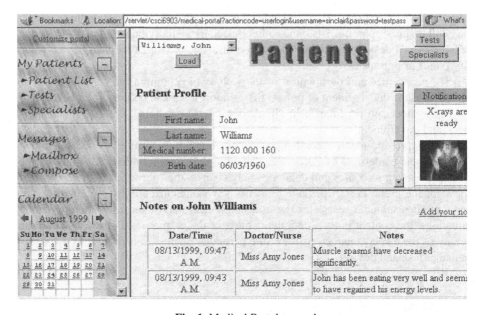

Fig. 1. Medical Portal example

We defined adaptive portals as a class of web portals that are proactive in their support of complex tasks, specific to the task at hand, and somewhat independent of the display device. These portals integrate the activities of managing data, for both individuals and groups. For example, while a corporate portal provides access links to corporate data, an adaptive portal would provide customization of that data based on task, personal, and device characteristics. This might mean that the data selected for display is different for different users and different tasks and that the data selected for display is tailored to use for the particular user and the particular device the user is at, from desktop to head set. The challenge is to exploit characteristics of the task, device, and user in the generation of instances of such a portal.

The growth in interest in mobile devices is substantial [Clar99]. As wireless technology provides a more substantial backbone for mobile mail, ftp, and internet access, users can expect an integration of mobile and fixed access for applications. Many applications, such as emergency medicine, clinical medicine, sales, and education, are ideal scenarios for the integration of fixed wire and wireless devices. Furthermore, individuals need the flexibility to migrate between devices in the course of a session.

For example, a physician may begin treatment while in transit and follow up in the office or at the hospital.

From the user's perspective, even though a range of devices may be available there needs to be continuity of task focus. Our approach is that the task is supported by data and the view of this data is tailored to the device rather than the task tailored to the device. This means that task is supported in a consistent manner independent of the actual device and that the user can move (reasonably) seamlessly from one device to another in connection with that task. This transparency of device means that software is required to track the task parameters from device to device, be knowledgeable about the device characteristics, and interpret the portal characteristics within the context of each device.

The simplistic approach of providing an internet browser on each device does not take into account what is known about the performance characteristics of users using data on small devices. Several studies have shown that screen size *does* have an effect on performance [KamE96]. A recent study by Jones et al [JonM99] examined the effect of screen size on the overall metric of task performance and they found that the smaller screen size impeded task performance. Several factors have been identified. First, line width has been shown to effect performance more then number of lines. Duchnicky and Kole [DucK83] showed that width was more important than height for comprehension of text on a screen. Of course, accessing data of any kind on a smaller display may involve additional scrolling, which has a mixed review on user task performance.

Second, studies, such as Reseil and Schnederman [ReS87], show that smaller screen sizes result in slower reading time of textual material. Dillon [Dill90] showed that smaller screens result in many more page forwards and backwards interactions. Third, the organization of menus has an effect on performance. Han and Kwanhk [HanK94] showed that searching through menus on smaller displays is much slower than on conventional displays. It is interesting to note that this reduction in menu based access does not affect hierarchical menus as much [Swie90]. Fourth, the use of search functions, like "find" in Windows, increases as users get into smaller and smaller displays. Jones et al [JonM99] found that small screen users followed shorter paths and used search facilities much more (double the rate) of the large screen users. Not too surprisingly, small screen users had to use scroll right and down extensively to read the data.

Not only is screen size and input functionality restricted on smaller devices but, at least to-date, bandwidth is also likely to be lower. This means that care must be taken to minimize lag times and maximize the impact of data transfers. Promises of 3G networks [Clar99], providing 144-384 Kbps, compared to the 14.4 Kbps of current wireless, will change the nature of these constraints. The challenge is to recognize these limitations and intelligently compensate by tailoring data presentation to minimize negative performance effects resulting from smaller screen displays.

3. Architecture

An agent-based architecture has been developed that supports adaptive portals for a broad range of complex tasks across a range of devices. Such an architecture would provide a (relatively) seamless device transition for the user, identifying the current device and adapting the presentation and content to reflect that context while maintaining a consistent task view.

The administrative and management software is independent of the actual task and context while the agents incorporate specific rules for handling the particular context and task of the application. The software functionality includes the following:

- Manage task procedures - Tasks have characteristic sequences of actions or inter-relationship of actions and data that need to be managed by the portal operation.
- Allow collaboration - For group related tasks, individuals can join in activities and their input is integrated with the task data. Additionally, notification of task related activities may be pushed to group members as needed. Group members need to be able to "join" on going sessions and "leave" as needed.
- Personalize - Individuals maintain control over many aspects of presentation, content, and may assume levels of privileges such as updates or deletion of data.
- Device independent - Drivers are used for device specific software so that devices can be added or removed by simply adding or removing device drivers.
- Device migration within a session- users move from one device to another during a session without any loss of current state of the session.
- Device recognition - The form and content of data should reflect the realities of band width and screen real estate of the receiving device.

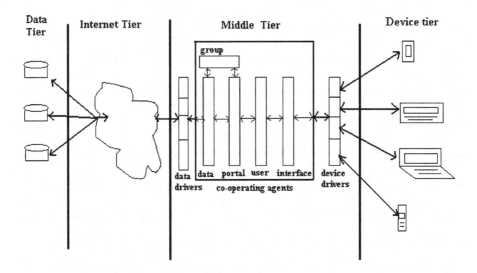

Fig. 2. Adaptive Portal Architecture

The Adaptive Portal is based on a multi-tier architecture, as shown above: data tier, internet tier, middle tier, and device tier.

Data Tier The data tier is the domain of documents, databases, and other data available to the system. The data may be proprietary or public, in files or in database management systems, real-time, triggered or generated as needed.

Middle Tier The middle tier is server(s) side software that provides the adaptive portal functions. This tier manages the administration functions of maintaining user, group and task profiles including definition and updates. The software in this tier manages task sessions, from both the individual and the group perspectives and includes data and device drivers. Data drivers facilitate access to particular data sources, providing a degree of data independence. This includes the specifics of access and updates to distributed databases and/or database management systems. Device drivers facilitate communication with particular devices, both wired and wireless.

The middle tier software has three main functions: administration, task management, and session management. The administration function is to manage the personal characteristics, task parameters and processes, and group characteristics. The task management function is to control the flow of task processes, including sequencing and completion of subprocesses. The session management function maintains the current state for a task over the period of a session, where a session may involve members joining and leaving the session during its course.

The middle tier software is designed as a layered architecture [Wool99] of cooperating agents, shown in Figure 2, where the following agent types are defined:

- Data agent - interact with remote data source
- Portal agent - manage portal tasks (e.g. for a Physician, CEO, etc.)
- Personal agent - manage personal profile characteristics
- Interface agent - manage migration of data to given device within contraints of device and personal portal characteristics
- Group agent - manage data and task agents with respect to the group characteristics

Group agents oversea the members of the group and manage the contribution of individuals to on-going activities within the context of a given task. *Portal agents* are responsible for following the task agenda, spawning off sub-tasks as needed, and maintaining the current state of the task. *Personal Agents* manage the activities of individual users, ensure compliance with personal preferences, and maintain personal information resources. *Data agents* are responsible for access protocols for data sources. *Interface agents* are responsible for data transformations appropriate for devices. Agents communicate in two ways: access to a common XML data set and KQML messages for direct communication.

The interface agents are responsible for intelligent transformation of display data characteristics and functionality to fit the target device. Rules are built into these agents to transform the data so that it makes the best use of the available screen space and makes accommodations that reflect the reality of the screen and device functionality within the context of the task and personal preferences.

Device Tier The device tier interacts with the middle tier via device drivers specific to each device used. These device drivers are independent of the device agent and ensure that any device specific protocols are satisfied. As new devices are made available, only the device driver is added to the system.

Message Standards

One of the most interesting principles of an agent architecture is the notion of agents working together, sharing information and delegating tasks. Agent communication is a critical consideration in adaptive portal development. KQML, Knowledge Query and Manipulation Language [HuhS99], is a recognized inter-agent messaging protocol that wraps around the actual message content. For our purposes we use the KQML to define the message structure and XML to define the message content. There are several reasons for us to use XML as the message content definition language: XML DTD's can be defined for individual and shared tasks, XML can be used to define both shared data (blackboard data) and agent message content, and XML has been proposed by others as an appliance independent interface language [AbrP99].

KQML messages are defined by type or performative plus attributes. The high level performatives used so far in our prototype are: ask, tell, and cancel. The attributes include: sender, receiver, language, ontology, and content. The language used for the content is currently always XML. The following is an example message:

```
(tell
        : sender Agent1
        : receiver        Agent2
        : language        XML
        : ontology        PatientID
        : content(<id>1234</id>
                        <Fname>Jane</Fname>
                        <Lname>Doe</Lname>
                        <birthdate><year>1962</year>
                                        <month>08</month>
                                <day>22</day>
                </birthdate>)
```

XML is currently the preferred semantic data description protocol for shared web data. In the prototype system XML is used to define profiles, shared data, and agent message content. Device-specific display units are created as needed from this shared data definition rather than converted from one form to another. Figure 3 shows the agent message protocols used in the prototype.

The use of KQML as the wrapper allows the potential interaction of our agents with agents from other co-operating applications.

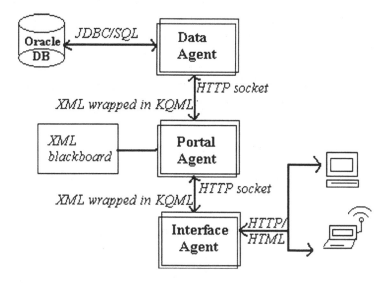

Fig. 3. Agent Communications in the Prototype

4. Device Migration and Prototype

Interface agents determine what data to send to a particular device, based on characteristics of the user and the device. The agents create appropriate navigational guides, such as menus or lists, based on the known aggregation hierarchy of the whole portal.

In theory, the same *content* would be available to the user no matter which device is currently in use. At a more practical level, knowing the screen and bandwidth constraints of the current device can be used intelligently, along with personal or task preferences to select appropriate data. For example, on a smaller device, in general;

- Lines of text should be short
- Concise/abbreviated and verbose versions are generated for use as needed
- the hierarchy of menu options or data choices is shown to reflect the aggregate view
- Thumbnail sketches may replace full images as default with full images by request
- Contextual information is included in each screen
- Data in tables is filtered at source

An important factor in the transformation of portals to smaller display units is knowledge about *functionality* or how users work within the confines of the smaller device. The search option becomes more frequently used as the amount of data per view is reduced and so this functionality is an automatic default on smaller screens. Many smaller devices have cumbersome text input capabilities and consequently entering text gets harder as the device gets smaller. Where possible, then the amount of free text input required from users is reduced and replaced with menus of "best guesses" to reduce the frequency and length of typed user input. The flow steps or sequences of processes related to a task is hard to maintain through a series of small screens, so, when possible, the "next" step in a sequence of task sub-processes is generated automatically for the user. Research has shown that even with context information on small screens, users increase the pattern of going back pages more frequently as the screen gets smaller and so including "bookmarking" and "back" options as part of the transformation algorithm makes sense.

Our prototype uses desktop, laptop, and handheld PC's, where CDPD is used for Internet access for the handheld device (a Casio Cassiopeia). The prototype implements the portal architecture with personal agents, group agents, task agents, data agents and several device agents. We show only one of the generic transformations used, that for lists.

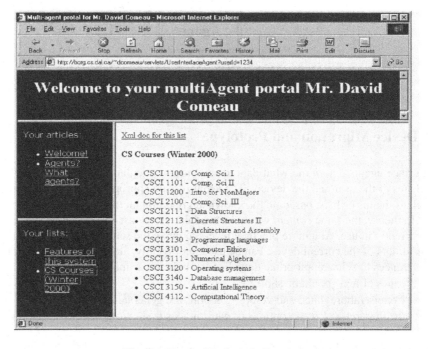

Fig. 4a. Laptop Display of a list

Figures 4a and 4b show an example of list transformation from the laptop (4a) to the handheld device (4b). Notice that the 4 frames of the laptop display are collapsed into 2 for the handheld. The list is broken into viewable chunks (scrolling is a personalized option) with context markers prominent for the user, such as fixed heading and current position within the list. In addition, the additional functionality of text search and back/next have been added as these are known to be heavily used by people on small screen displays.

Fig. 4b. Handheld Display of List

5. Conclusions

Adaptive portals managed by agents show promise of customizing web applications on several dimensions: task, user, and device. We continue to work on several areas related to this work. First, classes of interface agents for a wider range of mobile devices are being designed. Second, the maintenance of state for groups of users which was part of an earlier prototype is being reimplemented as group agents. Finally, the techniques used here for the automatic transformation of data for display on smaller devices are somewhat domain specific and we are exploring the applicability to the general web browser display problem on smaller and smaller devices.

References

[AbrP99] Abrams, M., C. Phanouriou, A.L.Batlongbacal, S. Williams, and J.E.Schuster. (1999) UIML: an appliance independent XML user interface language. Proceedings of the WWW8 Conference, Toronto, Canada. May 11-14. p. 617-30.

[Clar99] D.Clark Preparing for a new generation of wireless data. IEEE Computer 32(8): 8-11.

[Dill90] A. Dillon, J.Richardson, and C.McKnight. 1990. The effect of display size and text splitting on reading lengthy text from the screen. *Behavior and Information Technology*, 9(3) 215-227.

[DucK83] R.L.Duchnicky and J.Kwahk. Readability of text scrolled on visual display terminals as a function of window size. *Human Factors* 25. 683-92.

[HanK94] S.H.Han and J.Kwahk. 1994. Design of a menu for small displays presenting a single item at a time. *Proc. Human factors and Ergonomics Society 38th Annual Meeting.* 360-364.

[HuhS99] M. Huhus and L. Stephens. Multiagent systems and societies of agents. In *Multiagent Systems*, Ed. G. Weiss. MIT Press, Cambridge, USA. 1999. p. 79-120.

[JonM99] Jones, M., G. Marsden, N. Mohd-Nasir, K.Boone, and G. Buchanan. 1999. Improving Web interaction on small displays. Proceedings of the WWW8 Conference, Toronto, Canada. May 11-14. 51-59.

[KamE96] T.Kamba, S.Elson, T.harpold, T.Stamper, and N.Piyawadee. 1996. Using small screen space more efficiently. *Proc. CHI'96*. 383-390.

[ReiS87] J.F.Resiel and B. Shneiderman. 1987. Is bigger better? The effects of display size on program reading. In G.Salvendy (Ed.) *Social, Ergonomic and Stress Aspects of Work with Computers*. Elsevier, Amsterdam. 113-122.

[Swie90] S.J.Swierenga. 1990. Menuing and scrolling as alternative inforamtion access techniques for computer systems; interfacing with the user. *Proc. Human Factors Society 34th Annual Meeting*. 356-359.

[WatS99] Watters and Shepherd Adaptive Medical Portals. *ACM SIGIR Customized Information Delivery Workshop Proceedings*. San Franscisco. August 19, 1999.

[Wool99] M. Wooldridge. Intelligent Agents. In *Multiagent Systems*, Ed. G. Weiss. MIT Press, Cambridge, USA. 1999. p. 27-78.

An Evaluation of Formalisms for Negotiations in E-commerce*

Morad Benyoucef and Rudolf K. Keller

Département d'Informatique et de Recherche Opérationnelle
Université de Montréal
C.P. 6128, succursale Centre-ville, Montréal, Québec H3C 3J7, Canada
{benyouce, keller}@iro.umontreal.ca
http://www.iro.umontreal.ca/~labs/gelo

Abstract. The diversity of negotiation types in e-commerce calls for a clear description of the rules that govern them. The participant has to know the rules before engaging in a negotiation, and to this end, a formalism is needed which allows for the serialization and visualization of the rules. Furthermore, this formal description should be executable, in order to simulate the negotiation process and investigate its compliance with the underlying requirements. As a consequence of such formalization, the negotiation process and the software supporting it may be separated. This paper discusses the requirements for a formalism that is appropriate for capturing negotiation processes. It then presents five major techniques and formalisms for describing such processes and evaluates them according to the requirements. The paper concludes that the Statechart formalism is most suitable for the negotiation types considered.

1 Introduction

According to the Object Management Group (OMG) and CommerceNet whitepaper on electronic commerce (e-commerce) [1], commerce is at its heart an exchange of information. To obtain something of value from someone else you need to: (1) find a person who has what you want and communicate your desire, (2) negotiate the terms of a deal, and (3) carry out the deal. Each of these activities involves an exchange of information. Negotiation can be defined as "mechanisms that allow a recursive interaction between a principal and a respondent in the resolution of a good deal" [2]. The principal and the respondent are usually a consumer and a supplier. In general, they need to negotiate the price, the delivery date, the conditions of the purchase, the terms of the guarantee, etc. If the negotiation is carried out automatically or semi-automatically, we talk of electronic negotiation (e-negotiation).

The diversity of negotiation types calls for a clear description of the rules that govern them. The participant has to know the rules before engaging in a negotiation, and to this end, a formalism is needed which allows for the serialization and visualization of the rules. Furthermore, this formal description should be executable, in order to simulate the negotiation process and investigate its compliance with the

---

* This research is supported by Bell Canada, BCE Emergis, NSERC (National Sciences and Engineering Research Council of Canada), and CIRANO (Centre Interuniversitaire de Recherche en Analyse des Organisations).

P. Kropf et al. (Eds.): DCW 2000, LNCS 1830, pp. 45–54, 2000
© Springer-Verlag Berlin Heidelberg 2000

underlying requirements. Note that "negotiation rules" denote the rules governing the negotiation, whereas "negotiation strategy" describes the rules used by an individual participant during the negotiation in order to make the best out of her participation.

Our research focuses on *combined negotiations*, and we are currently studying concepts and architectures to support them [3]. We will rely on formal descriptions of negotiation rules to describe, understand, and test the different negotiation types that make up a combined negotiation. We propose a tool called Combined Negotiation Support System (CNSS). Its architecture is based on workflow technology, negotiating software agents, and decision support systems. A workflow that models a combined negotiation will be constructed to reflect the constraints and dependencies that exist among the individual negotiations. Software agents will be instantiated and assigned to the individual negotiations. They will be actors in the workflow, and the user can monitor them via the administration tool of a workflow management system. The CNSS will be similar to a decision support system, by supporting the user in controlling and tracking the progress of the combined negotiation [3].

This work is being conducted as part of the TEM (Towards Electronic Marketplaces) project. The project addresses market design issues in respect to resource allocation and control and reward mechanisms, investigates open protocols for electronic marketplaces, and explores concepts and tools for e-negotiations. As a common infrastructure of TEM, we are developing a generic negotiation platform (GNP) [4]. GNP is meant to support various types of negotiations. The GNP architecture assumes that the different negotiation types are described in a uniform and formal way, and that the descriptions can be serialized for exchange in the e-marketplace.

The contributions of this paper are threefold. First, we discuss a list of requirements for a formalism that is appropriate for capturing negotiation processes. Second, we review five major techniques and formalisms for describing such processes. Third, we evaluate these formalisms according to our requirements and summarize our findings in tabular form.

Section 2 of the paper briefly introduces the concept of negotiation. Sections 3, 4, and 5 present the three main contributions of the paper. Finally, a short conclusion is given in Section 6.

2   Negotiations

"Negotiating takes place when, based on offers made in the information phase, an agreement cannot be reached or the agreement has potential for optimization and the parties intending to carry out the transaction want to discuss their offers" [5]. The information phase is the period that precedes the negotiation and during which the participant gathers information about products, market participants, etc.

A considerable research effort is being dedicated to the subject of negotiations [6, 7, 8, 9, 10, 11, 12, 13, 14]. As described by Kumar and Feldman [6, 7], the simplest form of negotiation is no negotiation at all (also called fixed-price sale) where the seller offers her goods or services through a catalogue at take-it-or-leave-it non-negotiable prices. Auctions are one simple form of negotiation and are at present the most visible type of e-negotiations on the internet. Negotiations can take a more complex form called bargaining. It involves making proposals and counter-proposals until an agreement is reached or until the negotiation is aborted [15]. The OMG considers bargaining as a bilateral or multi-lateral negotiation depending on whether there are two parties (one-to-one bargaining) or many parties (many-to-many bargaining) involved in the negotiation [2]. Negotiations are further classified as distributive or integrative [5]. In distributive negotiations, only one attribute is negotiable (usually the price). The parties have opposing interests, that is, one party tries to minimize (e.g., the buyer) and the other party tries to maximize (e.g., the seller) the price. In integrative negotiations, multiple attributes of the item are negotiable. Furthermore, combinatory negotiations [16] are a form of negotiation that involves making bids on combinations of goods or services, and one of the main challenges is for the auctioneer to determine the winning bid. In a combined negotiation, finally, the user engages in many negotiations for different goods or services. The different negotiations are independent from each other, whereas the goods and services are typically interdependent. A more detailed and complete description of negotiation types can be found in [17].

3   Requirements for Negotiation Formalism

Before we discuss formalisms and techniques for describing the variety of negotiation types presented in the above section, we need to define the criteria we will use in evaluating these approaches. We have come up with a non-exhaustive list of eight interdependent criteria.

3.1 Formal Basis

If we are to make buying and selling decisions based on automated negotiations, then it is important that we have high confidence in the software involved in this activity. Cass et al. [18] suggest that an automated negotiation must have four necessary properties. It must be: (1) *Correct*: an automated negotiation must not contain errors such as deadlocks or incorrect handling of exceptions; (2) *Reasonable*: it must allow adequate time for bids to be made; (3) *Robust*: it should continue to function properly after an improper action by the user; and (4) *Fast*: it has to execute and respond quickly. We believe that there should be a fifth property. An automated negotiation must also be *traceable*. In order to be trusted, the software must be able to justify its actions to the user if necessary. This may be done by tracing the execution and by showing the decisions taken together with their rationale. In order to achieve these five properties, we need to formally describe negotiation processes. We agree with Cass et al. [18] that "a notation with well-defined, well-formed semantics can facilitate verification of desirable properties". Formalization will enable us to separate the process of negotiation from the other parts of the software. We believe that the rules governing the negotiation should not be hardcoded. The software tool supporting the negotiation should be able to pick one type (style) of negotiation from a repository and use it. This will lead to efficient implementation and easy testing and, last but not least, will encourage reuse. We can actually benefit from the fact that negotiation processes contain parts that are common to all of them.

3.2 Serialization

Negotiation rules should be known to the participant (human, software agent, proxy negotiation server, etc.) and to anyone who wants to consult them before engaging in the negotiation. Their rendering should be intuitive and flexible in order to cope with various audiences. We believe that the rules are as important as, or perhaps even more, than the other information describing the good or service that is the object of the negotiation. We agree with Wurman et al. [8] that "implementing auction mechanisms in a larger context will require tools to aid agents in finding appropriate auctions, inform them about auction rules, and perform many other market facilitation functions". It should therefore be possible to serialize the negotiation rules and transfer them over the network.

3.3 Visualization

Visualization (graphical if possible) is important to the user of the negotiation tool because humans are known to understand visual information better than textual information. Furthermore, animation possibilities can make the execution (if supported) more attractive and easier to follow by the user. The developer of the negotiation tool should also be able to visualize and eventually animate the negotiation rules, for instance for prototyping and testing purposes.

3.4 Executability

If the formalism chosen to describe the negotiation rules is executable, the negotiation process can be simulated. Simulation may support the verification of the formal description in respect to correctness, consistency, completeness, absence of deadlocks, and alike. Furthermore, it will help analyzing and validating the description against the underlying requirements.

3.5 Other Criteria

A good description approach should be *well-established* for at least two reasons: first, it will already have passed the test of time, and, second, software tools supporting the approach may be available. Moreover, it should be *easy to understand*. This criterion is important for the person who consults the negotiation rules before engaging in it. This consultation should be effortless and quick. If it is not, the user might dislike the negotiation tool, or even worse, she might use it without really understanding it. The description must also be *complete*. The formalism chosen to describe the negotiation rules should allow for capturing all the details of the negotiation type at hand. Otherwise, we would have to complement the description using natural language or another formalism. Finally, we believe that it should be possible to *automatically convert* the description to other existing formalisms. This criterion suggests the smooth transfer of the description to platforms supporting other formalisms.

4   Candidate Formalisms

We have identified five major description techniques and formalisms for negotiations. They are described below.

4.1 Natural Language

Bidding is a popular form of negotiation. Among the many definitions we found the following one [15]: "bidding is when the consumer specifies what she wants and the suppliers make their bids. Based on their bids, the consumer selects a supplier from whom to order the good or service". This definition is correct, but it can be confusing if we compare it to an alternative definition of the same term. In fact, it is widely known that "bidding" means "proposing a price on an item, and committing to take the item for that price if the seller agrees, or, in the case of an auction, if there are no higher bids than the proposed price". We can see that the use of natural language leaves the door open to dangerous ambiguities. It is this and other examples that call for a formal description of negotiation processes.

4.2 Agent Coordination Language

Little-JIL is an agent co-ordination language realized at the University of Massachusetts at Amherst. Programs written in Little-JIL describe the coordination and communication among agents which enables them to execute the process in question [19]. It is a graphical language in which processes are broken down into steps. The steps are connected to each other by edges that represent control flow and data flow. Each step is assigned to an agent to execute. A program in Little-JIL has a root that represents the entire process, and the root itself is decomposed as necessary into steps. Visually, a step is a rectangle with many tags associated to it (the name of the step, the resources necessary to execute it, the parameters, the exceptions that the step might raise, etc.).

Little-JIL was used to describe a set of negotiation processes [18]. The resulting programs define the coordination and communication between agents involved in the negotiation. An agent might be a seller or a buyer, and each agent is assigned a number of steps to perform. Describing a negotiation process in terms of steps and edges between them simplifies reasoning by following the flow of control and the flow of data in the tree of steps. Since a negotiation typically involves multiple participants, it is convenient to model it using Little-JIL by decomposing it into steps to be carried out by the participants and by providing coordination and communication between them.

A sealed-bid auction and an open-cry auction are described in [18] using this mechanism. The authors claim the following benefits from using Little-JIL: ease of understanding, the possibility to compare negotiation processes, to analyze them, to separate the process of negotiation from the application, and to execute a negotiation process. The ease of understanding is not as evident as the authors claim. The notations are quite exotic and the bigger the process gets, the harder it is to understand what it does. We do not know if a description using this formalism can be serialized or converted to other formalisms, but we do know that it is complete.

4.3 Finite State Machines

Kumar and Feldman [6] use Finite State Machines (FSMs) to model a negotiation. The states of the FSM are the states of the negotiation, and its input alphabet is the set of messages sent by the participants. A message is expressed as a pair < p , m > where p is the sender of the message and m is the message sent out. The output alphabet of the FSM is the set of messages sent to the participants. These messages are expressed as pairs << p , m >> where p is the subset of all the participants that will receive the message and m is the message itself. The process flow of the negotiation maps into the transitions of the FSM. The messages make the negotiation go from one state to another. Figure 1 gives a description of an English auction using this notation. The four states of Figure 1 can be found in the FSMs describing most of the other types of negotiations. This suggests that a great deal of common features can be isolated using the FSM description.

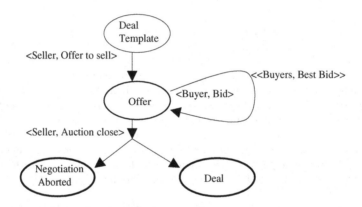

Fig. 1. Finite State Machine description of an English auction [6].

A FSM description alone is not sufficient to fully capture a negotiation process. It has to be complemented in order to answer the following questions: (1) what information should be made available to the participants and what should be hidden, (2) what is the minimum starting bid, (3) what are the rules for closing the auction, etc.

In another study, Su et al. [15] use a FSM to model bilateral bargaining. Here again, the states are the states of the negotiation and the transitions between states are labeled with "send" and "receive" primitives (e.g., send a call for proposal, receive an acceptance, etc.). The result looks similar to Kumar's and Feldman's FSMs, but the diagram produced is more complex and uses numerous states. According to Cass et al. [18], FSMs are used mainly to classify negotiations. They describe how the state of the negotiation changes in response to events, yet fail to describe the order of these events. This notation is purely a modeling notation and is not directly executable.

4.4 Statecharts

The FSM formalism alone cannot evidently capture a complete negotiation process. We propose to extend it by using Statechart diagrams [20] as adopted by the UML [21]. Statecharts are well-established, widely used, and are semantically rich enough to formally describe and visualize various kinds of processes. As a further important feature, Statechart diagrams can be serialized in XMI [22]. Finally, off-the-shelf simulation and analysis tools are available for Statecharts, such as *Statemate* [23], which will help to validate and render the descriptions being investigated. Below, we first discuss the OMG Negotiation Facility, which relies on a restricted form of Statecharts. Then, we present the fine-grained formalization which makes full use of the expressive power of Statecharts and which we adopted for our work.

4.4.1 The OMG Negotiation Facility

We present a proposal made by OSM [2] in response to the RFP for a Negotiation Facility issued by the OMG. The proposal contains three negotiation models described using three Statechart diagrams, respectively. The three models aim to cover all the negotiable aspects of an e-commerce transaction and introduce two new concepts: (1) negotiation through the introduction of motions, looking for consensus through voting, and (2) dealing with what comes after a deal is reached. For our work, only the bilateral negotiation model is relevant. It is defined as a collaborative process dealing with interactions between two participants (see Figure 2).

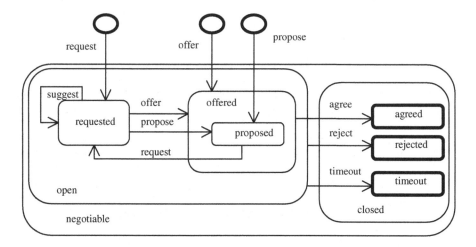

Fig. 2. The OMG Bilateral Negotiation Model [2].

The proposal considers a negotiation as a "give-and-take" process where two (or more) parties try to make concessions until they reach a deal. The OSM models are not well suited for describing auctions as they are intended to be generic at the cost of being precise. In a bidding situation, a bid can be thought of as an offer because it represents an engagement by the bidder to be honored if her bid is a winner. The OSM models, however, are based on the idea that a proposition is to be discussed until it becomes an offer, and then it can be agreed upon or not. Finally, since the

OSM models are designed to capture all major negotiation types, the corresponding diagrams are hard to understand. Note that the models do not make full use of the Statechart formalism, in that, for instance, neither guard conditions nor actions appear in the diagrams.

4.4.2 Fine-Grained Formalization

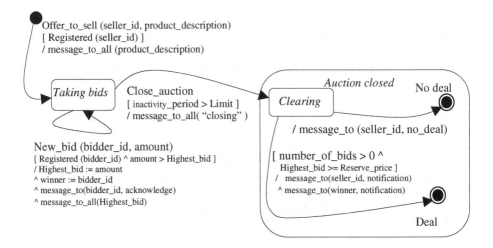

Fig. 3. Statechart description of an English auction.

We propose to use the full expressive power of Statecharts, in particular the Event-Condition-Action strings provided for specifying transitions. We also suggest to describe each negotiation type separately. Figure 3 shows our Statechart description of an English auction. The main states are "Taking bids" and "Auction closed". When the auction is closed, it goes to the "Clearing" state where the auctioneer has to determine if there is a deal or not. The two possible final states are "Deal" and "No Deal". In the first case the seller and the buyer are notified. In the second case only the seller is notified. The transitions are labeled with the string *event[guard-condition(s)]action(s)*. So far, we have used Statecharts to describe some popular types of negotiations like the fixed-price sale, the Dutch auction, the bilateral bargaining, etc. We feel that the formalism is powerful enough to capture entire negotiation processes.

5   Comparison of Approaches

Table 1 summarizes our evaluation of description approaches. A + means that the description approach verifies the corresponding criterion, a - means that it does not, and a ? means that we could not confirm either case. The table shows that Natural Language is the big looser and that Statecharts satisfy all of our requirements. OMG's Negotiation Facility lacks clarity, mainly because the models try to capture all types of negotiations in single diagrams. Furthermore, the OMG descriptions do not reach the level of detail and completeness of the (full) Statechart approach. FSMs are highly rated, but they do not permit a complete description of negotiation processes and are less popular than Statecharts. Agent Coordination Languages are even less popular and, to our knowledge, the descriptions cannot be serialized nor converted to other formalisms. We therefore adopted Statecharts as the formalism for describing negotiation rules.

Table 1. Comparison of the five description approaches considered.

	Formal Basis	Serial-ization	Visual-ization	Execut-ability	Popu-larity	Clarity	Complete-ness	Convert-ibility
Natural language	-	-	-	-	+	-	+	-
Agent coordination language	+	?	+	+	-	+	+	?
Finite state machines	+	+	+	-	-	+	-	+
OMG negotiation facility	+	+	+	+	+	-	-	+
Statecharts	+	+	+	+	+	+	+	+

6 Conclusion

In this paper we demonstrated the need for a formal description of negotiation rules, and to this end, we reviewed and evaluated five different description approaches. The evaluation led us to suggest Statecharts as the best choice. They have a good formal basis and can be serialized, visualized, and executed. They are also well-established, are easy to understand, are complete, and can be converted to other formalisms. Our research relies on Statecharts to describe the individual negotiations that make up a combined negotiation. This will enable us to understand, implement and test the different negotiation types more thoroughly before using them in a combined negotiation. So far, we have used Statecharts to describe several popular negotiation types. Our future plans include modeling all the types described in [17], and leveraging available Statechart tools for setting up the envisioned combined negotiation support system.

References

1. ECDTF Reference Model. Technical report, OMG, 1997. http://www.oms.net/ecdtf.html.
2. OMG Negotiation Facility final revised submission. Technical report, Object management Group, March 1999. http://www.oms.net.
3. Morad Benyoucef and Rudolf K. Keller. A conceptual architecture for a combined negotiation support system. Tech. Rep. GELO-118, Montreal, Canada, February 2000.
4. Morad Benyoucef, Rudolf K. Keller, Sophie Lamouroux, Jacques Robert, and Vincent Trussart. Towards a Generic E-Negotiation Platform. In Proceedings of the Sixth

International Conference on Re-Technologies for Information Systems, pages 95-109, Zurich, Switzerland, February 2000. Austrian Computer Society.

5.   M. Strobel. Effects of electronic markets on negotiation processes - evaluating protocol suitability. Technical Report 93237, IBM, Zurich Research Laboratory, Switzerland, 1999.

6.   Manoj Kumar and Stuart I. Feldman. Business negotiations on the internet. In INET98 Conference of the Internet Society, Geneva, Switzerland, July 1998.

7.   Manoj Kumar and Stuart I. Feldman. Internet auctions. Technical report, IBM Institute for   Advanced Commerce, Yorktown Heights, NY, November 1998.

8.   Peter R. Wurman, Michael P. Wellman, and William E. Walsh. The Michigan internet AuctionBot: A configurable auction server for human and software agents. In 2nd Intl. Conf. on Autonomous Agents, pages 301-308, Minneapolis, MN, May 1998.

9.   S. Lamouroux and R. Gérin-Lajoie. Le serveur de négociation électronique GAMME. Technical report, CIRANO, Montreal, Canada, 1999.

10.- C. Beam and A. Segev. Automated negotiations: A survey of the state of the art. Technical Report 97-WO-1022, Haas School of Business, UC Berkeley, 1997.

11. C. Beam, A. Segev, and G. Shanthikumar. Electronic negotiation through internet-based auctions. Tech. Rep. 96-WP1019, Haas School of Business, UC Berkeley, Dec 1996.

12. Pattie Maes, Robert H. Guttman, and Alexandros G. Moukas. Agents that buy and sell. Communications of the ACM, 42(3):81-91, March 1999.

13. Efraim Turban. Auctions and bidding on the internet: an assessment. International Journal of Electronic Markets, 7(4), December 1997.

14. Michael P. Wellman and Peter R. Wurman. Real time issues for internet auctions. In IEEE   Workshop on Dependable and Real-Time E-Commerce Systems, Denver, Co, June 1998.

15. S. Y. Su, C. Huang, and J. Hammer. A replicable web-based negotiation server for e-commerce. In Proc. (CD-ROM) of 33rd Intl. Conf. on System Sciences, Hawaii, 2000.

16. Tuomas Sandholm. An algorithm for optimal winner determination in combinatorial auctions. In Intl. Joint Conference on Artificial Intelligence, Stockholm, Sweden, 1999.

17. Morad Benyoucef. Support for combined E-negotiations: Concepts, architecture, and evaluation. Technical Report GELO-122, Université de Montréal, Montréal, Québec, Canada, May 2000. Thesis proposal. In preparation.

18. Aaron G. Cass, Hyungwon Lee, Barbara Staudt Lerner, and Leon J. Osterweil. Formally defining coordination processes to support contract negotiation. Technical Report UM-CS-   1999-039, University of Massachusetts, Amherst, MA, June 1999.

19. A. Wise. Little-JIL 1.0 language report. Technical Report 024, Department of Computer Science, University of Massachusetts at Amherst, 1998.

20. David Harel and Eran Gery. Executable object modeling with statecharts. In Proc. of 18th Intl. Conference on Software Engineering, pp. 246-257, Berlin, Germany, March 1996.

21. J. Rumbaugh, I. Jacobson, and G. Booch. The UML Reference Manual. Addison-Wesley, 1999.

22. XMI Metadata Interchange Specification. ftp://ftp.omg.org/pub/docs/ad/98-10-05.pdf.

23. D. Harel, H. Lachover, A. Naamad, A. Pnueli, M. Politi, R. Sherman, A. ShtullTrauring, and M. Trakhtenbrot. STATEMATE: A working environment for the development of complex reactive systems. IEEE Transac. on Software Engineering, 16(4):403-414, 1990.

Building Intensional Communities
Using Shared Contexts

John Plaice[1], Paul Swoboda[2], and Ammar Alammar[1]

[1] School of Computer Science and Engineering
University of New South Wales
UNSW SYDNEY NSW 2052, Australia
{plaice,ammara}@cse.unsw.edu.au
[2] Department of Computer Science, University of Victoria
P.O. Box 3055, Victoria, B.C., Canada V8W 3P6
paul@i.csc.uvic.ca

Abstract. Intensional communities are composed of intensional programs sharing a common context, implemented using a networked context server, called the AEPD aether process daemon. The programs are written in the ISE intensional imperative scripting language, which is illustrated through versioned assignments in undergraduate classes. Using this model of intensional communities, two examples are developed: a Web-based class in which a teacher leads a student through a multidimensional page, and the programming of chatrooms.

1 Introduction

In their position paper [3], Plaice and Kropf argue that building distributed communities requires that objects within a community share a common explicit context. As such, standard object-oriented methodology, which implicitly assumes that outside of the objects there is nothing, is not capable of creating real communities, despite the claims put forward by various practitioners.

The position paper goes further and states that evolution of a community should take place through the transformation of the shared context by the objects that it includes, as well as by the changes forced upon the objects by a changing environment.

However, no implementation details are given for how such a shared context can be built. In this article, we describe a mechanism by which network-aware ISE programs [7] can share contexts and give two examples of how this context-sharing can be used. We begin with a brief introduction to ISE, then explain how shared contexts can be built with the Aether Protocol Daemon, first presented in Swoboda's M.Sc. thesis [6].

2 The ISE Language

Intensional programming [4] corresponds to building programs whose behavior depends on an implicit multidimensional context; changing a context may influence the behavior of a program, which can test the current context to adapt its

P. Kropf et al. (Eds.): DCW 2000, LNCS 1830, pp. 55–64, 2000.

behavior or modify the context as it sees fit. *Intensional versioning* [5] is the dual to intensional programming; the definitions of all identifiers are assumed to vary through the set of possible contexts; we say that the identifiers are *versioned*.

ISE is an attempt to create the first imperative scripting language that combines intensional programming and intensional versioning. The basic notion in ISE is that everything that can be identified, including user-defined functions, can also be defined in multiple versions. When constructs such as variables and functions are accessed in expressions, intensional best fits are used to find the appropriate version of the entity referred to. A thread of execution carries with it a "current version", against which best fits can be made.

ISE's syntax is similar to that of Perl and C, and all variables, including scalars, arrays and hashes (and version-hashes), can be defined in multiple versions. Function definitions are similarly versionable. ISE uses an identical versioning algebra and best-fit scheme compatible with the `vmake` intensional-make tool and the `ircs` intensional repository system [6]. For a detailed description of this scheme, refer to `http://i.csc.uvic.ca/ise_docs` .

In terms of syntax, ISE is similar to a cut-down and modified version of Perl4, with version expressions and a modified function-definition structure. Variables in Perl can refer to scalar values (integers or strings, with automatic conversion), arrays (mapping integers to scalars) or associate arrays (mapping scalars to scalars — also called hashes). Scalar variables are written var, array variables as @var, and hash variables as %var. In addition to these, ISE also uses version hashes (mapping versions to scalars), written *var.

The set of possible versions uses the following syntax:

$$V ::= \epsilon$$
$$| \quad scalar$$
$$| \quad scalar : V$$
$$| \quad V + V$$

There is a partial order defined on the set of versions, including identities:

$$V : \epsilon \equiv V$$
$$V + \epsilon \equiv V$$
$$V + V' \equiv V' + V$$
$$V + (V' + V'') \equiv (V + V') + V''$$

$$\epsilon \sqsubseteq V$$
$$\frac{m \leq n}{m \sqsubseteq n}$$
$$V \subseteq V : V'$$
$$V \subseteq V + V'$$
$$\frac{V \sqsubseteq W \quad V' \sqsubseteq W'}{V + V' \sqsubseteq W + W'}$$

An example version is

```
<z+a:(b:1+c:(d:2+e)+f)+a:g:3>
```

which is equivalent to

```
<z+a:b:1+a:c:d:2+a:c:e+a:f+a:g:3>
```

as well as

```
<z+a:(b:1+c:(d:2+e)+f+g:3)>
```

The versioning of variables and functions is generally effected through the (potential) insertion of a versioning expression, immediately following the expression's identifier. Absolute-version expressions — called *vsets* — are denoted with angle brackets, while version-modifier (of the current version) expressions — called *vmods* — are denoted within square brackets.

Below we give some examples of versioned expressions in ISE.

- The (absolute) vanilla version of scalar `$var1` :

  ```
  $<>var1
  ```

- The `<nice>` version of array `@array1` :

  ```
  @<nice>array1
  ```

- The current version (plus a vmod of `[a:1]`) of hash (or associative array) `%hash1` :

  ```
  %[a:1]hash1
  ```

- The `<abc>` version of version-hash `*vhash1` :

  ```
  *<abc>vhash1
  ```

- A function call to the current version plus a vmod of `[dim1:abc]`, of function `function1`, with the (passed) argument expressions equal to the `<a:1>` version of `$var1` and the `[a:2]` vmod-version of array `@array1` :

  ```
  function1[dim1:abc]($<a:1>var1, @[a:2]array1)
  ```

An ISE script is started with an initial *current version*, which may be changed at different times during the execution of the script, using explicit `vset` or `vmod` instructions. The block structure of the language ensures that if changes are made to the current version within a block, then the version upon entry to the block is restored upon exit from the block.

Function calls are a bit tricky. When a function identifier appears, then a best-fit lookup for the appropriate function definition is undertaken. When it has been found, then there are three different possibilities for the version to run the function code: the current version, the (found) best-fit version, or the requested version, specified separately.

Flow of control can also be affected by `vswitch` and `vcollect` conditional statements, which test the current context. For example,

```
vswitch {
  <@[follow:]@> {
    print("Dimension follow is not set\n");
  }
  <@[follow:on]@> {
    print("Dimension follow is set\n");
    }
  }
};
```

tests the `follow` dimension to see if its coordinate is equal to `on` in the current context. The `vcollect` statement gathers all of the branches that are acceptable.

Function definitions are somewhat more limiting in ISE than in Perl, due to their use of an explicit list of formal arguments which are type-checked at runtime. Although not strictly necessary, this enforcement of the passing of the correct number and types of parameters helps debugging, since differing versions of the same routine are followed to have differing formal-argument lists; a function-call that behaves well under one version-environment may fail under another, due to argument discrepancies.

ISE currently has only a small number of built-in routines, including a print statement, some basic file handling and system calls, and a collection of math-routines. Currently, the implementation causes each of the built-in functions to occupy all versions associated with the function's identifier; the behaviour of the built-in routine can then vary with the specific version of the routine executed.

3   Example: Versioned Assignments

It is crucial when teaching software engineering to ensure that each and every student actually works on all aspects of software development and release. The only way to impose this requirement is to hand out relevant individual assignments, and then to weight these assignments sufficiently highly, in order for the students to take them seriously.

The problem with this approach is that it then becomes very difficult to assess the exact contributions of the student, because the student will be in continual contact with other students, possibly copying parts of or even the entire solution.

One possible 'solution' is to inform the students that they are not to interact with their colleagues when working on the assignments. Apart from being naive, this is not a useful recommendation, since in the real world, we would expect someone to ask for help from their colleagues if they actually needed it.

A more realistic approach is currently being taken in a Software System Design and Implementation class currently being taught at UNSW. This class, taught by Plaice with the support of Alammar, uses *versioned assignments*. For every assignment, midterm and exam, each student receives a slightly different assignment, produced by an ISE script. The idea is that the assignments are sufficiently close that students can talk among themselves and help each other at the conceptual level, but that the assignments are sufficiently different that each student will have to do the hard work of getting the assignment to work.

Because versions and their components can be explicitly manipulated in ISE, it is relatively straightforward to produce, in addition to the actual assignment statements, the appropriate marking schemes as well as version annotation, for further perusal in the future.

4   The AEP Daemon

If intensional programming refers to programming in a context, it was unclear what it meant to put several objects in the same context, and to allow each of them to change the context, thereby affecting the other. It is by studying this problem that the concept of *intensional communities* [3] was first proposed.

Using a *shared context*, where two or more executing processes, presumably coded in a contextually sensitive language such as ISE, operate under the same global context, or at least share a mutually-modifiable context that each can periodically refer to, then they can synchronously affect their respective behaviours.

Work has already begun on a network daemon for managing such distributed contexts, termed "aethers", under a simple context-management protocol called AEP, for AEther Protocol. The daemon, aepd (AEP daemon), has been constructed using a threaded implementation, and is accessible by arbitrary numbers of clients from anywhere on the Internet.

The current ISE interface to the AEP and daemon is provided in a small collection of extension routines, which closely resemble the AEP commands they invoke over the network. When the aepd-connection routine is invoked in ISE, an aepd-monitoring thread is spawned, directly in the interpreter, which waits for context changes. Although future versions of ISE AEP support might allow for the aepd's control of the global ISE context in a client, the current implementation simply keeps a separate (aepd) context in each of the participating interpreters, which does not directly affect the ISE clients' behaviours. Clients are left to decide exactly when and how the shared context is to affect them; a current demonstration program simply loops after waiting for broadcast context changes from a controlling ISE process, and dispatches various actions based on best-fits against each new broadcast context. Below are simple descriptions of the current ISE extension routines for AEP support:

– aepd_connect(*hostname, port*)
  Connects to an aepd daemon at the given host and port number. Returns zero on success.
– aepd_disconnect()
  Disconnects from the current aepd connection and cancels the associated monitoring thread. Returns zero on success.
– aepd_create(*aether name, initial context*)
  Creates a new aether with the given name and given initial (version) context. Returns zero on success.

- aepd_delete(*aether name*)
Deletes a given aether, thereby causing all participating clients who have not exited from the aether to do so, first. Returns zero on success.
- aepd_enter(*aether name*)
Causes the caller to enter a aether, which must have been created, first. Returns zero on success.
- aepd_exit()
Causes the caller to exit the current aether. Returns zero on success.
- aepd_vmod(*version*)
Broadcasts a version modifier to the current aether. Returns zero on success.
- aepd_vset(*version*)
Broadcasts an absolute version change to the current aether.i Returns zero on success.
- aepd_query()
This simply returns the current context from the current aether of the caller. The context can have been seen before.
- aepd_wait()
This returns any previously-unseen context from the current aether of the caller, and causes the caller to be suspended until a context change is broadcast, if the caller has already seen the current context.

The basic idea of an aether server and its protocol is that clients have the ability to create, manage, destroy and participate in aethers, each of which is a single context, or intensional version. When a change is made to an aether (i.e. a version modifier or an absolute version setting, as in ISE) by one of its participant processes, that change is immediately broadcast to the other participants. Typically, if a version modifier is sent to an aether, only the modifier, and not the resulting total context, need be re-broadcast to the participants. This saves on the networking overhead of maintaining large, shared contexts. An important feature of the daemon is that commands from various participants in an aether be serialized and processed atomically.

A practical implementation of such a context server needs to be multi-threaded, with a request-processing thread for each participant client, as well as a thread for each of the instantiated aethers in the server. The current implementation of the aepd also has front-door and connection-manager processes, whose purpose is to quickly accept successive connections without dropping new ones. Figure 1 shows the overall structure of the aepd daemon.

The front door waits for incoming connections on the server's main port, queueing new connections as soon as they are detected for the connection manager to process. The connection manager is responsible for spawning client-handling threads for each connection it finds in its queue; these threads then simply loop on incoming commands until the connection is terminated, spawning aether-controller threads whenever clients create new aethers. Each aether-controller thread has a queue of serialized commands sent to it from client-handling threads, which the controller processes. It is the aether controller that broadcasts outgoing data to the aether's participants. Needless to say, the re-

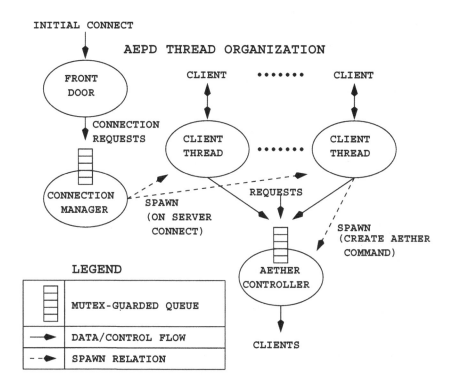

Fig. 1. AEPD Daemon Thread Structure

sulting group of threads and its various critical sections has to be carefully coordinated with semaphores, mutexes and thread conditions.

5   Example: Multilingual Education

Many universities are investing increasing sums into various forms of distance and online education. As the reach of these programs extends across national borders, there are more and more students who are 'attending' classes that are not being given in their native languages. It would be interesting to be able to deliver the content of lectures in the native language of the student, even if the instructor is not familiar with that language.

A prototype session for this sort of education has been prepared, using ISE and AEPD. A multidimensional Web site [8,1] is prepared. This page includes dimension lg for language (possible values are en for English and fr for French), along with a number of Boolean dimensions to control stretchtext and pop-text [2]. This Web site collectively forms all of the versions of a single Web page. This Web page is written as a single ISE script, and an Apache Web server, capable of understanding versioned URLs, passes on the version information to the ISE script.

This page, `content.ise`, can be perused all by itself, but it becomes much more interesting when it is accessed through a wrapper script, `class.ise` that can facilitate the teacher-student dynamic. The code for `class.ise`, remarkably short, is given below:

```
if (aepd_connect("localhost", "4949")) {
  error("couldn't connect to aepd");
} elsif (aepd_enter("demo")) {
  error("couldn't enter aether: \"demo\"");
}
vswitch {
  <@[follow:]@> {
    aepd_vset([follow:-]);
    system<[]>("./content.ise");
  }
  <@[follow:on]@> {
    if (~($version = aepd_query())) {
      error("bad initial version!");
    }
    print("Content-type: multipart/x-mixed-replace;");
    print("boundary=---ThisRandomString---\n\n");
    print("---ThisRandomString---\n");
    while (1) {
      system<$version + []>("./content.ise");
      print("---ThisRandomString---\n");
      $version = aepd_wait();
    }
  }
};
aepd_exit();
aepd_disconnect();
```

Suppose the teacher is English-speaking and the student is French-speaking. Then the teacher points her browser to `http://localhost/class.ise<lg:en>`, and the student `http://localhost/class.ise<lg:fr+follow:on>`. By adding the `follow:on` information, the student is informing the `class.ise` script that his browser should follow the lead.

The teacher's ISE script will run every time the teacher clicks in the page, then will inform the aether daemon sitting on machine `localhost` at port 4949 that aether `demo` should be updated with the teacher's current version. The student's ISE script will loop, waiting for changes to that aether; should it change, then the page is refreshed, to where the teacher moved to, with the added provision that the student will always see the French version of the page.

6   Example: Programming Chatrooms

After email, chatrooms are probably the most commonly used Internet application, and it can be argued that are the paradigm for intensional communities.

In an experimental class on Programming Languages at the Department of Computing and Software, McMaster University, Canada, ISE and AEPD were taught together. The class assignment was to build a chatroom. All the students were able to build chatrooms, and some were quite sophisticated. The standard mechanism was to use one aether for one chatroom, and that the last message sent by user `Fred` would be stored as the coordinate of dimension `Fred`. More sophisticated mechanisms, keeping track of entire histories, were developed as well, as were entire universities of chatrooms!

7   Conclusion

The idea behind intensional communities is that we are interested in creating a new model of computation that is more powerful than the current object-oriented paradigm. It should be clear from the example descriptions given above that the introduction of shared contexts, using the `aepd` daemon, allows for the very rapid production of a number of networked applications that would otherwise take much more time and energy.

There is much future research to be undertaken. First, at the implementation level, the current aether daemon is not sufficiently robust to be able to deal with thousands of simultaneous threads. Second, at the semantics level, there are probably more generalizations to be undertaken, such as versioned aether servers.

Acknowledgments

None of the work in intensional communities and aethers would have ever taken place without the continual discussions with Bill Wadge (University of Victoria, Canada) about the role of atomism in the development of twentieth-century science. Bill Wadge also first thought of the multilingual Web page.

Much of this work took place when the first author was on sabbatical leave at McMaster University, Canada. Many thanks to David Parnas who persuaded me to go there, and to the very energetic software engineering students at McMaster who attended my class.

Thanks also go to Peter Kropf (Université de Montréal, Canada) for his support through the WOS^{TM} project.

References

1. m. c. schraefel and W. W. Wadge. Putting the hyper back into hypertext. In *Intensional Programming II.* World-Scientific, Singapore, 2000.
2. T. H. Nelson. *Literary Machines.* Mindful Press, Sausalito CA 94965, 1993.

3. J. Plaice and P. Kropf. Intensional communities. In *Intensional Programming II*. World-Scientific, Singapore, 2000.
4. J. Plaice and J. Paquet. Introduction to intensional programming. In *Intensional Programming I*, pages 1–14. World Scientific, Singapore, 1995.
5. J. Plaice and W. W. Wadge. A new approach to version control. *IEEE Transactions on Software Engineering*, 3(19):268–276, 1993.
6. P. Swoboda. Practical languages for intensional programming. Master's thesis, University of Victoria, Canada, 1999.
7. P. Swoboda and W. W. Wadge. Vmake, ISE and IRCS: General tools for the intensionalization of software systems. In *Intensional Programming II*. World-Scientific, Singapore, 2000.
8. W. W. Wadge, G. D. Brown, m. c. schraefel, and T. Yildirim. Intensional HTML. In E.V. Munson, C. Nicholas, and D. Wood, editors, *Principles of Digital Document Processing*, volume 1481 of *Lecture Notes in Computer Science*. Springer-Verlag, 1998.

DSM-Communities in the World-Wide Web

Peter Schulthess, Oliver Schirpf, Michael Schoettner, and Moritz Wende

Distributed Systems Laboratory, Ulm University
schulthess@informatik.uni-ulm.de

Abstract. Distributed shared memory is an interesting alternative to message-based construction of distributed systems. We contemplate extending the applicability of our current implementation of a DSM operating system from the locally connected PC cluster to large scale intranets and multiple federated DSM domains in a global network context. Telecooperation and collaborative browsing in a DSM domain are discussed and may constitute useful communication tools within a community. Potential gains in functionality, speed, consistency and elegance are expected

1   Introduction

The grand vision of a globally interconnected information space has found its preliminary implementation in the world-wide-web. However, there is room for improvement in several aspects (aspects revisited in the paragraph "Perspective"):
 – connection oriented protocols do not efficiently transfer single information pages,
 – www information pages are burdened with irrelevant advertisements,
 – the consistency of the URL-pointers is currently not guaranteed,
 – the world-wide connectivity represents a security hazard,
 – there is no logical concept of a closed user group,
 – world-wide web pages are read-only items,
 – the world-wide web is too slow.

We certainly are enthusiastic about the advent of internet services and the word-wide web in particular and feel that our development in the area of distributed shared memory (DSM) might present a partial solution to the problems quoted above. We suggest a multitude of separately managed special interest domains, so called DSM-communities (Figure 1). Topics for such communities might range from "Scientific Computing Resource Pool" or "Twenty First Century Lifestyle Conversion" or "North American Baseball News" to "Bavarian Octoberfest Attractions" or "Sears Roebuck Departments Stores" or "Distributed Data of Peter Schulthess".

The information for a community might be stored in a single distributed memory space and the links between information texts (hypertext) can be regular pointers. Within each address space browsers, information retrieval and distributed applications are easily programmed obeying a simple sequential execution model. Appropriate transaction protocols guarantee the consistency of objects in the distributed shared memory space. We suggest that each station is permitted to write to exactly one DSM community at one instant - information from other domains may be copied but not

P. Kropf et al. (Eds.): DCW 2000, LNCS 1830, pp. 65-73, 2000
© Springer-Verlag Berlin Heidelberg 2000

written. Objects from other domains (or in other DSM-Communities respectively) are accessed using "copy semantics" rather than "shared object semantics" (Figure 1). "Copy semantics" means to create a new instance of an object and sending the created copy to the requestor. The copy and the original instance are no longer kept synchronized as it would necessarily be done for an object shared by more than one user. Readers interested in current DSM research and implementation are encouraged to consult references [1] to [7] and the literature in general. However, we assume in the context of this paper an application-level perspective on the subject of DSM operation.

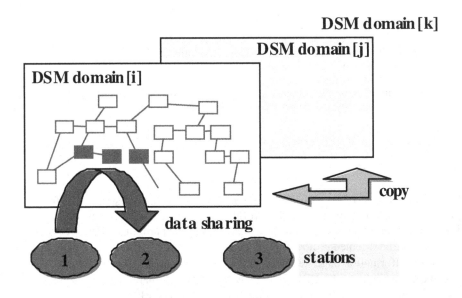

Fig. 1. Federated DSM-Communities

2   Mode of Operation

The envisaged DSM-communities in the world-wide web shall be implemented as multiple disjoint DSM address spaces. DSM (Distributed shared memory) is an interesting alternative to message-based construction of distributed systems. A major challenge lies in keeping the objects in DSM storage consistent according to some selected consistency model [1]. As long as a DSM page remains unmodified copies may be kept at individual nodes. This is particularly convenient for web pages and program code. The copies are discarded at the discretion of the containing node or when they are invalidated by the DSM management protocol. We imply that if a web space is realized as a DSM community it will work faster, more securely and offer additional functionality.

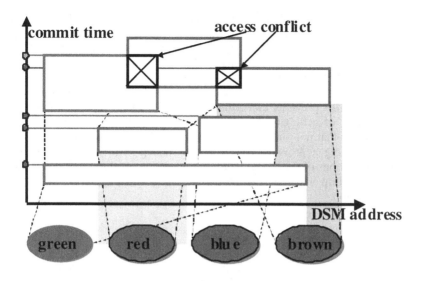

Fig. 2. Transactional DSM Storage

Our Plurix operating system uses the model of transactional consistency [7] for the DSM storage areas: Competing transactions in different nodes write to local copies of DSM storage and attempt to commit their actions at the end of each transaction. A commit request distributes its read/write-set onto the network invalidating all modified pages in eventual partner nodes if it is successful. Because the system consists of a small set of light-weight Java classes the user interactions tend to be comparatively short transactions. In case of a collision with another transaction the aborted transaction is automatically restarted.

Figure 2 shows four stations operating in a common DSM area and issuing transactions. On the horizontal scale the accessed DSM addresses are shown and on the vertical scale we find the completion moments for each transaction. In a first step the green station successfully completes a transaction using a broad range of DSM addresses. For this transaction no concurrency is observed and it can complete without conflict. In a second step two competing transactions with non intersecting read/write-sets are issued by the stations red and blue. Both transactions will complete without conflict. In a third phase three concurrent transactions are shown with an inherent conflict. The brown transaction attempts to commit first and the conflict between red and brown is detected. As a consequence the red transaction is restarted (for example). Please note that a conflict does not arise if two transactions overlap with respect to their read-set only.

3   Limitations of Domain Size

A major limiting factor for the geographical and numerical size of a DSM domain is the propagation delay in the network and consequently the achievable transaction rate. Transactions on individual stations will execute concurrently but commission of the modified pages must be propagated to all participating nodes. In a local PC-cluster the propagation of commit requests to all stations is fast and in the order of 50 microseconds - leading to a limit of 20000 transactions per second. In a wide-area cluster, however, the propagation delay may be 50 milliseconds or higher. The resulting rate of 20 transactions per second is clearly unacceptable. Therefore in a wide-area DSM domain each node should overlap his current transaction with the commit request of his previous transaction (Figure 3). These pipelined transactions carry the potential of achieving high transaction rates even in a wide-area DSM domain but require that not only the current but also the previous transaction is kept restartable. Restarting a previous transaction of node[i] will automatically restart subsequent transactions of this node. Pending transactions within other nodes are not affected and cascading aborts are confined to the node which attempts to commit the pipelined transaction.

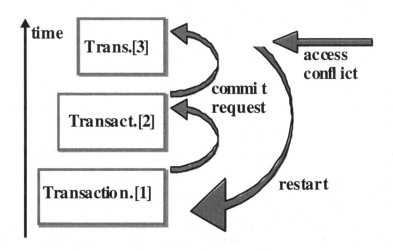

Fig. 3. Pipelining the transactions of a node

The maximum memory size of a DSM domain is given by the address length in the pointers. The current implementation therefore limits its domain size to 4 Gigabytes. By using separate segment descriptors current Intel CPUs can extend their addressing capability to 46 bit. However, since segment descriptors are not supported by the virtual memory mechanism we decided against including a segment selector in pointers of our prototype. In the future with the advent of 64 bit architectures all practical addressing limitations will be removed. Instead of a physical addressing restriction the desire of the owning institution to control content and access rights of a DSM domain will most likely limit its size to less than a 2**64 bytes.

4   Protecting a DSM Community

After a successful logon a user is given pointers to his personal object collection and to selected common resources. Within the Java language framework forging of pointers and tampering with memory structures is not possible. Additionally Java attributes like "private", "protected" and "final" will protect important operating system structures. Thus the strong typing of the language represents a first line of defense against DSM inconsistencies introduced by non malicious users.

A user might only be authorized to participate in a DSM community as a reader of common resources but not as a writer. This read-only mode is most conveniently enforced at commit time and the user will not be allowed to commit write operations to a common resource. Unauthorized users will never be allowed to commit. Their requests are ignored and no one should exchange pages with them. To which extent it will be possible to circumvent authorization procedures and to manipulate pages in transit is determined by the effort spent on encryption. Ideally encryption should be strong enough to withstand an attack for at least a few transaction times – until the page in question is obsolete.

If a participating station inadvertently shuts off all the memory portions owned by it are temporarily lost. Stations requesting the lost pages will fail to receive an answer and must trigger recovery actions. In due time the lost memory pages will be invalidated and then reinserted into the DSM heap. If later the deceased station restarts it will have to resynchronize to the current state of the DSM domain. Serialized backup copies of objects may be kept on ftp-servers.

5   Advanced Application #1: Telecooperation

Telecooperation (within a DSM Community) might serve as an example of the applicability of our approach beyond traditional web browsing. Transactional structures are natural for telecooperation scenarios. Often several participants will jointly edit a document. Sharing of the document residing in DSM storage is depicted in Figure 4.

The Node1 and Node2 both possess a pointer to access and to display relevant portions of the shared document. Modifications are directly written to the document and propagated to all participants during the commit phase. Conflicting transactions are detected and restarted in their updated context. Depending on the modification history reformatting on the screens is initiated. The encapsulation properties of our DSM transactions are helpful when implementing floor control policies to avoid unstructured interleaving of input from different stations.

The telecooperation scenario might be a teleconference, windows on the screen may be shared or the shared object may be a document or an application service [8]. Cooperative scenarios are useful within a research team, for teleworkers, for business meetings, for teaching courses and for a plethora of other situations. Beyond editing of shared documents DSM storage can hold the video frames and the audio samples augmenting the scenario. Sharing video frames in DSM often creates less overhead than conventional streaming techniques - which must encapsulate a video stream into a sequence of carefully compressed, paced and buffered messages.

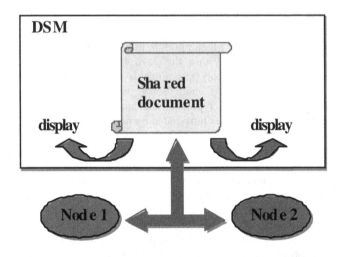

Fig. 4. Document sharing in a DSM environment

6   Advanced Application #2: Collaborative Browsing

The CoBrow project [9] implements a communication model which deviates from the traditional connection setup paradigm. Meetings in "cyberspace" occur spontaneously and not by explicit invocation of a telecooperation session. People accidentally meet when visiting specific web pages and the presence of other people near the current page is indicated by appropriate applets or plug-ins. Personal contacts are made possible using chat-, voice- or video tools. DSM storage may hold additional dialog boxes for video, audio and chat communication.

Figure 5 shows a web space with three users (drawn as ellipses). The user in the center is displaying two documents and from the collaborative browsing subsystem he automatically gets an indication of the presence of two other users in his vicinity. The CoBrow subsystem uses a distributed database storing the location, the preference profiles and the personal communication page of individual users. Based on this information the virtual distance between user pairs is computed and an appropriate subset is displayed to each participant. This vicinity database need not conform to a strict consistency scheme and may be kept in DSM - thus eliminating a bottleneck in the current version of CoBrow.

7   Plurix Implementation Status

The Plurix project at Ulm University implements a native DSM operating system [10]. The resources of a cluster of PC machines and its distributed shared memory are managed by a set of approximately 20 Java core classes (Figure 6 below). All objects reside in persistent DSM storage and can be accessed via regular pointers. A native

Java compiler [11] compiles application classes and operating system classes directly to 32-bit Intel code. Additional Java language constructs simplify the programming of drivers and interrupts and provide direct access to the hardware. The core classes support transactions in the DSM context and will soon support the splitting and fusion of separate domains. The overall system structure is patterned after the archetypal Oberon system developed by Wirth & Gutknecht [12]. It uses a central event loop in each station and a simple cooperative multitasking concept. Currently a single station will only support one DSM domain within a 32 bit address space. The system has been successfully demonstrated at various trade fairs and proved to be fast, compact and reliable.

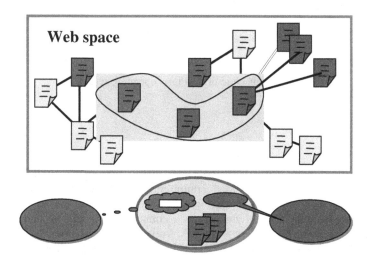

Fig. 5. Vicinity in "Cyberspace"

The Plurix DSM operating system is intended as a generic operating system including special support for distributed operation within multiple separate domains. Stations supporting preemptive tasking might participate in several DSM domains simultaneously. Current work concentrates on streamlining the current prototype and extending the address space to 64 bit. This implies a rewrite of the compiler and of the memory management component. Experience with the current prototype in a local environment and with real programs will help to decide on an implementation strategy for a wide-area DSM prototype. In particular the question should be answered whether pipelined transactions are really required.

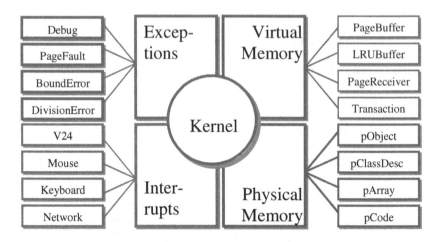

Fig. 6. Architecture of the Plurix operating system

8   Perspective

Based on the discussions above we expect that "life in cyberspace" will be become easier with the introduction of DSM communities. Specifically we refer to the potential improvements quoted in our introductory paragraph: the transfer of an information page within a DSM domain is a connectionless request and therefore more efficient than page transfers via TCP. Irrelevant advertisements and general information dilution may be avoided by carefully selecting the users for a given DSM community., thus guaranteeing The consistency of the hypertexts in the DSM heap is guaranteed by replacing traditional URL-references by Java object references which are inherently safe and "non-dangling". The world-wide-web security hazards are reduced by partitioning the global information space in separate domains. If the operator of an intranet wishes to offer services to a closed user group he might provide services to the user group of a DSM community.

DSM systems can easily cache read-only pages without precluding their occasional modification. CGI-scripts, however, are inadequate to introduce interactivity into the web. Compared to standard web browsing a substantial speed-up of hypertext access is expected in a DSM community because addressing and communication are simplified and because there is the option for integral resource management within a cluster. Further evolution of the Internet will introduce negotiable quality of service and permit communication with an upper bound on latency time. To boost the transaction rate in a wide-area DSM the concept of pipelined transactions and more elaborate DSM protocols are considered.

Introducing DSM communities requires a migration path from the current world-wide web to a more integrated solution. Initially DSM operation might be embedded in commercially available browsers. Later on partitions of the internet might develop which are entirely based on the principle of DSM-storage, -interaction and -

consistency. On a longer time scale identifying and managing individual domains in the context of a consistent network operating system will be more realistic and acceptable than a uniform global information space.

References

1. Mosberger, D.: "Memory consistency models"; Operating Systems Review, Volume 27. No. 1 pp. 18-26. ACM press.
2. Tanenbaum A. S.: „Verteilte Betriebssysteme"; Prentice Hall 1995.
3. Keleher P.: „TreadMarks: Distributed Shared Memory on Standard Workstations and Operating Systems"; USENIX Winter 1994, 1994.
4. Speight E., Bennett J.: „Brazos: A Third Generation DSM System"; USENIX-NT W`shop, 1997.
5. Traub S.: „Speicherverwaltung und Kollisionsbehandlung in transaktionsbasierten verteilten Betriebssystemen"; Dissertation, Universität Ulm, 1996.
6. Yu & Cox: „Java/DSM: A Platform for Heterogeneous Computing"; Workshop on Java for Science and Engineering Computation, 1997.
7. Schoettner M., Traub St., Schulthess P.: "A transactional DSM Operating System in Java"; Proceedings of the 4th International Conference on Parallel and Distributed Processing Techniques and Applications, Las Vegas, USA, 1998.
8. Dermler G., Froitzheim K.: "JVTOS - A Reference Model for a New Multimedia Service"; 4th IFIP Conference on High Performance Networking (hpn 92). Liège, 1992.
9. Sidler G., Scott A., Wolf H.: "Collaborative Browsing in the World Wide Web"; Proceedings of the 8th Joint European Networking Conf., Edinburgh, May 12.-15. 1997.
10. Recent Plurix status: http://www-vs.informatik.uni-ulm.de/projekte/plurix. html
11. Schoettner M., Schirpf O., Wende M., Schulthess P.: "Implementation of the Java language in a persistent DSM Operating System"; Proceedings of the 5th International Conference on Parallel and Distributed Processing Techniques and Applications, Las Vegas, USA, 1999 .
12. Wirth, N., Gutknecht J.: Project Oberon. ACM Press, Addison-Wesley, New York 1992.

A Resource Classification System for the WOS

Simon Schubiger

IIUF, Université de Fribourg, Chemin du Musée 3, CH-1700 Friburg
simon.schubiger@unifr.ch

Abstract. There are many standardized communication protocols that define the interaction between entities, but often they fall short in providing clues about the meaning of the data exchanged and the service provided. In order to enhance interaction between WOS nodes, an agreement on the meaning of data and services is required.

The impossibility to classify resources on the Web in a reasonable amount of time asks for support of multiple classifications that can evolve locally and independently.

This paper introduces classifiers that together with local ontologies add semantics to resources. It looks at the problem of merging multiple ontologies as it might be necessary in communities of WOS nodes. The design of a WOS warehouse based upon classifiers and ontologies is presented.

1 Introduction

There are many standards in use on the Internet for data transmission between active entities such as RPC [4], CORBA [1], RMI [13], HTTP [7] and other protocols, but once communication is established, what should the entities talk about? In fact, if they do not agree on the meaning, is interaction even possible? Communication protocols like the WOSP [2] define very well the interaction between the entities for establishing communication as well as specifying the *structure* of the data exchanged. However, they often fall short in providing clues about the meaning of the *content* or explicitly do not address content at all. What is needed for higher level interaction is an *agreement* on that meaning. This is, what is usually captured by the notion of *ontology*.

Both data and active entities are referred as "resources", because they are addressed in the same way by URI's (Universal Resource Identifiers) [3]. Furthermore, since only invariant parts of resources are of interest here[1] data and active entities are not distinguished.

In [11] it is stated that: "The rapid development and the heterogeneous nature of the Web ensures that it is impossible to develop a complete catalog of all resources available on the Web.". In this context, we would like to extend this statement. Building a catalog is only concerned about *instances* (physical versions) of resources. But in the ever changing environment of the Web, we claim

---

[1] State changes over time as it is the case for active entities are not addressed by an ontology.

P. Kropf et al. (Eds.): DCW 2000, LNCS 1830, pp. 74–81, 2000.
© Springer-Verlag Berlin Heidelberg 2000

that it is even impossible to build a complete *classification* of resources on the Web, at least within a reasonable time. As a consequence, we need support of many different (versioned) ontologies that can emerge and evolve independently of each other, logically close to the resources that are related to the problem domain they are concerned with.

Having versioned ontology support at hand helps building and structuring WOS warehouses as well as specifying the interaction requirements of active entities. The WEBCOM system [12] for example requires the possibility to express a precondition in order to validate the data used to trigger an action. These preconditions are expressed in an agreed vocabulary of terms that form an ontology.

The notion of ontology, although aiming at normalizing things, is not very well defined throughout the literature. Its meaning differs largely between the different usages in the philosophical and computer science domains. A widely used definition is given in [8] by T. R. Gruber: "An ontology is a specification of a conceptualization". Unfortunately, this definition is not oriented towards the goal of entities that communicate, the goal we seek for the WOS. Therefore, the following more informal definition of ontology will be used throughout this paper that is more directed towards a usage for the WOS:

Definition 1 *An* ontology *is an agreed vocabulary of common terms and their meaning within a community of communicating entities.*

In a more practical sense, entities that agree with an ontology, will use the same terms for making assertions and queries with respect to the same meanings of the terms. This definition opens several new questions that are addressed throughout the rest of this paper. An example in section 2 illustrates the use of ontologies and introduces the notions of terms and concepts. Section 3 deals with the question, how *meaning* (semantic) is introduced into an ontology. The (syntactical) *representation of terms* is examined in section 4. A simple definition of *communities* is given in section 5. It is intended to adapt this definition to the upcoming community model of the WOS. *Communication* is not further investigated in this paper, since there is a sufficient number of widely accepted data exchange and representation standards available, as stated before. Section 6 illustrates the design of a resource classification system which will be used by our WEBCOM system.

2   Ontologies

Ontologies used in the context of the WOS are always associated with a WOS warehouse that is in turn located in a WOS node [9]. An ontology is sourced and versioned [11], thus globally uniquely identifiable.

According to definition 1, an ontology defines a vocabulary of terms. Terms stand for a concept that is relevant[2] for the domain addressed by the ontology.

---

[2] Relevant in this context means that the warehouse using that ontology accommodates resources that are instances of the concept expressed by that term.

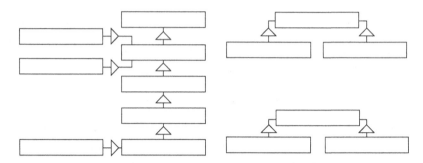

Fig. 1. An example ontology

Definition 2 *A concept is a collection of attributes and actions. Attributes form the state of an instance of a concept. The Actions can be invoked on an instance of a concept. A concept has a semantic.*

A concept is therefore very similar to a class known from object oriented programming. The main difference is that the only relation defined between classes is the subclass (specialization, is-a) relation, whereas concepts are open to be interrelated by other means than just specialization.

See section 3 for how semantic is associated with a concept.

Definition 3 *An instance of a concept is a resource identified by its URI that has the semantics of the concept.*

A resource may be an instance of zero or more concepts at the same time. A LATEX document for example is not an instance of any concepts of the ontology in figure 1. A pizza compiler in contrast is an instance of the concepts "Pizza Compiler", "Java Compiler", "Compiler", "Executable", "File", "Byte Stream" and it might be very well be an instance of "Solaris" and "Platform" as well as "Sparc" and "Architecture".

Definition 4 *A term stands for a concept or is a relation of concepts.*

A term such as "HTML File" stands for the concept that is referred as "HTML File" in computer science. This concept may be related to other concepts (by terms) for example: a "HTML File" *is-a* "File" that *is-a* "Byte Stream". Atomic terms (terms that are not a relation) are usually human readable identifiers.

Figure 1 shows several concepts (depicted as rectangles) and terms consisting only of *is-a* relations (depicted as arrows) forming an ontology.

3   Semantics of Concepts

In order to give meaning to a *concept*, terms either state explicitly the relation of that concept with other concepts or *classifiers*[3] implicitly give the meaning. Classifiers are active entities[4] that given a resource and an ontology, output concepts specified in that ontology. Basically this means that a classifier associates one or more concepts with that resource, therefore marking the resource as an instance of these concepts.

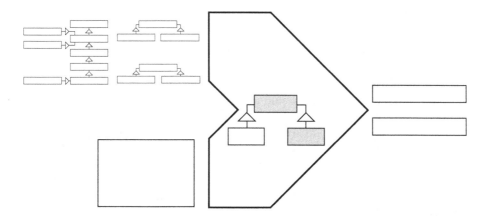

Fig. 2. An example of a classifier

Figure 2 gives an example of a classifier that classifies Win32 and Solaris executables. The classifiers takes an ontology and a resource as input. In this example it is the ontology from figure 1 and a pizza compiler located on local file system. The input ontology is either a superset of the classifiers ontology or contains concept that are equivalent with the classifiers concepts. The classifier outputs zero or more concepts of the input ontology that the resource is an instance of. In this example, the pizza compiler is an instance of the concepts "Platform" and "Solaris".

Classifiers have their own ontology, i.e. the domain they are able to classify. Concepts of classifier ontologies are usually merged to yield the ontology required for a WOS warehouse. A warehouse may also define its proper ontology and

---

[3] The use of classifiers in the knowledge representation domain is not new. For example the LOOM System[5] includes a classifier but for a different reason and there is only *one* single classifier in contrast to the multiple classifier approach presented here.

[4] Classifiers are considered as a special kind of resources, for the moment JAVA classes that implement the classifier interface. A version of the WOSP will be defined for classifier access as soon as the interface requirements of classifiers are fully understood.

declare some concepts in that ontology equivalent with concepts of a classifier's ontology.

We can think of a classifier managing a *conceptual version space*, defined by the ontology of that classifier and the set of classified resources as the *physical version space* [11]. For the example given in figure 1, possible classifiers are:

- **Win 32, x86** A classifier that looks for and examines the PEF header.
- **Solaris, Sparc, x86** A classifier that looks for and examines the ELF header.
- **Java Compiler** A test suite of JAVA files that should compile without errors.
- ...

4 Representation

The representational requirements of a resource classification system are twofold. On the one hand, the system should accommodate assertions about the domain in question, providing a representation of the ontology. On the other hand, the system should provide sophisticated access to the ontology, ranging from simple matching to complex queries that require inference mechanisms.

We use a minimal but extensible language for representing ontologies. The language so far only allows to express hierarchical classification of resources (subsumption of concepts) and concept equivalence but is open for adding new inter-concept relations.

This hierarchical *is-a* classification can easily be mapped to JAVA interfaces and classes. Every concept is translated into a JAVA interface and a corresponding implementation. The interface is the "term" that stands for the concept. The implementation holds the attributes and actions of the concept. Attribute access is provided by appropriate methods added to the interface.

5 Communities and Ontologies

The services provided by a WOS node are usually of basic nature such as providing information or transforming data, for example converting a Word document to postscript or postscript to GIF. To provide higher level services such as converting from Word documents to GIF directly, WOS nodes may form communities.

Definition 5 *A* Community *is a collection of interacting* WOS *nodes that provides a service.*

As far as every node in the community commits to the same ontology, interoperation of WOS nodes is not a problem. Disagreement occurs as soon as there is more than one ontology present in the community. Several solutions to this problem are possible:

- **Merging the concept name spaces.** Despite the fact that this is very simple and might even make sense for some domains, it may result in conflicting semantics for some concepts.
- **Mutual resource classification.** WOS nodes merge resources stored in warehouses but classify these resources according to their proper ontology. This approach may be very expensive if classification is expensive and there is a large number of resource to exchange while there is no community wide ontology at the end of the process.
- **Explicit declaration of concept equivalence.** Meta ontologies may be used to explicitly state equivalence of concepts in different ontologies. These meta ontologies will require careful maintenance, likely done by humans.
- **Proving of concept equivalence.** A very clean solution would be proving equivalence of concepts. Unfortunately concepts are partially captured inside classifiers and thus not easy accessible. Nevertheless, this solution might be practicable if the WOS community shares a pool of classifiers that are used for different ontologies. A possible scenario would be one ontology in French and one in English sharing a subset of classifiers. Starting from the classifiers, at least partial equivalence of the two ontologies can be proved.
- **Inferring concept equivalence.** Concept equivalence may also automatically be inferred by observing classifiers by so-called meta-classifiers. That is, the automated version of building meta ontologies. Concepts may be considered equivalent as long as different classifiers consistently output the same concepts for all resources exchanged in the community. For example, this might be the case for file types. Even if the concept "HTML file" might be known as "html", "HTML Document" or "HTML File" by different classifiers, these classifiers are likely to react consistently, always producing the same output, for a set of HTML files.

Although no final answers to the problem of ontology merging can be given here, several solutions are possible. Experiments have to show which ones are practical in terms of efficiency and implementation complexity. Even more important is the question, which of the above solutions are finally useful for WOS applications.

6   Implementation Design

Figure 3 gives an overview of the design of the implementation of a WOS warehouse as it is used inside the WEBCOM project. The basic design of the WOS warehouse [6] was extended by an ontology of the resource domain known by the warehouse and a resource classification system.

There are basically three operations supported by this kind of warehouse:

- **Ontology extension** results in adding new concepts to the ontology. Adding new concepts usually implies new classifiers or the extension of existing classifiers. Concepts are extracted from an ontology file and translated to JAVA classes and interfaces. The resulting class files are cached in the file system, represented by the "Concepts" database in figure 3.

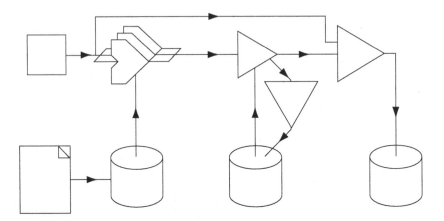

Fig. 3. Overview of the WEBCOM WOS warehouse design.

- **Resource insertion** starts with a given URI. This URI is passed to all known classifiers in parallel which return a set of concepts. This set of concepts is translated into a set of corresponding JAVA interfaces. Because a resource might be an instance of any number of concepts, the system must be able to synthesize an appropriate version by combining the interfaces and classes of the concepts in question. This task is handled by the wrapper generator which produces for each combination of concepts an appropriate wrapper class that delegates the implementation to the classes generated from the ontology file. Instances of wrapper classes are created with the initial URI as argument and stored for resource query and action triggering.
- **Query facilities** are still under development and we do not know yet to which extend queries will be supported by the warehouse. Proposal range from simple matching to inference and proof techniques. Application requirements and implementation efficiency will define the final query capabilities. Query capabilities largely depend on the power of the ontology representation that is still limited.

7   Conclusion

Although several questions still have to be answered, ontologies together with classifiers give a sound base for:

- Shifting from name based addressing of resources (URI) towards concept (semantic, content) based addressing.
- Local creation and extension of ontologies.
- Classification tailored to the requirements of the resources available at a specific WOS node.
- Implementation of a WOS warehouse.

- An experimental framework for testing different query and ontology merging approaches.

A prototype implementation of a WOS warehouse for the WEBCOM project will show the usability of these concepts.

References

1. Object Request Broker Architecture. Technical Report OMG TC Document 93.7.2. Technical report, Object Management Group, 1993.
2. Gilbert Babin, Peter Kropf, and Herwig Unger. A Two-Level Communication Protocol for a Web Operating System (WOS). In *Euromicro Workshop on Network Computing*, pages 939–944, Vsteraas, Sweden, August 1998.
3. Tim Berners-Lee. Axioms of Web Architecture. Technical report, W3C, December 1996. http://www.w3.org/DesignIssues/Axioms.html.
4. A.D. Birrell and B.J. Nelson. Implementing Remote Procedure Calls. *ACM Transactions on Computer Systems*, 2:39–59, 1984.
5. David Brill. *Loom Reference Manual, Version 2.0*. University of Southern California, December 1993.
6. WOS Community. `package wos.comm.warehouse`. http://paradis.ift.ulaval.ca/~alice2/wos.comm.javadoc/Package-wos.comm.warehouse.html.
7. D. Ragget. HyperText Markup Language Specification Version 3.0. Technical report, W3C (World-Wide Web Consortium), 1995.
8. T.R. Gruber. A Translation Approach to Portable Ontology Specifications. *Knowledge Acquisition*, 5:119–220, 1993.
9. Peter Kropf. Overview of the Web Operating System (WOS) project. In *Advanced Simulation Technologies Conference (ASTC1999)*, pages 350–356, San Diego, California, USA, April 1999.
10. Peter Kropf, John Plaice, and Herwig Unger. Towards a Web Operating System (WOS). Technical report, Université Laval, Département d'Informatique, Sainte-Foy (Québec), Canada, G1K 7P4, 1997.
11. Slim Ben Lamine John Plaice. Simultanous Multiple Versions: The Key to the WOS. In *Proceedings of Workshop on Distributed Computing on the WEB*, Rostock, Germany, June 22-23 1998.
12. S. Schubiger, O. Krone, and B. Hirsbrunner. WebComs: Transactions as Object-Flow Networks for the WOS. In *Proceedings of Workshop on Distributed Computing on the WEB*, Rostock, Germany, June 21-23 1999.
13. Sun Microsystems, Inc. *Java Remote Method Invocation TM Specification , Revision 1.50, JDK 1.2*, October 1998.

Intensional Markup Language

William W. Wadge

Department of Computer Science, University of Victoria,
P.O. Box 3055, Victoria, B.C., Canada V8W 3P6
wwadge@csr.uvic.ca

Abstract. IML is a simple markup language that extends HTML. IML makes it practical for even unskilled authors to produce multiversion Web pages. The form and content of a particular version of a page are determined by the settings of a collection of parameters that specify (for example) layout, in terms of font and size, color, and background color; they can determine sections to be included or omitted, in particular, as droptext; which of a series components to present, and in which order; or they can determine a choice of language. An important advantage of the parametric approach is that members of a community can share pages by sharing parameters.

The IML implementation uses ISE, a Perl-like CGI language with run time parameterization. The IML source is translated (once) into a corresponding ISE program which, when run with specific parameter settings, produces the appropriate HTML.

1 Introduction

Diversity is an integral part of community. In a real community, different members are allowed different points of view and the community is the result of sharing these points of view.

Computer systems have a reputation of hostility to diversity; of imposing a single uniform reality on all their users. Most systems are still at the level of Henry Ford's model T, offered (in Ford's own words) in "any color you want, as long as that color is black".

There is, however, no inherent reason why computer systems should be so inflexible, a fact recognized by John McCarthy as early as 1966, in his introduction to the classic Scientific American book, *Information* [2]:

> The speed, capacity and universality of computers make them machines that can be used to foster diversity and individuality in our industrial civilization, as opposed to the uniformity and conformity that have hitherto been the order of the day. Decisions that that now have to be made in the mass scan in the future be made separately case by case. A piece of furniture, a household appliance, or an automobile can be designed to the specification of each user. The decision whether to go on to the next topic or review can be made in accordance with the interests of

P. Kropf et al. (Eds.): DCW 2000, LNCS 1830, pp. 82–89, 2000.

the child rather than for the class as a whole. In other words, computers can make it possible for people to be treated as individuals in many situations where they are now lumped in the aggregate.

It is now thirty years later, computers are thousands of times more powerful than they were in 1966, but McCarthy's vision is still far from being realized. What we might call "diversity engineering" has proved far more difficult than anticipated.

Our Intensional Markup Language is a modest step towards making practical computer-supported diversity, in what should be an ideal application domain — Web authoring. (Incidentally, in the same article McCarthy gives an astonishingly accurate prediction of the Web).

In theory, Web pages, being purely electronic, can be updated frequently and provided in customized versions on demand. In practice, however, this is rarely the case. The cost of delivering a new or customized version is near zero, but the maintenance is a real problem. HTML itself provides very little support for the production and maintenance of multiversion sites. The problem is that different versions of the same site cannot share pages except through links; but then they have to share all the pages accessible from the shared page. Furthermore, pages with analogous layout cannot share the markup that describes the layout.

As a result, authors of multiversion sites are forced to create separate copies by cloning and editing — just like authors of hard-copy documents. And, just like hard copy authors, they are faced with maintaining the consistency of many separate but parallel pages.

Clearly, what is needed is an authoring formalism in which one can specify whole families of related pages/sites with only a modest effort additional to that required to specify a single page/site.

2 Intensional HTML

Any systematic approach to the engineering of diversity requires a framework or paradigm, so authors can specify families of diverse entities without having to construct them one by one. The traditional approach in software and other kinds of engineering is modularity/hierarchy. We provide a stock of basic components and modes of combining components. These selections implicitly define the family of all entities that can be using these components and combination modes.

This approach is limited, however, in the forms of diversity that can be easily produced. Differences between conceptually close versions cannot always be localized in one component. The deluxe model of a car, for example, may differ in many places (color, trim, upholstery, suspension, engine, etc.) from the standard one. The French version of a web page will differ in many places from its English counterpart. We cannot change the car or the page by swapping a single component. Our approach to diversity is based a parametric model first presented by J. Plaice and the author in [3]. The members of a family are determined by (and can be generated from) the values of a collection of parameters. These parameters (also called dimensions) are global — in principle, any component can be sensitive to (altered by changing) any of the parameters.

The first Web authoring system based on the parametric approach was Intensional HTML (IHTML) [5]. IHTML allows the author to create source files for pages and parts of pages which, in general, are generic — valid for a whole family of versions of the component in question. When a request for a particular version of a page is received, the source for that particular version is assembled from the results of specializing the relevant source files for the components. The assembling work is done by a plug-in for the Apache server; the output generated is standard HTML, and thus no special browser software is required.

The different versions of a document are specified by the parameter settings, represented by expressions in a simple algebraic version language. A request for an IHTML page consists of two parts, a conventional URL indicating the name of the page requested, and a version expression indicating which version of the page is requested.

The simplest version expressions consist of a dimension (parameter) identifier and a corresponding value, separated by a colon. For example, the expression `lg:fr` specifies that the value of the `lg` parameter (which might denote the document language) is `fr` (which might denote French). More generally, we can form sums of such expressions, specifying that each of the given dimensions has its respective value. For example,

`lg:fr + size:a4 + mod:ml4 + lv:expert`

might stand for the French language A4 manual for the ML4 model, written at the expert level.

IHTML gains its leverage from the general phenomenon that a particular component of a document typically depends only on a subset (often a small subset) of the collection of parameters. For example, the image on a page giving operating instructions for a copier might depend on the `model` parameter, but not on the `language` parameter; whereas the instructions for loading paper will depend on the `language` parameter but perhaps not on the `model` parameter (because they are all loaded the same way). In this situation an IHTML author most provide an image for each model, and a paragraph of loading instructions for each language, but not a separate entire page for each combination.

3   Intensional Markup Language

Experience with IHTML revealed a serious shortcoming: lack of modularity.

The extra markup required for even simple effects (such as droptext) can be rather intricate. However IHTML, like HTML itself, provides no facility for encapsulating this complexity. The (I)HTML author has no way of defining new modes for combining markup.

The situation clearly calls for the extensible markup, i.e. XML. Ideally, the author could define a new tag `<drop>` and then write

```
<drop text="Contact Numbers">
 office: 555-1234<br>
 fax: 555-4321
</drop>
```

This markup would render to text consisting of the heading `Contact Numbers`, which when clicked would drop the indicated information below.

(A droptext section is an example of an intensional component: it has two different renderings, depending on the value of the parameter controlling the presence/absence of the droppable text. Readers do not explicitly provide values to these parameters. Instead, in its closed form the heading is anchored to a version of the surrounding page identical to the current one except that the droptext parameter is toggled. To the reader, it seems that the heading acts like a button which, when pressed, causes the text to drop).

Unfortunately, XML tools are (currently) not easy to find and use. We therefore adopted an almost laughably simple yet surprisingly powerful substitute: troff macros. Troff is a pioneering computer typesetting package no longer used much but nevertheless still distributed with every flavor of UNIX. It has a simple but powerful macro facility which can be used in a stand alone mode — by turning off all line-filling and the like, and requesting ASCII output.

The troff macros allow us to encapsulate the intensional markup (as described below), and write

```
.bdrop "Contact Numbers"
 office: 555-1234<br>
 fax: 555-4321
.edrop
```

The addition of a macro processing stage made a huge difference in the usability if IHTML, because it was now possible to combine the parametric and modular approaches to diversity. In particular, constructs (such as droptext) can be nested, so that (for example) the text that drops from a heading may itself contain drop sections.

4   From IHTML to ISE

Experience with the first form of Intensional Markup Language (i.e. IHTML plus troff macros) soon revealed other limitations, this time more fundamental.

The basic problem is that IHTML is not a programming language. There are no provisions for evaluating expressions — this rules out constructs such as a slide show because the author cannot generically specify a link in which a parameter is incremented. There is no iterative construct, so that sequences of similar marked-up copy have to be (re)produced by hand. And there are no functions, and this means (among other things) that copy must appear on the rendered page in the same order it appears in the marked-up source.

IHTML does have a simple conditional construct (the `iselect`) and this allows copy to be selectively hidden and revealed. It also has an `include` feature, which can be used as a crude macro definition facility. However these are completely inadequate as a substitute for the power of a real programming language.

Paul Swoboda's 1999 Masters thesis [4] remedies the situation. He devised (in collaboration with the author) and implemented the Intensional Sequential Evaluator, a full-featured Perl-like scripting language that incorporates a (run-time) parametric versioning system. Briefly, this means all entities in the language (variables, arrays, functions, etc.) can be versioned; that programs execute in an implicit context, which determines which versions of the relevant entities are used; and that there are also explicit mechanisms for accessing and modifying the context.

Now, instead of representing a multiversion page as an IHTML file, we represent it as an ISE program which, when called with the required parameter settings, produces (as output) the HTML source for the appropriate version. Here is the ISE source for a simple personalized bilingual greeting page:

```
#!/usr/bin/ise
print("Content-type: text/html\n\n");
print("<html> <title>Page</title> <body>\n");
$happy<><lg:en> = "happy";
$happy<lg:fr> = "content";
$happy<lg:fr+sx:fe> = "contente";
vswitch{
<lg:fr>  {
        print(@[Bonjour, ##nm##, es-tu $$happy$$]@);
        print(" avec cette page Web?\n");
        }
<lg:en><>{
        print(@[Hi, ##nm##, are you $$happy$$]@);
        print("with this Web page?\n");
        }
};
print("</html>\n");
```

The HTML produced as the output of this program depends on the value of three parameters: nm (name), which is required; the optional lg (language), which is en or fr (English or French); and the optional sx (sex), which (if present) is fe.

To use ISE as a cgi language (using Apache on Linux), we need only a simple plug-in, which extracts the name of the script and the version expression. The ISE program is executed with the given version as the (initial) context, and the output is sent directly to the client. For example, entering the URL

```
http://i.csc.uvic.ca/page.ise<nm:Soizic+lg:fr+sx:fe>
```

would display a page with the greeting

```
Bonjour, Soizic, es-tu contente avec cette page Web?
```

The program given above illustrates several important ISE features: the string variable $happy exists in three versions; the vswitch chooses the language of the greeting; and the @[ ]@ string construct allows references to the values of dimensions and variables.

5 Basic Document Macros

Once ISE was available, we reimplemented IML as a front end for ISE rather than IHTML. This is the version of IML about which we now provide a few illustrative details.

Consider first the simplest case of intensional authoring: a plain HTML page with no versioning whatsoever. Converting such a page to an ISE program is easy: we place standard boilerplate at the beginning, and make the actual copy into a quoted string to be printed. Here is a "Hello World" page as an ISE program:

```
#!/usr/bin/ise
print(@[
Content-type: text/html
<head><title>Greeting</title></head>
<body>
<h1>A Greeting</h1>
<hr>
Hello World!
</body>
</html>
]@);
```

Notice that ISE's @[ ]@ construct allows embedded newlines. As a result, the conversion involves nothing more than adding a few lines at the beginning and end. We can define two macros that encapsulate these texts:

```
.de bdoc
#!/usr/bin/ise
print(@[
Content-type: text/html
..
.de edoc
     ]@);
..
```

An author can then convert a standard HTML file into IML by adding the lines

```
.bdoc
```

and

```
.edoc
```

at the top and bottom respectively of the HTML file.

Here are the definitions for the (extremely simple) form of droptext described above

```
.de bdrop
<h3>
.balink pop:on
\\$1
.ealink
</h3>
]@);
vswitch{
  <pop:> { }
  <pop:on>{print(@[
..
.de edrop
]@);}
};
print(@[
..
```

(Note that the bdrop macro closes off the preceding print statement, while the edrop begins the next one). This cross-version link described above is produced by the balink/ealink macros (definitions not given).

(Realistic droptext macro definitions we actually use a more complex, because we allow any number of retractable sections, arbitrarily nestable.) Macros for stretchtext and other constructs described in [1] are equally straightforward.

6   Beyond IHTML

It should be clear by now that IML is potentially far more powerful than IHTML. Macro definitions can contain arbitrary ISE code; in particular, this code can extract the values of parameters from the current context, perform arbitrary calculations with them, invoke computations in a temporarily different, local context, or update the context. For example, there is no particular difficulty in defining macros for an arbitrarily long sequential presentation. We use a single parameter that counts the progress, and at stage n the current page links to a version of the same page identical to the current one except that the counting parameter is increments (after being tested for overflow).

Probably the most important advantage, in the long run, is the fact that the copy need not appear in the browser window in the same order as it appears in the source. We have already seen that simple HTML data is turned into a command (a print command). These commands can be packed as ISE functions and called in any order, and/or repeatedly.

Furthermore, ISE functions can be versioned like everything else. We can give a standard, generic definition, then incrementally add special cases and subcases which, when relevant, override the more general definitions. This should allow the IML author to (for example) define inheritance hierarchies of template pages. We are currently investigating these possibilities.

Acknowledgement

This was made possible by generous support form the Canadian Natural Sciences and Engineering Research Council (NSERC).

References

1. m. c. schraefel and W. W. Wadge. Putting the hyper back into hypertext. In *Intensional Programming II*. World-Scientific, Singapore, 2000.
2. J. McCarthy. Information. In Gerard Piel, Denis Flanagan, and Francis Bello *et. al*, editors, *Information*. Scientific American, 1966.
3. J. Plaice and W. W. Wadge. A new approach to version control. *IEEE Transactions on Software Engineering*, 3(19):268–276, 1993.
4. P. Swoboda. Practical languages for intensional programming. Master's thesis, University of Victoria, Canada, 1999.
5. W. W. Wadge, G. D. Brown, m. c. schraefel, and T. Yildirim. Intensional HTML. In E.V. Munson, C. Nicholas, and D. Wood, editors, *Principles of Digital Document Processing*, volume 1481 of *Lecture Notes in Computer Science*. Springer-Verlag, 1998.

Towards a Logical Basis for Modelling and Querying Multi-dimensional Databases

Mehmet A. Orgun

Department of Computing, Macquarie University, Sydney, NSW 2109, Australia
mehmet@ics.mq.edu.au

Abstract. This paper presents a formalism for modelling and reasoning about multidimensional databases. It is supported by a rule-based system based on a multidimensional logic, which we call ML(ω), extended with aggregation meta-predicates. The system supports a hierarchy of aggregation dimensions by mapping those dimensions to actual dimensions of ML(ω), and aggregation meta-predicates basically perform data transformations over specified aggregation dimensions. We demonstrate that the rule-based system can be used as a deductive front-end to a multidimensional database stored in a data warehouse and can be used as an aid in decision suport systems.

1 Introduction

In many computer applications, we deal with multidimensional information, for example, time series, spatial information, and data warehousing data. It is not surprising, therefore, that a recent development in database systems is the emergence of multidimensional database systems to store multi-dimensional information in order to provide support for decision support systems [4,9].

Most of the recent approaches to multidimensional data models offer hypercube-based data models. For instance, Agarwal *et al* [1] proposed a simple hypercube data model oriented towards a direct SQL implementation into a relational database. Libkin *et al* [6] defined a query language based on multidimensional arrays, which is oriented towards physical implementation. Cabibbo and Torlone [2] proposed a multidimensional data model based on *f*-tables, a logical abstraction of multidimensional arrays. These approaches, among others, are steps towards a systematic approach to modelling mutidimensional information in the database context. However, the current multidimensional databases are still not as powerful and widely accepted as relational databases, partly because they are not based on an application-independent formal basis, in which each dimension is treated uniformly, whose model generalized the relational model, and which enables the declarative specification and optimization of queries.

In this paper, we advance the thesis that multidimensional logics (logics with multiple dimensions such as time, location and so on) [8], enriched with features to cater for the special requirements of OLAP technology, have the potential to provide such a basis for multidimensional databases. We in particular propose

P. Kropf et al. (Eds.): DCW 2000, LNCS 1830, pp. 90–99, 2000.

a rule-based multidimensional programming language, called MLP, which can be used as a powerful tool for representing and manipulating multidimensional objects found in multidimensional database systems and data warehousing naturally. A program of the language is a rule-based system, deductively formalizing our knowledge of a multi-dimensional target application. The language is based on an executable subset of multidimensional logic[8].

In the following, section 2 summarizes the multi-dimensional logic we use in our formalism and gives a brief introduction to multidimensional logic programs. Section 3 outlines an approach for modelling multi-dimensional databases using multi-dimensional logics. Section 4 proposes aggregation hierarchies over given dimensions of interest so that complex aggregation operations can be supported in the system. Section 5 concludes the paper with a brief summary.

2   Multi-dimensional Programming

This section discusses multi-dimensional logic we use in our formalism and multidimensional logic programs. It also presents an example program, that of the Sieve of Erastosthenes for generating prime numbers.

2.1   Multi-dimensional Logic

Here we consider a multi-dimensional logic in which the set of possible contexts (possible worlds) is modeled by $\mathcal{Z}^\omega$ (the countably infinite Cartesian product $\mathcal{Z} \times \mathcal{Z} \times \mathcal{Z} \times \cdots$) where $\omega = \{0, 1, 2, \ldots\}$. For a given $x \in \mathcal{Z}^\omega$, we write $x = \langle x_0, x_1, x_2, \ldots \rangle$ where each x_k is the coordinate (index) for the kth dimension. For each dimension $k \geq 0$, there are three contextual operators: init_k, prior_k, and next_k operating on that dimension. Informally, init_k refers to the origin along dimension k; prior_k the previous point along dimension k; and next_k the next point along dimension k.

The syntax of multi-dimensional logic extends that of first-order logic with three formation rules: if A is a formula, so are $\text{init}_k\, A$, $\text{prior}_k\, A$, and $\text{next}_k\, A$, for all $k \geq 0$. Note that contextual operators are applied to formulas, not to terms of the language. For any given $m \geq 0$, we write $\text{prior}_k[m]$ and $\text{next}_k[m]$ for m successive applications of prior_k and next_k. In case $m = 0$, $\text{prior}_k[m]$ and $\text{next}_k[m]$ are the empty string.

We write $\text{ML}(\omega)$ for the multi-dimensional logic with countably infinite dimensions. We are especially interested in multi-dimensional logics with a finite number of dimensions. For instance, $\text{ML}(n)$ is a logic with n dimensions (for $n \in \omega$) for which $\mathcal{Z}^n$ is the set of possible contexts.

The meaning of a formula is naturally context-dependent, provided by multidimensional interpretations [8] over $\mathcal{Z}^\omega$. A multidimensional interpretation assigns meanings at all possible contexts to all the basic elements of the language such as function and predicate symbols, and variables.

2.2 Multi-dimensional Logic Programs

We start by defining a multi-dimensional logic program as a set of program clauses. The basic building blocks in a multi-dimensional logic program are *contextual units* defined inductively as follows:

Definition 1.

- *All atomic formulas are contextual units.*
- *If A is a contextual unit and $\triangledown$ is a contextual operator of ML, then $\triangledown A$ is a contextual unit.*

We adopt the clausal notation [5] for multi-dimensional logic programs. For convenience, we use upper-case letters for variables, and lower-case letters for function and predicate symbols.

Definition 2.

- *A program clause is the universal closure of a clause of the form $A\text{<-}B_0,\ldots,$ B_{m-1} ($m > 0$) where each B_i and A are contextual units.*
- *A unit clause is a program clause with an empty body of the form $A\text{<-}$.*
- *A goal clause is the universal closure of a clause of the form $\text{<-}B_0,\ldots,B_{m-1}$ ($m > 0$) where each B_i is a contextual unit.*

The informal semantics of a program clause $A\text{<-}B_0,\ldots,B_{m-1}$ is defined as follows: at all contexts $x \in \mathcal{Z}^\omega$, for each variable assignment, if all of $B_0,\ldots,$ B_{m-1} are true, then A is true. Then a multi-dimensional logic program consists of (the conjunction of) a set of program and unit clauses regarded as axioms true at all contexts in $\mathcal{Z}^\omega$. Goal clauses are also called queries.

For practical purposes, we restrict the following discussion to MLP with a finite number of dimensions. There is a dimensionality analysis technique to determine the dimensionality of a given MLP program. The dimensionality of P is determined by the dimensionalities of the contextual operators that appear in it. If the dimensionality of P is n, then we say it is in MLP(n). We refer the reader to [8] for details.

We now give an example program. The Sieve of Erastosthenes is a popular prime number generation technique. It operates by putting all of the natural numbers from 2 onwards into a "sieve". We then perform the following steps ad infinitum:

- Remove the smallest number from the sieve. This is our prime number; and
- Remove all the multiples of this number from the sieve.

Each step naturally corresponds to a moment in time. We can model the notion of time using dimension 0. The positive fragment of the dimension 0 can be regarded as representing a set of moments in time. All program clauses are interpreted as assertions true at all points in the hyperfield of contexts.

A solution for generating prime numbers using the Sieve of Erastosthenes is discussed in [7]. Here we present a solution in MLP(2) (call the program P):

```
init₁ ints(2) <- !.
next₁ ints(X) <- ints(Y),X is Y+1.

init₀ sieve(X) <- ints(X),!.
next₀ sieve(X)<- init₁ sieve(Y),smallest(X),(X mod Y) =\= 0,!.

init₁ smallest(X) <- newsmallest(X).
smallest(X) <- next₀ prior₁ sieve(Y),newsmallest(X),X =\= Y.

newsmallest(X) <- sieve(X).
newsmallest(X) <- next₁ newsmallest(X).

prime(X) <- init₁ sieve(X).
```

As shown in Figure 1, at each moment in time, the sieve predicate represents all the natural numbers left in the sieve, along dimension 1. The prime predicate just picks the smallest number from the sieve at each moment in time (at each point along dimension 0). The sieve predicate varies in both dimensions, whereas the prime predicate varies along the dimension 0 because its definition involves the use of init₁. In other words, sieve/1 can be regarded as a two-dimensional object, whereas prime/1 is a one-dimensional object.

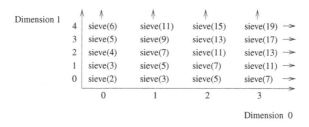

Fig. 1. The sieve/1 relation in two dimensions

3 Modelling Multi-dimensional Databases in ML(ω)

A multidimensional relation of a multi-dimensional database looks like a hypercube defined over a number of dimensions of interest. Each dimension may represent a perspective to data stored in say a (relational) database. For *sales* data, the dimensions of interest may be: product, time, location and so on. A sales value (eg., quantity sold) is stored in a cell in the hypercube indexed by the actual values of all the perspectives to the database. Figure 2 shows the sales hypercube in three dimensions. Each cell in the cube represents a sales data identified by index values for all three dimensions. In the figure, not all the sales values are shown.

A multidimensional database is a collection of data cubes (multidimensional relations), each of which is defined over a set of perspectives (dimensions). Re-

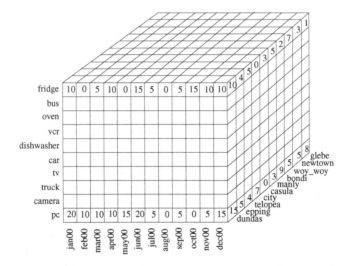

Fig. 2. Sales data cube over 3 dimensions

call that, in MLP, each predicate naturally represents a multidimensional relation over $\mathcal{Z}^\omega$. Then there is a natural correspondence between multidimensional relations of MLP and those of multidimensional databases. If we assume that we are given a multidimensional database, we can easily provide a mapping between the database and a collection of relations in MLP. Therefore MLP can be used to provide a deductive capability on top of multidimensional databases. However, it is possible that an MLP program can be viewed as a (deductive) multidimensional database on its own right.

In a multidimensional database, each dimension is normally defined over a finite domain of values (eg., products), which can be easily mapped to an actual dimension in MLP(n) using enumerated types as follows.

> Dim $time = \{jan00, feb00, mar00, apr00, may00, jun00, jul00, \ldots\}$
> Dim $product = \{fridge, oven, dishwasher, car, truck, bus, tv, vcr, \ldots\}$
> Dim $location = \{dundas, epping, telopea, city, casula, bondi, \ldots\}$

Here time 0 is represented by `jan00` and so on.

We can easily provide a mapping from the dimensions given above to dimensions in MLP(n) by providing a function, say `actual`, as follows:

> `actual=` $\{$`time` $\mapsto 0,$ `product` $\mapsto 1,$ `location` $\mapsto 2\}$

The mapping is determined by the programmer. In a given program, the contextual operators may be indexed by numeric dimension values or by symbolic names of the dimensions involved, eg., the operator init_0 is identical to $\text{init}_{\text{product}}$.

One could imagine another hypercube for *price* data over dimensions *product*, *location* and *time*. One could also imagine other hypercubes representing some other critical decision support information defined over a different set of dimensions and so on. By mapping hypercubes (or multi-dimensional relations in a multi-dimensional database) such as sales values to relations in $ML(\omega)$, we are making the logical tools and techniques in MLP available in the decision making process.

We now give a few examples of MLP that may be useful in OLAP applications. Vector operations are naturally supported in MLP and they can be applied to multi-dimensional relations of any dimensionality (here by the term *dimensionality* we are referring to the *actual* dimensions in which a relation varies). In the following example, price and sales data are combined into a binary relation called price_sales.

```
price_sales(X, Y) <- price(X), sales(Y).
```

The dimensionality of the defined relation is always the union of the dimensionalities of the relations used in the right hand side. We can easily reduce the dimensionality of a multi-dimensional relation using contextual operators. The following clause defines feb00_sales relation where the contextual operators $init_{time}$ $next_{time}$ always moves the time index to February 2000 with the assumption that time 0 (the initial time the operator $init_0$ refers to) is represented by jan00.

```
feb00_sales(X) <- init_{time} next_{time} sales(X).
```

A distinctive feature of the data model for OLAP is its stress on aggregation of perspectives by one or more dimensions as a key operation [3]. For example, we may want to compute the total sales values for a particular product over *all* locations at a particular time. Note that aggregating over all indices of a given dimension is only possible if there are finitely many indices associated with that dimension. We may also want to use complex aggregation operations such as aggregation over selected indices in a given dimension (with finitely or infinitely many indices) or aggregation over another aggregated predicate over the same dimension and so on.

In short, we are looking at extensions of MLP to support aggregation operations. However, MLP, as outlined earlier, does not support aggregation which is basically a second-order operation (it would take a predicate of $ML(\omega)$ and a dimension as parameters and produce another predicate as output).

4   Aggregation Hierarchies

We now outline an extension of the above multidimensional database model to support complex aggregation operations. We start from a small set of predefined dimensions which may be defined in a given multidimensional database. We can aggregate over a predefined dimension, say time, by assigning indices of that dimension into finite groups. For instance, we could define a year dimension (whose indices are say, years 2000, 2001, 2002 etc) by assigning all the months in a given year to the indices in the year dimension. Of course, we do not need to stop there as we also could define, say, a 10 year dimension by assigning the indices of the year dimension into 10 yearly groups. We could then define aggregation operations over those aggregation dimensions (say total sales over years, 10 years and so on) and all the corresponding values would be computed from the values in the base relations according to their groupings.

In other words, we have a hierarchy of aggregation dimensions and any dimension in a given level in the hierarchy (that is not a base dimension) is built up from a dimension in the level immediately below it. This approach is in line with some of those other approaches in the OLAP and multidimensional database literature.

We now make our approach more concrete. Let D_0 represent those dimensions that are predefined for the relations in a given multidimensional database; for the example given above, if we have the sales relation in the database and no other relation, then $D_0 = \{time, product, location\}$. A dimension $d \in D_0$ is a sequence of identifiers (representing indices) defined as follows:

$$d : \omega \rightarrow index(d)$$

where $index(d)$ is the set of identifiers for dimension d. We have the restriction that d is a total, one-to-one mapping (in case the corresponding dimension has a finite number of indices, we assume that it is extended with infinitely many additional distinct identifiers). We also use the following sequence notation $d = \langle d_0, d_1, d_2, \ldots \rangle$ where d_i is the element of d whose index is i.

An aggregate dimension $d \in D_{i+1}$ is built on top of a dimension $e \in D_i$ as follows: $d : \omega \rightarrow index(d)$ and it is associated with a mapping α that assigns each element of d a subset of the indices of e

$$\alpha(d) : index(d) \rightarrow \mathcal{FP}(index(e))$$

where $\mathcal{FP}(S)$ is the set of all finite, non-empty subsets of a given set S. We require that indices of d are mapped to finite, non-empty subsets so that the aggregated value will be defined and can be computed. At this stage, we impose no restrictions on the way in which the subsets of S are allocated to indices of d.

Then, with the requirement that D_i's are disjoint sets (so that dimensions are uniquely identified), the dimensions over which a multidimensional database is defined is obtained as follows:

$$\mathcal{D} = D_0 \cup D_1 \cup D_2 \cup \ldots$$

We can provide a mapping from the dimensions in $\mathcal{D}$ to dimensions in MLP(n) by extending the definition of the `actual` function.

Note that, although the relations in the given multidimensional database will be defined over the dimensions in D_0, aggregated relations may be defined over any number of dimensions in $\mathcal{D}$. In other words, not all relations vary over all dimensions. However, in MLP, *every* relation is defined over *all* dimensions. This would not create any problems, because the dimensionality analysis would tell us over which dimensions a multidimensional relation actually varies. Also, we stipulate that defined relations are always *aggregation-stratified*, in other words, when a relation is defined using aggregation meta-predicates over some given dimensions all of which defined over the same base dimension, it is always defined in terms of other relations that are defined over dimensions at the same level or at a lower level of the aggregation hierarchy.

A given aggregation operation, say max, over a given aggregate dimension is then performed as follows: The value at a particular element of dimension $d \in D_{i+1}$ is defined as the maximum of the values over the elements of dimension $e \in D_i$ that correspond to the element of d. We can imagine that some other aggregation functions such as avg, sum, min and so on can also be used in a similar fashion.

Suppose that we want to find the maximum number of cars sold in a month in each season by rolling up sales values. We first define a dimension called *season* (representing seasons) over the time dimension where:

$$season = \langle winter00, spring00, summer00, fall00, winter01, spring01, \ldots \rangle$$

and it is associated with a mapping α that assigns each element of *season* a non-empty, finite subset of the elements of *time*.

$\alpha(season) = \{$
    $winter00 \mapsto \{jan00, feb00\},$
    $spring00 \mapsto \{mar00, apr00, may00\},$
    $summer00 \mapsto \{jun00, jul00, aug00\},$
    $fall00 \mapsto \{sep00, oct00, nov00\}, \ldots\}$

Then the following clause would define the desired result (see Figure 3):

```
max_sales(X) <-
    aggregate(sales(X), max, season/time).
```

Note that it would actually suffice to list the name of the tagret dimension (season) only as it is obvious over which dimension the aggregation will be performed and how, because season dimension is in fact defined over time dimension.

Note that the contextual operators init_{season}, prior_{season}, and next_{season} all operate on that dimension. For instance, if the current index for season dimension is, say, $winter00$, then the next index along season dimension is $spring00$.

We might also want to aggregate sales data over years and product groups. Say for instance, we would like to get total sales over years for the product groups of automotives and white-goods. We define a dimension called *product_groups* as follows:

$$product\_groups = \langle automotives, white\_goods \}$$

and it is associated with a mapping α that assigns each element of *product_groups* a non-empty, finite subset of the elements of *product*.

$\alpha(product\_groups) = \{$
    $automotives \mapsto \{car, truck, bus\},$
    $white\_goods \mapsto \{fridge, oven, dishwasher\}\}$

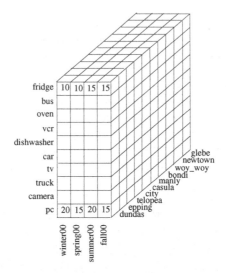

Fig. 3. Max sales data cube over season dimension

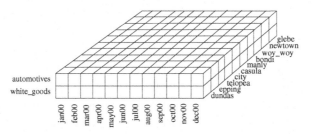

Fig. 4. Aggregate sales data cube over product_groups dimension

We also need another dimension called years: $years = \langle 2000, 2001, 2002, \ldots \rangle$ with its associated mapping:

$$\alpha(years) = \{2000 \mapsto \{jan00, \ldots, dec00\}, 2001 \mapsto \{jan01, \ldots, dec01\}, \ldots\}$$

Then we first aggregate sales data over products:

```
group_sales(X) <-
    aggregate(sales(X), sum, product_groups/product).
```

The resulting relation varies over time, location and product_groups (see Figure 4). The following clause gives yearly sales data over product groups.

```
yearly_sales(X) <-
    aggregate(group_sales(X), sum, years/time).
```

Note that as far as the resulting relation is concerned, the the order of aggregation does not matter; we could aggregate sales data over years first and then over products. However, the former order of aggregation would be more efficient as it directly focuses on the product groups we are interested in.

5   Concluding Remarks

We have presented a deductive formalism which can be used to model and reason about multidimensional objects naturally. We have shown the utility of our formalism in modelling and querying multidimensional databases found in OLAP technology [4]. The formalism provides an application-independent and sound basis for reasoning about multidimensional properties of certain applications, which has been lacking in many approaches reported in the literature. However, not all the standard OLAP facilties are yet supported and they will be considered as future work. The declarative and operational semantics of MLP with aggregation operations (and other OLAP facilities) will also need to be investigated in the context of meta-programming and higher-order logic programming. When coupled with a programmable visual user interface such as the one defined in [8], the implementation of MLP will allow the user to view and analyse a multidimensional relation from different perspectives by providing facilties for OLAP slice and dice operations.

Acknowledgments

This research has been supported in part by an Australian Research Council (ARC) grant. Thanks are also due to Weichang Du for many fruitful discussions.

References

1. S. Agrawal, A. Gupta, and S. Sarawagi. Modeling multidimensional databases. Technical report, IBM Almaden Research Center, San Jose, California, 1995.
2. L. Cabibbo and R. Torlone. Querying multidimensional databases. In *Proceedings of the Sixth Workshop on Database Programming Languages*, 1997.
3. S. Chaudhuri and U. Dayal. An overview of data warehousing and OLAP technology. *SIGMOD RECORD*, 26(1):65–74, 1997.
4. G. Colliat. OLAP, Relational, and multidimensional database systems. *SIGMOD RECORD*, 25(3):64–69, September 1996.
5. R. A. Kowalski. *Logic for Problem Solving*. North–Holland Publishing Company, Amsterdam, 1979.
6. L. Libkin and L. Wong. A query language for multidimensional arrays: Design, implementation and optimization techniques. In *Proceedings of the 1996 ACM SIGMOD International Conference on Management of Data*, pages 228–239. ACM Press, 1996.
7. W. H. Mitchell. Intensional Horn clause logic as a programming language – it's use and implementation. Master's thesis, Department of Computer Science and Engineering, Arizona State University, Tempe, Arizona, 1988.
8. M. A. Orgun and W. Du. Multidimensional logic programming: Theoretical foundations. *Theoretical Computer Science*, 185(2):319–345, 1997.
9. Kenan Technologies. An introduction to multidimensional database technology. http://www.kenan.com/acumate/mddb.htm.

Multidimensional XML[*]

Yannis Stavrakas[1], Manolis Gergatsoulis[1], and Panos Rondogiannis[2]

[1] Institute of Informatics & Telecommunications,
National Centre for Scientific Research (N.C.S.R.) 'Demokritos',
153 10 Aghia Paraskevi Attikis, Greece.
{ystavr,manolis}@iit.demokritos.gr
[2] Department of Computer Science
University of Ioannina,
P.O. Box 1186, GR45110, Ioannina, Greece.
prondo@cs.uoi.gr

Abstract. The Extensible Markup Language (XML) tends to become a widely accepted formalism for the representation and exchange of data over the Web. A problem that often arises in practice is the representation in XML of data that are context-dependent (for example, information that exists in many different languages, in many degrees of detail, and so on). In this paper we propose an extension of XML, namely *MXML or Multidimensional XML*, which can be used in order to alleviate the problem of representing such context-dependent (or *multidimensional*) data. Apart from its usefulness in the semistructured data domain, MXML also reveals some new and promising research directions in the area of multidimensional languages.

1 Introduction

The Extensible Markup Language (XML) [1,6,19,11] is a data description language which tends to become standard for representing and exchanging data over the Web. Although elegant and concise, the syntax of XML does not allow for convenient representation of multidimensional information. Suppose that one wants to represent in XML information that exists in different variations (for example in different languages, in various degrees of detail, or in different time points). With the current XML technology, a solution would be to create a different XML document for every possible variation. Such an approach however is certainly not practical, because it involves excessive duplication of information (especially if the number of variations is high and there exist large identical parts that remain unchanged between variations).

In this paper we propose a solution to the above problem, based on ideas that originate from the area of *multidimensional programming languages* [4,14]. More

---

[*] This work has been partially supported by the Greek General Secretariat of Research and Technology under the project "Executable Intensional Languages and Intelligent Applications in Multimedia, Hypermedia and Virtual Reality" of $\Pi ENE\Delta$'99, contract no 99EΔ265.

specifically, we propose the language *Multidimensional XML (MXML)* which extends traditional XML with the capability of representing context dependent information in a compact way. The development of MXML was influenced by the ideas behind the design of *Intensional HTML* [20,8,7]. In contrast to IHTML, which aims at handling multidimensional information at a document level, the goal of MXML is to provide a formalism for representing and exchanging context-dependent data over the web. Apart from its applications in the XML domain, the study of MXML revealed new ideas that are of interest in the area of multidimensional languages.

2 Preliminaries

2.1 Extensible Markup Language

The basic component in XML is the *element*, which is a piece of data bounded by matching tags (markup) of the form <element-name> and </element-name>, called *start-tag* and *end-tag* respectively. Element names in XML are defined at will so that they best represent data domains. Inside an element we may have other elements, called *subelements*.

Markup encodes a description of the storage layout and the logical structure of the document. An XML document [6,19] consists of nested element structures, starting with a root element. The data in the element are in the form of character data, subelements, or attributes.

XML allows us to associate *attributes* with elements. Attributes in XML are declared within element start tags and have the form of a sequence of name-value pairs. The value of an attribute is always a string enclosed in quotation marks. Unlike subelements, where a subelement with the same name can be repeated inside an element, an attribute name may only occur once within a given element.

Example 1 shows a piece of XML document that contains information about a book.

Example 1. A sample XML document.

```
<bibliography>
    <book isbn="12345678" publisher = "pb1">
        <author>
                <firstname> Manolis </firstname>
                <lastname> Gergatsoulis </lastname>
        </author>
        <author>
                <firstname> Panos </firstname>
                <lastname> Rondogiannis </lastname>
        </author>
        <title> Multidimensional Programming Languages </title>
        <price currency = "USD"> 100 </price>
```

```
        <year> 2000 </year>
</book>
...other book elements ...

<publisher id = "pb1">
        NCSR Demokritos
</publisher>
...other publisher elements ...
```

`</bibliography>`

In this example, the element book has the attributes isbn and publisher. It also has five subelements. The first two represent the authors of the book, while the rest represent the title, the price and the publication year of the book. The attribute publisher of the book element refers to the publisher element.

A key feature of XML is the capability to specify the structure of XML documents through the use of *Document Type Definitions* (DTDs). A DTD declares constraints on elements and attributes and can be viewed as a context free grammar for XML documents, or as a kind of schema for XML data. A document may refer to a DTD to which it conforms.

2.2   Multidimensional Formalisms

The idea of "dimension enabled" languages is not new. Possibly the first multidimensional programming language is the (functional) language GLU [3,4]. GLU allows the user to declare dimensions, and to define multidimensional entities that vary across these dimensions. So, a two-dimensional entity can be thought as an infinite table, a three-dimensional one as a cube extending infinitely across the three dimensions, and so on. One can perform various operations with arguments such higher-dimensional entities, or even define functions that take them as parameters and return new entities as results. Moreover, the language supports intensional operators that work along each different dimension. A language in the spirit of GLU has also been developed in the logic programming domain [14].

An area in which multidimensionality appears to offer significant benefits is the area of *version control* [16]. The intensional versioning approach described in [16] has recently found applications in the evolving area of Internet computing. One example application in this domain is the development of the language IHTML (Intensional HTML) [20,8,7,18], a high-level Web authoring language. The main advantage of IHTML over HTML is that it allows practical specification of Web pages that can exist in many different variations. Web sites created by IHTML are easier to maintain and require significantly less space when compared to the sites created by cloning conventional HTML files.

Finally, we should mention the language ISE [17] which is a multidimensional version of Perl. ISE is more general purpose than IHTML and it is expected to have a broader range of applications.

3   Multidimensional XML

When modelling the real world, the same entity may often have multiple facets. For example, a technical document concerning a car may vary according to the language, the metric system (i.e. miles, or kilometres), the price currency, etc. of the potential customer. In classical XML one has to write different XML documents, each one representing a possible variation. In multidimensional XML we are allowed to specify elements that may exhibit varying content and structure, by assigning them dimensions. This is done by extending the syntax of XML.

3.1   Syntax of Multidimensional XML Documents

A Multidimensional XML document (MXML document) is presented in example 2.

Example 2. A sample multidimensional XML document:

```
<bibliography>
    <book isbn="12345678" publisher = "pb1">
        <author>
                [language = English]
                    <firstname> Manolis </firstname>
                    <lastname> Gergatsoulis </lastname> [/]
                [language = Greek]
                    <firstname> Μανόλης </firstname>
                    <lastname> Γεργατσούλης</lastname> [/]
        </author>
        <author>
                [language = English]
                    <firstname> Panos </firstname>
                    <lastname> Rondogiannis </lastname> [/]
                [language = Greek]
                    <firstname>Πάνος</firstname>
                    <lastname> Ρουτογιάννης </lastname> [/]
        </author>
        <title>
            [language = English]
                Multidimensional Programming Languages [/]
            [language = Greek]
                Πολυδιάστατες Γλώσσες Προγραμματισμού[/]
        </title>
        <price currency= "USD">
            [period = discount client = regular]
                100 [/]
            [period = normal client = regular]
                120 [/]
```

```
                  [period in {discount, normal} client = special]
                      100 [/]
              </price>
              <year> 1999 </year>
          </book>
          ...other book elements ...

          <publisher id = "pb1">
              [language = English] NCSR Demokritos [/]
              [language = Greek] ΕΚΕΦΕ Δημόκριτος [/]
          </publisher>
          ...other publisher elements ...


</bibliography>
```

The document in example 2 is a multidimensional extension of the document
in example 1. The elements **author** and the elements **title** and **publisher**
have two versions each. One corresponding to the value **English** of the dimension
language and the other corresponding to the value **Greek** of the same dimension.

The element **price** depends on two dimensions namely **period** and **client**.
Notice that in general an element or an attribute may depend on zero, one or
more dimensions. The dimensions are considered orthogonal in the sense that
the value of one dimension does not depend on the values of another dimension.
Each dimension may be assigned to more than one elements or attributes.

By the term *context* we refer to a set of dimension-value pairs assigned to a
given element or attribute.

The syntax of XML is extended as follows in order to incorporate the use of
dimensions. In particular, an element in MXML has the form:

```
      <element_name attribute_specification>
          [context_specifier_1]
              element_contents_1
          [/]

                  .
                  .
                  .

          [context_specifier_n]
              element_contents_n
          [/]
      </element_name>
```

where element_contents_i, with $1 \leq i \leq n$ is the contents of the element
for the context specified by context_specifier_i. Note that all the alternative
element_contents_i above, are within the same element "element_name". In
addition, all contents of an element must occur inside a context specifier; in other

words context specifiers cannot occur freely inside element contents, instead they are "attached" to element names. A *context specifier* is of the form:

dimension_1_specifier,...,dimension_m_specifier

where dimension_i_specifier, for i = 1 to m is a *dimension specifier* of the form:

dimension_name specifier_operator dimension_value_expression

A *specifier_operator* is one of =, ! =, in, not in. If the *specifier_operator* is either = or ! = then the *dimension_value_expression* consists of a single dimension value. Otherwise, if the *specifier_operator* is one of in, not in then the *dimension value expression* is a set of the form $\{value_1, ..., value_k\}$, with $k \geq 1$.

For example the following expressions are valid context specifiers:

[language in {Greek, English, French}]
[language = Greek]
[language != French]

Note that we assume that the dimension-value expressions that correspond to a specific element must be formulated in such a way so as no two of them are concurrently satisfied.

An attribute may also depend on dimensions, in which case, the syntax is similar to that of elements. Thus, the attribute_specification is of the form:

attribute_name =
        [context_specifier_1]
                attribute_value_1
        [/]

                .
                .

        [context_specifier_n]
                attribute_value_n
        [/]

4   On the Semantics of MXML

In this section, we discuss in brief some points related to the semantics of MXML.

4.1   Scoping of Dimensions

A dimension assigned a value in an element retain its value in all the descendant elements of this element. However, if a dimension which has been assigned a value in an element E, is assigned a new value in a descendant E1 of E, then the active value of that dimension for E1 and its descendants is the value of the dimension assigned in element E1.

Dimensions for attributes are independent of the dimensions of elements. Moreover, the values of the dimensions of an attribute apply only to the specific attribute.

4.2 Multidimensional OEM

Object Exchange Model (OEM) is a simple graph-based data model for semi-structured data designed at Stanford as a part of the Tsimmis project [9]. Due to the semistructured nature of XML, it has also been adopted for modelling XML documents. In OEM, an XML document is represented as a graph with a single root. The nodes represent the element contents while the edges represent the element names, with leaves holding character data. Attribute values are given on corresponding nodes, and attribute references are depicted as dashed lines [2].

In order for OEM to model MXML documents we have to adapt it so as to represent elements and attributes whose contents vary according to dimension values. For this, we extend OEM by introducing another type of node-edge pair, which is represented by a thick line departing from a square. The square is called *context node* while the thick line is called *context edge*. The MOEM model of the MXML document of example 2 is shown in figure 1.

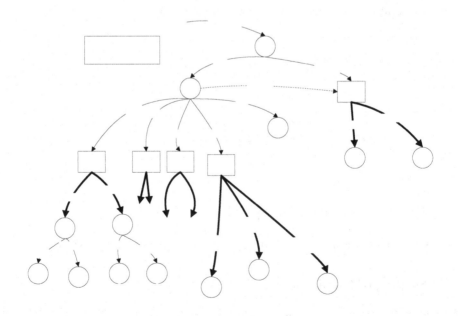

Fig. 1. The Multidimensional OEM model for example 2.

For each multidimensional element (whose value depends on a number of contexts), there corresponds a context node and a set of context edges departing from this node. Each context edge represents a possible context and leads to the content of the element for the specific context.

Attributes whose values depend on contexts are represented in a similar way. Attribute values qualified by the dimension values are given on corresponding nodes. In the case of attribute references, the dashed line of the OEM model leads to a context node from which context attribute edges depart (denoted by thick lines). Each context edge leads to the element node to which the attribute refers for the specific context.

It is easy to see that, from a given MXML document we can obtain a set of ordinary XML documents, each one corresponding to different combination of choices of context edges.

5   Discussion and Future Work

The MXML formalism presented in this paper attempts to remedy what seems to be a shortcomming of XML, namely its inability to represent context-dependent information in a concise way. Although MXML has inherited many features from existing multidimensional formalisms, it also appears to lead to new interesting and unexplored issues of multidimensionality. In the following we discuss the relationship of MXML with other formalisms and also outline new directions for future research.

Relationships with Existing Formalisms: MXML has been mainly influenced from the work on IHTML [20,8,7] (Intensional HTML). In fact, the work on MXML started as an attempt to transfer the research results of the IHTML project, to the more data-oriented formalism of XML. The main difference between IHTML and MXML is a projection of the difference between HTML and XML. IHTML is focused on the composition and presentation of hyperdocuments while MXML is focused on data representation mainly for information exchange purposes. In this context MXML has to deal with problems such as assigning dimensions to the arbitrary structure of XML data. Other XML-ralated issues such as DTDs and XML query languages give an interesting research direction to XML.

Future Research Problems: There are many aspects of the MXML formalism that the authors would like to further investigate. In the following we list some of them:

- In the current discussion we have made the assumption that a MXML document exists without reference to an existing DTD (Document Type Definition). DTD are formalisms similar to *types* in programming languages and their purpose is to impose restrictions on what a particular document can contain. For example, a DTD can specify that a document describing a book can only contain a single <title> element. In this paper we have not considered DTDs with respect to MXML documents. It is quite possible that MXML will require the definition of MDTDs (Multidimensional DTDs).

- We have not considered any particular query language for MXML. Research in query languages for XML is especially active [12,13,5]. We believe that a query language for MXML would have to take *contexts* into account.
- A potential application of MXML which we are currently investigating concerns the representation of time-dependent information. Much work has been carried out in the past on temporal databases [15]. The need to incorporate time information is also present in the case of semistructured data [10]. However to the best of our knowledge, no such extension has been considered for XML.
- There is currently no existing implementation of the ideas presented in this paper. The authors plan to undertake such an implementation of MXML together with an associated query language.

We believe that further research in the relationships between semistructured data and multidimensionality, will reveal many issues from which both worlds will gain significant benefits.

References

1. S. Abiteboul, P. Buneman, and D. Suciu. *Data on the Web: From Relations to Semistructured Data and XML*. Morgan Kaufmann Publishers, 2000.
2. Serge Abiteboul. On views and XML. In *Proceedings of the 18th ACM SIGACT-SIGMOD-SIGART Symposium on Principles of Data Base Systems*, pages 1–9. ACM Press, 1999.
3. E. A. Ashcroft, A. A. Faustini, and R. Jagannathan. An intensional language for parallel applications programming. In B.K.Szymanski, editor, *Parallel Functional Languages and Compilers*, pages 11–49. ACM Press, 1991.
4. E. A. Ashcroft, A. A. Faustini, R. Jagannathan, and W. W. Wadge. *Multidimensional programming*. Oxford University Press, 1995.
5. A. Bonifati and S. Ceri. Comparative analysis of five XML query languages. *SIGMOND Record*, 29(1), March 2000.
6. T. Bray, J. Paoli, and C. M. Sperberg-McQueen. Extensible markup language (XML) 1.0. http://www.w3.org/TR/REC-xml, 1998.
7. G. D. Brown. IHTML 2: Design and Implementation. In W. W. Wadge, editor, *Proceedings of the 11th International Symposium on Languages for Intensional Programming*, 1998.
8. G. D. Brown. Intensional HTML 2: A practical Approach. Master's thesis, Department of Computer Science, University of Victoria, 1998.
9. S. Chawathe, H. Garcia-Molina, J. Hammer, K. Ireland, Y. Papakonstantinou, J. Ullman, and J. Widom. The TSIMMIS project: Integration of heterogeneous information sources. In *Proceedings of IPSJ Conference, Tokyo, Japan, October*, pages 7–18, 1994.
10. S. S. Chawathe, S. Abiteboul, and J. Widom. Representing and quering changes in semistructured data. *Theory and Practice of Object Systems (TAPOS)*, 2000. Special Issue on Object-Oriented Technology in Advanced Applications (to appear).
11. Sudarshan S. Chawathe. Describing and manipulating XML data. *Bulletin of the IEEE Computer Society Technical Committee on Data Engineering*, 22(3):3–9, September 1999.

12. A. Deutch, M. Fernández, D. Florescu, A. Levy, and D. Suciu. XML-QL: A query language for XML. http://www.w3.org/TR/NOTE-xml-ql, 1999.

13. A. Deutsch, M. Fernández, D. Florescu, A. Levy, D. Maier, and D. Suciu. Quering XML data. *Bulletin of the IEEE Computer Society Technical Committee on Data Engineering*, 22(3):10–18, September 1999.

14. M. A. Orgun and W. Du. Multi-dimensional logic programming: Theoretical foundations. *Theoretical Computer Science*, 158(2):319–345, 1997.

15. G. Ozsoyoglu and R. T. Snodgrass. Temporal and real-time databases: A survey. *IEEE Transactions on Knowledge and Data Engineering*, 7(4):513–532, August 1995.

16. J. Plaice and W. W. Wadge. A New Approach to Version Control. *IEEE Transactions on Software Engineering*, 19(3):268–276, 1993.

17. P. Swoboda and W. W. Wadge. Vmake and Ise General Tools for the Intensionalization of Software Systems. In M. Gergatsoulis and P. Rondogiannis, editors, *Intensional Programming II*, pages 310–320. World Scientific, 2000.

18. W.W. Wadge, G. D. Brown, m.c. schraefel, and T. Yildirim. Intensional HTML. In *Proceedings of the Fourth International Workshop on Principles of Digital Document Processing (PODDP '98)*, Lecture Notes in Computer Science (LNCS) 1481, pages 128–139. Springer-Verlag, March 1998.

19. Norman Walsb. A guide to XML. *World Wide Web Journal "XML:Principles, Tools and Techniques"*, 2(4):97–107, 1997.

20. T. Yildirim. Intensional HTML. Master's thesis, Department of Computer Science, University of Victoria, 1997.

Application Programming Interface for WOSP/WOSRP

Gilbert Babin[1], Hauke Coltzau[2], Markus Wulff[2], and Simon Ruel[1]

[1] Département d'informatique, Université Laval,
Sainte-Foy (Québec) Canada G1K 7P4
{babin,ruelsimo}@ift.ulaval.ca
[2] Fachbereich Informatik, Universität Rostock,
18059 Rostock, Germany
{django,mwulff}@informatik.uni-rostock.de

Abstract. The Web Operating System (WOS™) allows for a user to submit a service request without any prior knowledge about the service and to have it fulfilled according to the user's desired constraints/requirements. Such services may be specialized hardware or software, or both. The WOS considers the communication layer to be the centralized part. The communication protocols may thus be seen as the "glue" of the WOS architecture. This paper presents an Application Programming Interface (API) to access WOS communication services. In order to present how the communication layer works, we introduce all the concepts related to the communications in the WOS and will show how these components are put together to support communication.

1 Introduction

The Web Operating System (WOS™) [3,4,5] was developed to provide a user with the possibility to submit a service request without any prior knowledge about the service (where it is available, at what cost, under which constraints) and to have the service request fulfilled within the user's desired parameters (time, cost, quality of service, etc.). In other words, the WOS is designed to enable transparent usage of network-accessible resources, whenever a user requires a service, wherever the service is available. These services may be specialized hardware or software, or a combination of both. A user needs only to understand the WOS interface, and does not need to known how the service request is fulfilled. Therefore the WOS provides a computation model and the associated tools to enable seamless and ubiquitous sharing and interactive use of software and hardware resources available on the Internet.

The WOS is designed as a fully distributed architecture of interconnectec nodes where the communication protocols are considered to be the centralized parts. The communication protocols may thus be seen as the "glue" of the WOS architecture. Communication between nodes is realized through a simple discovery/location protocol, the WOS Request Protocol (WOSRP), and a generic service protocol, the WOS Protocol (WOSP). The WOSP protocol is in fact

P. Kropf et al. (Eds.): DCW 2000, LNCS 1830, pp. 110–121, 2000.

a protocol language with a corresponding parser and serves to easily configure service-specific protocol instances. For example, one WOSP instance could implement an interface to XML, CBL (Common Business Library) or GIOP/IIOP of CORBA. At the lower levels of the protocol stack, we assume the usage of the TCP/IP protocol family.

This paper describes an Application Programming Interface (API) to access WOS communication services provided by WOSP/WOSRP. The need for new mechanisms to use communications in the WOS has arisen from WOS application developers who wanted to have a better control over communications. Many versions of WOSP may exist. Each version supports the communications for one class of services provided by the WOS. All these versions, however, share a common syntax. From a pure object-oriented perspective, we clearly see that a single class (*WOSP_Parser*) can manage syntax processing, while multiple classes are required to process the semantics. This is exactly what was done in the first implementation of the WOS communication layer [1,2]. To make this possible, we had defined a class (*WOSP_Analyzer*) which was specialized for each version of WOSP. Once a message was processed for its syntax, the *WOSP_Parser* class would locate the appropriate specialization which would process the semantics.

We identified two majors problems with this approach:

1. The service classes could not be developed independently from the communication layer, because they had to specialize *WOSP_Analyzer*.
2. The communication layer was controlling the flow of processing for the whole system, since *WOSP_Parser* was explicitly calling the specialized *WOSP_Analyzer*.

In addition, the initial design of WOSRP/WOSP assumed that a synchronous dialog was required between two nodes in the connection-oriented mode. It turns out that this requirement imposes too much constraints on the service class developer. For instance, the application developer must guarantee that all communications between clients and servers be synchronized.

The new API presented in this paper alleviates these problems by removing every aspects of the semantics processing from the communication layer. This should provide more flexibility to the service class developper. It also supports asynchronous communications between clients and servers. In order to present how the new communication layer API works, we first introduce all the concepts related to the communications in the WOS (Sect. 2). We will then show how these components are put together to support these communications (Sect. 3). We conclude this article in Sect. 4.

2   Communication Concepts for the WOS

This section presents some basic concepts required to understand communications in the WOS.

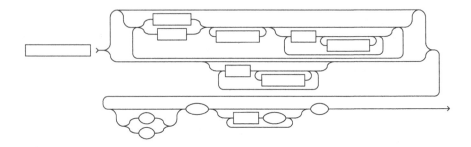

Fig. 1. WOSP generic syntax

2.1 WOSP Message

A WOSP message is a data stream that has the syntax illustrated in Fig. 1, where `<message>` may be a command or a reply. For a command, we provide the command type (execution, query, setup), the command name, and the command identifier. The command identifier is composed of the WOSP message identifier (see Sect. 2.4), the position of the command within the message, and the number of data and metadata elements describing the command. For a reply, we provide the identifier of the original command to which this reply is addressed and a command identifier.

Applications using WOSP to communicate do not create that data stream. Indeed, each element of the WOSP message syntax may be represented by a data structure called a triplet. A triplet contains three fields, as indicated by its name : a triplet type, a triplet name, and a triplet value. Table 1 shows how WOSP message information is stored in a triplet.

Table 1. WOS triplet structure

Type	Name	Value
EXECUTE	name of execution command	command identifier
QUERY	name of query command	command identifier
SETUP	name of setup command	command identifier
REPLY	identifier of command to which this is a reply	command identifier
DATA	name of data field	value of data field
METADATA	name of metadata field	value of metadata field
FILE	local name of data file	*not used*

A message is therefore composed of a list of triplets. When sending a message, the application composes a list of triplets that it provides to the WOS communication layer. When receiving a message, the application receives a list of triplets from the WOS communication layer.

Because all WOSP messages use the same syntax, a single module may be used to construct a data stream from the list of triplets and vice versa. The interpretation of the content of the message depends on the version of WOSP. Therefore, the different versions of WOSP correspond to the different semantics that we can associate to the basic syntactic elements presented here.

2.2 WOSRP Messages

The WOS Request Protocol (WOSRP) serves two purposes : locating versions of service families (i.e., specific WOSP versions) and transmitting WOSP messages to an appropriate server (version and service family). To locate services, two types of messages are used, namely WOSRP request and WOSRP reply message types.

Two modes are available to transmit WOSP messages : connectionless mode and connection-oriented mode. In connectionless mode, an application sends a single WOSP message to another application which acts as a server to a specific WOSP version, without establishing a long term connection with that node; once the message is transmitted, the connection is closed. In this case, the WOSRP message is used to identify the appropriate WOSP version server and to encapsulate the WOSP message.

In connection-oriented mode, the application must explicitly establish a connection with a specific WOSP version server. Once the connection is established, it can send and receive WOSP messages asynchronously, until the connection is closed or broken. In this case, the WOSRP message is used to establish the connection with the appropriate WOSP version server.

2.3 Message Queues

In order to enable fully asynchronous communications, WOSP and WOSRP messages must be queued at the receiving side of the communication link. Therefore, the WOS communication servers put the received WOSP and WOSRP messages into appropriate queues. Once an application is ready to process the next message, it requests it from a queue. A queue is uniquely identified by a Message Queue Identifier (MQID; see Sect. 2.4). We will now present the different queue types used by the WOS communication layer.

WOSRP Request Queue. Queues of this type contain WOSRP requests received by a WOS node. A given WOS node will have *only one* queue of that type.
WOSRP Reply Queue. Queues of this type contain WOSRP replies received by a WOS node. A given WOS node will have *only one* queue of that type.
WOSP Connectionless Queues. Queues of this type will contain WOSP messages received in connectionless mode by a WOS node for a specific WOSP version. A WOS node may therefore have *zero or more* such queues.
WOSP Connection Request Queues. Queues of this type will contain WOSP connection requests received by a WOS node for a specific WOSP version. A WOS node may therefore have *zero or more* such queues. However, there

will be *at most one* such queue for every WOSP version known by a WOS node.

WOSP Connection-oriented Queues. Queues of this type will contain WOSP messages received in connection-oriented mode by a WOS node. They are bound to a WOSP connection. There will be *one* such queue for every WOSP connection established with another WOS node.

2.4 Message Identifiers

One of the concerns in WOS communications is that every message is uniquely identified. We also want the identifiers used to support very fast CPUs, where a large number of messages may be generated by the same machine within a short time interval. The WOSP Message identifier is built with these constraints in mind. It is the concatenation of the following elements :

1. the domain name (or IP address) of the machine sending the message,
2. the port number where replies should be sent to,
3. the MQID where replies should be stored, and
4. a timestamp.

The MQID is a timestamp representing the moment where the queue was created. Timestamps (and MQIDs) have the following syntax :

1. the year (4 digits),
2. the month (2 digits),
3. the day of the month (2 digits),
4. the hour (2 digits),
5. the minutes (2 digits),
6. the seconds (2 digits),
7. a 5 character alphanumerical string (taken from a list of ASCII characters non conflicting with the communication layer).

Timestamps (and MQID) are provided by a single server running on the WOS node to avoid duplicates and therefore guarantee unicity.

2.5 WOSP Version Identifiers

Every version of WOSP must be uniquely identified. Furthermore, the possible number of existing versions may grow quite large. Consequently, the format of WOSP version identifiers must accommodate a potentially large domain of values. We chose to identify WOSP versions using a string of 448 Bytes, thus allowing for 2^{3584} ($\approx 10^{1079}$) distinct values.

2.6   Queue Servers

The WOS communication layer is responsible for receiving and placing into the appropriate queue all the WOSP and WOSRP messages addressed to a specific WOS node. However, the communication layer does not process these messages. This is accomplished by queue servers. A queue server is an application that informs the WOS communication layer that it will process messages put into a specific queue. We say that the application "registers" as the queue server.

A queue may have at most one queue server. However, an application may act as queue server for many queues. For each queue type, the communication layer knows one application that acts as default queue server for that queue type. This way, if a queue is not empty but no application has registered as queue server, the WOS communication layer can launch an application that will register as queue server (the default queue server).

3   Operation of the Communication Layer

The Communication Layer is responsible for the reception of incoming messages and the transmission of outgoing messages. In this section, we present how these two functions are achieved and how the user applications may access these services of the communication layer. The prototype of the communication layer was developed in JAVA. The communications between WOS nodes are achieved using TCP/IP while access to the API by a WOS application is achieved using the Remore Method Invocation package (RMI) supplied with Sun's JAVA Development Toolkit (JDK).

3.1   Registering Queue Servers

The registration process depends on the queue type. For WOSRP request queues (*WOS_RegisterRequestServer()*) and WOSRP reply queues (*WOS_RegisterReplyServer()*), the application selects the appropriate method. If an application is already registered for these queues, the registration will fail. Otherwise, the application will receive the MQID.

For WOSP connectionless queues, the application must provide the WOSP version (*WOS_RegisterConnectionlessServer(VersionID)*). Depending on which version of WOSP is used, many WOSP connectionless queues may be active for the same WOS node. On receiving a WOSP message in connectionless mode, the communication layer will dispatch the message parts to the appropriate queue (using the WOSP message identifier; not yet implemented).

For WOSP connection request queues, the application must also provide the WOSP version (*WOS_RegisterConnectionServer(VersionID)*). In this case, at most one application may register to act as connection request server for a specific WOSP version.

Applications do not need to register as WOSP connection-oriented queue server. This is done implicitly when the connection is acknowledged. When a connection request is made, the WOSP connection request queue server launches the appropriate application and supplies it the MQID of the corresponding WOSP connection-oriented queue. The queue is removed when the connection is closed.

3.2   Receiving WOSRP and WOSP Messages

Initially, no message queue is available. A queue is created by the WOS communication layer either when a new message of a specific type is received, in which case the corresponding default queue server is launched, or when an application registers as queue server.

For any new message it receives, the communication layer first determines its type. This type is used to place the message in the appropriate message queue. In the case of connectionless WOSP messages, a more detailed analysis of the message is needed. Since many applications may act as queue server for a specific WOSP version, the communication layer must dispatch replies to the appropriate queue by looking at the command identifier of each command contained in the message. This dispatch feature is not yet implemented; in the current implementation, connectionless messages are stored in the first queue found for the corresponding WOSP version.

Figure 2 illustrates in more details how a (WOSP or WOSRP) message is processed. In the first step, the relevant WOSRP Connection Server (either for TCP connections or UDP datagrams) retrieves the message from the network. The message is processed by the WOSP/WOSRP Message Manager (Step 2) which, in turn, issues a warehouse (cache) lookup request (Steps 3 and 4) to the Search Engine to determine whether this version is already served or not, and if not, to retrieve the command to launch the corresponding default queue server. The message is then stored in the appropriate queue.

The queue server eventually fetches a message (Step 6) with one of the following methods:

WOS_GetMessage(MQID). This method is used to retrieve the next available message in the message queue identified by MQID, if any message is available.

WOS_WaitForMessage(MQID). This method waits indefinitely for the next available message in the message queue identified by MQID.

WOS_WaitForMessage(MQID, t). This method waits at most t seconds for the next available message in the message queue identified by MQID.

The WOSP/WOSRP Message Manager locates the appropriate queue (Step 7) and returns the first message found (Step 8), if any, depending on the access method used.

3.3   Sending WOSRP and WOSP Messages

In general, all WOS messages are sent using the same mechanisms. However, variations exist which we will describe in details later in this section. Figure 3 presents an overview of the transmission process. Requests for sending messages are made to the WOS Communication API (Steps 1 and 2). The API accesses

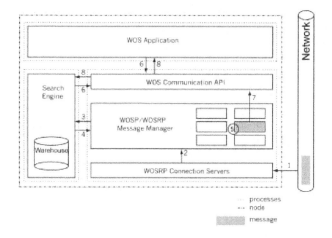

Fig. 2. Receiving messages at a WOS node

the appropriate module within the WOSP/WOSRP Message Manager to build either a WOSRP or a WOSP message (Step 3; see the following subsections), which, in turn, is sent to the network (Step 4).

Sending WOSRP Messages. Any application may send WOSRP requests and replies. Special commands are available for that purpose:

WOSRP_Request(...). This method is used to send WOSRP requests.
WOSRP_Reply(...). This method is used to send WOSRP replies.

Establishing WOSP Connections. For connection-oriented communications, a connection must first be established. An application sends a connection request message and waits for a positive acknowledgment (or a timeout) using the method *WOSP_SetupConnection(...)* with the appropriate arguments. On receiving such a request, a WOS node creates a WOSP connection-oriented queue and the connection request message containing the MQID of the newly created queue is put in the WOSP connection request queue for the appropriate WOSP version. The corresponding connection request queue server decides to accept (*WOSP_AcceptConnection(MQID)*) or not (*WOSP_RejectConnection(MQID)*) the connection. The communication layer may also throw a timeout exception if the connection request queue server takes too much time to process the connection request. In this case, the message is removed from the queue, a negative acknowledgment is sent to the requesting machine, and the WOSP connection-oriented queue is removed. The requesting application will then receive a null value to indicate that the request for connection failed.

When the connection is accepted, a positive acknowledgment is sent to the requesting node. On reception of the acknowledgment, a local WOSP connection-oriented queue is created and the MQID is supplied to the requesting application.

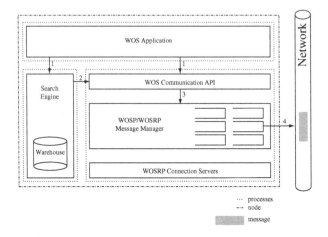

Fig. 3. Sending messages at a WOS node

Sending WOSP Messages. WOSP messages are sent directly to a remote host without establishing a connection or through an already established connection using one or the other form of the method *WOSP_SendMessage(...)*. We will now see how the communication layer transmits these messages.

WOSP Connectionless Messages. An application may send a WOSP connectionless message using one of two approaches :

1. by specifying the remote host IP address and port number (optional) of the remote WOS communication server. In this case, the WOSP message identifier is generated using the default WOSP connectionless queue for the specified WOSP version. If no such queue exists, one is created.
2. by providing a WOSP connectionless queue identifier, along with the remote host IP address and port number (optional) of the remote WOS communication server. In this case, the WOSP message identifier is generated using the MQID provided.

WOSP Connection-oriented Messages. Sending a WOSP message in connection-oriented mode requires that a connection be established. Access to the connection is given by the WOSP connection-oriented queue ID supplied to the application when then connection was created. Therefore, the application must only provide the MQID associated to the connection to send a message.

Furthermore, a node may request that the connection be closed. This information will be part of the WOSP message (the special "!!" command in the WOSP syntax). The other participant must acknowledge the termination of the connection. Again, this information will also be part of the WOSP message (the special "$!" command in the WOSP syntax). The connection is closed only when both sides have agreed on the termination of the connection. The communication layer keeps track of close-connection requests and acknowledgments.

3.4   A Complete Example

The WOS communication layer is accessed by using RMI services. It must therefore create a reference to an RMI registry, which will be used to locate the interface to the communication layer. A WOS application should have the following structure :

```java
import java.net.*;
import java.rmi.*;
import java.rmi.registry.*;
import wos.comm.interf.*;
import wos.comm.message.*;
public static void main ( String argv[] ) {
   Registry register;
   WOS_Client interface = null;
   try{
      String hostName = InetAddress.getLocalHost().getHostName();
      register = LocateRegistry.getRegistry(hostName);
      interface = (WOS_Client) register.lookup("WOS_Interface");
      // Your code is placed here
   } catch (java.net.UnknownHostException e){
   } catch (NotBoundException e) {
   } catch (RemoteException e) {
   }
}
```

The object *interface* will provide the access to all the methods of the communication layer.

We show here a complete communication cycle for a WOSRP request/reply (Fig. 4). The cycle comprises 4 sequences of actions, represented by the different dashed lines. Each sequence starts at a numbered circle, the number indicating the relative order of the sequence. We describe each of these sequences as follows :

1. A WOS application requests information about an available service class (i.e., a specific WOSP version). The information is not available locally, and a network search is initiated. The message is placed in the appropriate queue at the remote host. The call looks like this:

```java
try {
   InetAddress hostA = InetAddress.getByName("hostA");
   interface.WOSRP_Request(hostA,         // Recipient IP address
                           9671,          // Recipient port number
                           true,          // hostA speaks the version
                           true,          // Version ID included
                           1,             // Hop count
                           "versionID");  // Version looked for
} catch (java.net.UnknownHostException e) {
} catch (java.rmi.RemoteException e) {
}
```

2. The Search Engine fetches the next message in the WOSRP Request queue. This is done with the following call to the API:

```
try {
    String MQID = interface.WOS_RegisterRequestServer();
    WOS_Message msg;
    while ((msg = interface.WOS_WaitForMessage(MQID,60)) != null) {
        // Process msg
    }
    interface.WOS_Unregister(MQID);
} catch (java.rmi.RemoteException e) {}
```

3. An answer (a WOSRP Reply message) is produced and sent to the requesting node. The message is placed in the appropriate queue at the remote host. The JAVA code looks like this:

```
try {
    InetAddress hostA = InetAddress.getByName("hostA");
    InetAddress hostB = InetAddress.getByName("hostB");
    interface.WOSRP_Reply(hostB,        // Recipient IP address
                          9671,         // Recipient port number
                          hostA,        // Server IP address
                          true,         // hostA speaks the version
                          "versionID"); // Version spoken
} catch (java.net.UnknownHostException e) {
} catch (java.rmi.RemoteException e) {}
```

4. The Search Engine fetches the next message in the WOSRP Reply queue. The information is used to provide and answer to the WOS application and to update the local warehouse. This uses the same code as sequence 2, except that we register as reply queue server instead of request queue server.

4   Conclusion

This paper has described the concepts related to the WOS communication layer, required for the development of a new API. Furthermore, a description of the communication mechanisms was provided. This new API was developed using Java programming language. Access to the communication layer is provided by the Remote Invocation Method (RMI) package. In its current implementation, the API only supports queue servers developed in Java. It would be interesting to investigate other implementation approaches for the API that would allow for queue servers to be developed using other languages. One such approach is CORBA.

Although the new API provides a more flexible utilization of the WOS communication layer and supports asynchronous communications, some issues remain unresolved. For instance, a naming scheme (naming space, naming conventions, name assignment, distributed name management, etc.) still needs to be specified.

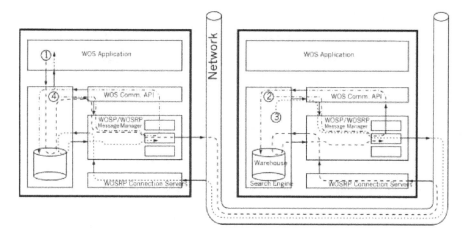

Fig. 4. A WOSRP request/WOSRP reply cycle

We also need to investigate the use of network and/or transport layer protocols other than the TCP/IP protocol family. This will require an extension of the WOSRP protocol to consider other transport mechanisms.

References

1. Gilbert Babin. Requirements for the implementation of WOS^{TM} protocols. In *Distributed Computing on the Web Workshop (DCW'98)*, pages 129–133, Rostock, Germany, June 1998.
2. Gilbert Babin, Peter Kropf, and Herwig Unger. A two-level communication protocol for a Web Operating System (WOS^{TM}). In *IEEE Euromicro Workshop on Network Computing*, pages 939–944, Västerås, Sweden, August 1998.
3. Peter Kropf. Overview of the WOS project. In *1999 Advanced Simulation Technologies Conferences (ASTC 1999)*, San Diego, CA, USA, April 1999.
4. P.G. Kropf, J. Plaice, and H. Unger. Towards a WEB operating system. In *Webnet '97*, Toronto, Canada, November 1997. Association for the advancement of computing in education.
5. John Plaice and Peter Kropf. WOS communities — interactions and relations between entities in distributed systems. In *Distributed Computing on the Web (DCW'99)*, Rostock, Germany, June 1999.

Message Chains and Disjunct Paths for Increasing Communication Performance in Large Networks

Markus Wulff[1], Peter Kropf[2], and Herwig Unger[1]

[1] Universität Rostock, FB Informatik, D-18055 Rostock, Germany,
{mwullf,hunger}@informatik.uni-rostock.de
[2] Université de Montréal, Montréal, Canada H3C 3J7, kropf@iro.umontreal.ca

Abstract. In this paper we propose a simple powerful method to increase communication performance in large networks such as the Internet. Our approach is based on the usage multiple disjunct paths for the transmitting data from one node to another one. The method exploits the dense connectivity of the Internet by making use of the different routes engaged in communications originating from different nodes to one target nodes. We show that depending on the bandwidth offered and the amount of data to be transfered, a linear speedup can be achieved. An experimental implementation of the method within the WOS framework confirms the theoretical analysis of the method.

1 Introduction

To access the huge amount of mostly inefficiently used hard- and software-resources in the Internet, new approaches to use and maintain this potential are needed. The complex, inhomogeneous and dynamic structure of the world-wide network requires decentral, adaptive mechanisms, that provide access to both local and global capacities in a efficient and transparent way [10]. For any system implementing such functionality, it is crucial to provide to the applications and users eased access to advanced network services. In particular, applications and users request for ever more bandwidth and high speed data transmission. However, it is acknowledged that despite the tremendous advances in network technology, there remains a high demand for even more communication capacity. While the network capacities in the context of the global communications infrastructure or the Internet appear to be insufficient, there exists still a potential of using this infrastructure more efficiently. In fact, when considering the traffic on the Internet, we observe that at the lower communication layers the various techniques of multiplexing (time-, frequency-, code-division, etc) are heavily used to maximize the efficient use of the communications infrastructure. As far as the data transfer is concerned, sophisticated compression techniques are applied to decrease communication times.

There exist however, other ways to increase communication speed as observed by an application or user. If we consider a file transfer, the transport layer will

P. Kropf et al. (Eds.): DCW 2000, LNCS 1830, pp. 122–132, 2000.
© Springer-Verlag Berlin Heidelberg 2000

usually set up an end-to-end connection. The network layer usually offers a connectionless packet switching service (e.g. IP). While it might be possible for the packets to travel along different routes, the data transfer still takes place within the scope of the connection set up at the higher level, thus realizing a sequential communication path. These different mechanisms do not improve communication speed (as seen by the application or user), but rather avoid communication bottlenecks. A simple way to increase communication speed would be to use different connections with different communication paths in parallel for different chunks of data from the same data stream.

This paper presents a method allowing to exploit this potential of parallel usage of the global communication infrastructure for a single data stream. First, we briefly present the Web Operating System (WOS™) [9] environment providing application and user support for the transparent use of the global information infrastructure. Sect. 3 introduces the concept of message chains and disjunct paths for parallel communication and formally analyzes the possible gain in communication speed. Finally, Sect. 4 discusses the implementation of the method within the WOS and presents first experimental results.

2   The Web Operating System – A Brief Overview

The Web Operating System (WOS™) [9] is an open middleware solution allowing for software services to be distributed over the Internet. It supports applications and users with mechanisms to offer own resources and to locate and use accessible remote resources while taking advantage of the ever changing software and hardware infrastructure of global systems. The WOS approach to support distributed computing relies on the widespread use of version control techniques. It is a decentralized system, for which there is no complete catalog of available services and resources. Such knowledge is rather dynamically built up and managed. Therefore, the central component of the WOS is a generic communication framework allowing for versioned protocols, used to support communication between components or nodes. Each node operates as a server and a client at the same time and maintains warehouses [14] with information about other nodes. This allows to considerably reduce the response time to requests because expensive search procedures may often be avoided while relying on the information present in the warehouses for fulfilling service requests. The information in these warehouses are continuously updated when new knowledge about other nodes becomes available through service requests issued by the node itself or by other nodes. A collection of such nodes form a WOSNet which is managed in a completely decentralized manner.

The WOS communication layer uses a two-level approach [2]. The first layer offers discovery/location services and the second one is used for service invocation. To build up the WOSNet and to locate requested services and appropriate resources, a search mechanism based on multiple sequential chains has been defined [2,15]. Based on the knowledge of the WOSNet a node belongs to, a set of search chains consisting in a sequence of nodes to visit along disjunct paths is defined prior to starting the search. The search along these chains is thereafter issued in parallel. Theoretical as well as practical investigations have shown the efficiency of this procedure [15].

A WOSNode is composed of different modules to handle communication, i.e. incoming and outgoing messages using the two WOS communication layers, and to process the associated requests for services, resources or system information. The node's information warehouses, which are some form of cache, store information about its own and other nodes' services and resources. In particular, this includes addresses of other known WOSNodes which thereby defines a WOSNet as a logical structure on top of the Internet. Fig. 1 shows an example for such a structure. A WOSNode usually knows the machines in its neighborhood. Other machines can be found through the search mechanisms mentioned above.

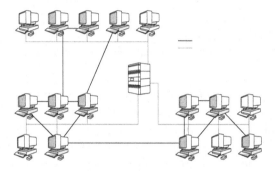

Fig. 1. The structure of the WOSNet.

The possibly large number of nodes, widely spread all over the Internet provide the precondition for new, efficient ways of communication between the machines belonging to the WOSNet by extending the WOS communication layer for exploiting multiple disjunct communication paths between two communicating nodes. The source node of a communication may contact other WOSNodes in his neighborhood which will act as starting or base nodes for using multiple disjunct communication paths to the destination. These multiple paths can be used in parallel and will therefore lower the overall communication time between the source and destination node. It must be noted, that only the source node, the base nodes and the destination node need to be part of a WOSNet. The intermediate nodes may be any node belonging to the Internet.

3   Message Chains and Disjunct Paths

3.1   Internet and Routing

In contrast to parallel and cluster computing systems exhibiting much potential to optimize the communication by different routing algorithms [1,3,4,16], distributed systems mostly just support point to point connections. In some cases, like in subnetworks, broadcasts and multicasts are possible [8]. Because of the large structure of the Internet, routing algorithms cannot be influenced by the user and are rather ruled by standard routing procedures [13]. Other approaches, like [6], try to improve the communication behavior between loosely coupled workstations through low level communication optimization. These approaches are only successful in local environments. Other communication systems like ATM and IPv6 use special mechanisms to provide efficient communication through Quality of Service (QoS) mechanisms and policies [7]. Only few works, such as [11], motivate that user- or application specific dispositions may require the use of disjunct paths in the Internet.

3.2   Multiple Sequential Search Chains

As mentioned in Sect. 2, a search and localization method based on multiple sequential search chains [2,15] has been applied to the WOS framework. This method basically consists in a combination of the broadcast and the serial search and request strategy. The broadcast strategy is used to perform searches in the local area (e.g. on a diffusion based subnetwork such as an Ethernet) and to concurrently initiate multiple serial searches at different nodes in the network. The serial searches are defined through lists of nodes to visit. These lists are built up based on the information available in the node's warehouse. The search for a service or resource consists thus basically in sending search lists to a set of nodes which then concurrently perform the search defined in the associated list for that node. This first step of distributing the lists follows thus conceptually a broadcast or multicast strategy. However, as opposed to pure broadcasting, the data sent to the nodes are individual data. Using a stochastic time estimation model, this strategy was shown to yield very favorable response times [15]. The performance of searching for services and resources can be further improved by using *Message Chains* [17].

3.3   Message Chains and Disjunct Paths

The concept of message chains is based on active messages [5]. Tokens are the basic components of a message chain. Beside the information to be transmitted, each token contains a set of addresses of machines, which must be visited one after the other, thus representing the lists introduced above. Each of those lists defines a *disjunct path* in the network from the source node to the destination node of a communication. The different communication daemons of the machines (way points) support an automatic active forwarding of any token to the next machine in the given chain. In addition, every machine may have to execute a service request as specified for the token processed before forwarding it to the next node. The output of such services is sent directly back to the requesting node or can be attached to the token. An example of such a service might be to provide information about the current load of the communication channels the visited node is connected to.

In complex networks like the Internet, almost every machine can be reached using more than one path. Therefore, two different nodes could use more than one route thereby improving performance. However, it is usually not possible for a user or an application to decide which route a packet (i. g. an IP datagram) should use. This is the responsibility of the lower protocol layers [8]. Furthermore, the default routing between two machines may change from time to time. But these changes of the standard routing paths usually do not occur very frequently, and it is possible to trace a route and to determine the average communication parameters for the transmission.

The message chains and disjunct paths approach takes advantage of the potential of multiple routes. Some selected nodes in the neighborhood of the source node act as base nodes from which the data is transmitted along their respective standard routes to the destination node. The standard routes for these base nodes to the destination node should of course be disjoint or at least differ considerably. This could for example be detected prior to any transmission using ICMP messages in a similar way the `traceroute` utility explores a route.

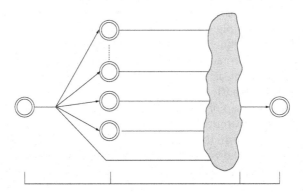

Fig. 2. Communication along disjunct paths.

Fig. 2 shows the principles of a communication using disjunct paths. The source node S can split the message to transmit into n pieces of different sizes and send them to T via the base nodes N_i using n disjunct paths offering the bandwidth $b_0 \ldots b_n$. The standard path with the bandwidth b_0 is the route from S to T without involving any base node. The transmission path from S to T can be divided into two local (near) areas in the vicinity of S and T, and a long distance area (far) between the base nodes N_i and the neighborhood of T.

This communication scheme requires the node S to know suitable base nodes N_i to use disjunct paths. The WOSNet introduced in Sect. 2 defines a logical structure over the Internet and provides the necessary mechanisms to find the nodes which may act as base nodes. Of course, the use of disjunct paths for data transmission makes sense only, if the amount of data to be sent is big enough.

The speedup gained with disjunct paths must be higher than the time necessary to find the bases and their alternate routes.

3.4 Analysis of the Communication Speedup

To analyze the performance of this method, we consider the case of a file transfer from a node S to node T such as illustrated in Fig. 2. There are $n + 1$ paths available with the bandwidth $b_0 \ldots b_n$ to transmit a file of size D. The bandwidth of the standard routing path between S and T is assumed to be b_0. The transmission time t is the total amount of time needed to transmit the data D. In order to achieve a transmission speedup, the time $t_{\text{near}} = t_{\text{near}_1} + t_{\text{near}_2}$ for all local connections from the source S to the bases N_i ($i = 1 \ldots n$) must be much smaller than the time t_{far} for the long distance connections within the network. In this case, the share of t_{far} in the total communication time t determines the potential for communication speedup using disjunct paths. The transmission time for sending the data using the standard route only (serial case) is

$$t_{\text{serial}} = t_{\text{near}} + t_{\text{far}} = \frac{D}{b_{\text{near}}} + \frac{D}{b_0}, \tag{1}$$

where b_{near} denotes the mean bandwidth available for the local communications near S and T ($b_{\text{near}} = (b_{\text{near}_1} + b_{\text{near}_2})/2$). Equation (1) makes clear, that a speedup can only be achieved, if $b_{\text{near}} \gg b_{\text{far}}$, e. g. the transmission of data to the bases $N_1 \ldots N_n$ is pretty fast. Depending on the bandwidth b_i, the whole amount of data D shall be divided into pieces $d_0, d_1, \ldots, d_n$ such that the transmission through all $n + 1$ different paths can be accomplished in almost the same time $t_{disjunct} = \frac{d_i}{b_i}, i = 0 \ldots n$. When transferring the data D in parallel along the $n + 1$ paths, the transmission time t_{far} becomes $t_{far} = \frac{d_i}{b_i}$ with $i = 0 \ldots n$:

$$t_{far} = \frac{D}{b_0 + b_1 + \cdots + b_n} \tag{2}$$

The size each piece of data ($d_0, d_1, \ldots, d_n$) for path i can be determined by

$$d_i = \frac{D}{b_0 + b_1 + \cdots + b_n} b_i \quad \text{with} \quad i = 0 \ldots n \tag{3}$$

The overall transmission time $t_{parallel}$ using disjunct paths becomes now

$$t_{\text{parallel}} = \frac{D}{b_{\text{near}}} + \frac{D}{\sum_{i=0}^{n} b_i}. \tag{4}$$

Let us assume $b_{\text{near}} = k_{\text{near}} b_0$, i.e. the bandwidth b_{near} is defined as the bandwidth of the standard path multiplied with some constant value. The bandwidth for the other paths is defined in a similar manner relatively to b_0 by $b_i = k_i b_0, i = 1 \ldots n$. The communication speedup using disjunct paths as compared to the use of single route only becomes

$$S_{\text{comm}} = \frac{t_{\text{serial}}}{t_{\text{parallel}}} = \frac{b_0 + k_{\text{near}} b_0}{b_0 + \frac{k_{\text{near}} b_0}{1 + k_1 + \cdots + k_n}} \tag{5}$$

By replacing $k_1 + \cdots + k_n$ in (5) by K with $k_i = \frac{b_i}{b_0}$, the speedup becomes

$$S_{comm} = \frac{1 + k_{near}}{1 + \frac{k_{near}}{1+K}} \quad \text{with} \quad K = \frac{\sum_{i=1}^{n} b_i}{b_0} \tag{6}$$

If the local communications times (t_{near}) are very fast, we have $k_{near} \to \infty$ which results in a speedup of K. On the other hand, if the accumulated bandwidth available along the disjunct paths $i = 1 \ldots n$ is small as compared to the bandwidth b_0 of the standard path, we have $K \to 0$, which results in a speedup of 1, i.e. there is no speedup at all. Fig. 3 visualizes the expected speedup S_{comm} as defined in (6), depending on k_{near} and K.

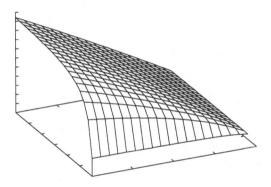

Fig. 3. Visualization of the speedup through disjunct paths.

A larger k_{near} represents a faster connection in the local area as compared to the long distance connection, resulting in a growing speedup. This growth is not linear, because the influence of b_{near} on the overall performance is small. After some point a faster local connection will therefore not increase the speedup any more. If further powerful disjunct paths are added, the growth of the speedup raises in a linear manner. It must be noted that throughout this performance analysis no overhead introduced by the method has been considered. The saturation of the speedup growth in a real system depends of course as well on such overhead times, which depend, as well as the latency introduced, on the size of the data subsets d_i. The following two assumptions should therefore be made in order to benefit from this method:

1. not every machine in the Internet tries to use disjunct paths at the same time (WOSNet $\subset$ Internet);
2. a sufficient amount of data D should be transmitted, and the data subsets d_i should not become too small.

4   The Realization in the WOS

4.1   The WOSForward Service

Message Chains are introduced in the WOS as a special service: WOSForward service (WFS). If a user or application wants to transfer data from one machine to another one using disjunct paths, he issues an appropriate request to his WOSNode. As described in Sec. 3.2, other WOSNodes are needed as base for this kind of service. The requesting user or application first searches the WOSNet for base nodes in its neighborhood. This search is made by calling the standard search and location services of the WOS using the WOS communication layer. If suitable nodes with a fast connection to the requesting node, i.e. with a high bandwidth b_{near1}, are found and the WOSForward service is available at all those nodes, the data to be sent is split into pieces depending on the number of paths and their bandwidth (see equation (3)). These pieces are then sent out in a quasi parallel manner on the disjunct paths.

At each base node the incoming data packets will be forwarded to the target machine using the standard routing path of that node. The flow of a service request at a base node is shown in Fig. 4.

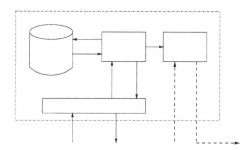

Fig. 4. The flow of a WOSForward request in a base WOSNode.

The incoming request (1) is passed directly to the module *Remote Resource Control Unit* (RRCU) (2). The RRCU looks up the requested WOSForward service in its local Service/Resource Warehouse (3) and (4). If this service is available on the node and is opened by the owner for public use, the WOSForward service (WFS) process is started by the RRCU (5'). In either case, whether the service is available or not, an answer is returned to the requesting node (5, 6). Then, assuming the service is available, the data can be transmitted. It will be directly forwarded by the WOSForward service, thus bypassing the WOS communication layer, which improves the communication speed by eliminating its protocol overhead.

4.2   Practical Results

First experiments have shown, that the expected speedup can be achieved. Fig. 5 shows the environment for the test. Files of $1, 2, 4 \ldots 64$ MB were first sent from the source machine S to the target machine T along the standard path without using any WOS services. Then, each file was split into two equally sized pieces and sent via two disjunct paths, the standard path and the path originating at machine R. Each machine is a WOSNode and at the base node R the WOSForward service was installed to pass the data from S to T.

Fig. 6 shows the result obtained with this experiment. The measurements confirm the speedup predicted in Sect. 3.4, equation (6). For larger file sizes, a linear speedup is observed, while the overhead introduced by the base node search and the splitting up of the files eliminates the speedup gained in the case of smaller files.

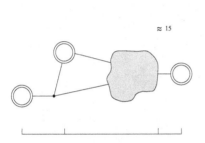

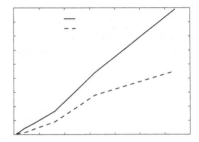

Fig. 5. Experimental setup for the communication with two disjunct paths.

Fig. 6. Transmission times for one path and two disjunct paths.

Further experimentation is currently under way. This involves in particular larger WOSNets as well as simultaneous use of the WOSForward service by different source nodes within the same WOSNet. Moreover, we will also investigate the influence of latency on the speedup achieved.

4.3   Future Developments

The search mechanisms for finding base nodes is one source of overhead introduced. While this method was already shown to be efficient [15], further work is necessary to optimize the management and maintenance of the warehouses, which store information about the WOSNet. Because there is no central catalog for a WOSNet, the concept of dynamically defined or versioned *communities* of components (such as WOSNodes) will be applied [12]. Components can adapt their behavior as they enter or leave a community, and may participate in several communities simultaneously. They can negotiate their relationship with other communities and may modify the shared context with other members of a community. This concept of communities may be well applied to the WOSForward service, where a suitable set of base nodes for possibly multiple source nodes may form a community who offers faster communications through its disjunct paths.

Splitting up data into different pieces to be transmitted along multiple paths exhibits as well a side effect concerning fault tolerance [11]. If one path brakes down, the data sent along the other ones still arrives and the receiving node may immediately request retransmission of the missing data along another path. This aspect of fault tolerance offered by the disjunct path communication will be further investigated.

5   Conclusion

This article shows that the concept of message chains and multiple disjunct paths can improve the performance of data transmission in the Internet. The Web Operating System (WOS™) provides all functionality which is necessary to realize this ideas. Together with an appropriate WOS service, this approach makes the working efficient and transparent for the user in many cases where a powerful search mechanism and a fast data transmission is needed.

References

1. G. R. Ash. *Dynamic Routing in Telecommunications Networks*. McGraw Hill, New York, 1998.
2. G. Babin, P. Kropf, and H. Unger. A Two-Level Communication Protocol for a Web Operating System (WOS). In *IEEE 24th Euromicro Workshop on Network Computing*, pages 934–944, Sweden, 1998.
3. D. Bertsekas and R. Gallagher. *Data Networks*. Prentice Hall, Englewood Cliffs, NJ, 2nd edition, 1991.
4. J. T. Brassil, A. K. Choudhury, and N. F. Maxemchuk. The Manhattan Street Network: A High Performance, Highly Reliable Metropolitan Area Network. *Computer Networks and ISDN Systems*, 1994.
5. R. Buyya. *High Performance Cluster Computing Vol 1*. Prentice Hall, Upper Saddle River, NJ, 1999.
6. G. Hipper and D. Tavangarian. Evaluating the Communication Performance of Beowulf- and FastCNA- workstation clusters through Low-Level Communication Benchmarks. In SCS A. Tentner, editor, *High Performance Computing*, pages 271–276, Boston, 1998.
7. G. Hommel. Quality of Communication-Based Systems. In *International Workshop on Quality of Communication-Based Systems*, TU Berlin, Germany, 1994. Kluwer Academic Publishers.
8. G. Hunt. *TCP/IP Network Administration, Second Edition*. O'Reilly, Cambridge, 1998.
9. P. Kropf. Overview of the WOS Project. In SCS A. Tentner, editor, *ASTC High Performance Computing*, pages 350–356, San Diego, CA, 1999.

10. S. B. Lamine, J. Plaice, and P. Kropf. Problems of computing on the Web. In SCS A. Tentner, editor, *High Performance Computing*, pages 296–301, Atlanta, 1997.
11. M. Lyubic and C. Cap. Enhancing Internet Security Through Multiple Paths. In *Distributed Computing on the Web (DCW'98)*, pages 55–60, Rostock, Germany, 1998.
12. J. Plaice and P. Kropf. Intensional Communities. In World Scientific Press, editor, *Intensional Programming II*, Singapore, 2000.
13. Y. Rekhter and T. Li. *A Border Gateway Protocol 4 (BGP-4)*. RFC 1771, Mar. 1995. http://info.internet.isi.edu/in-notes/rfc/files/rfc1771.txt.
14. H. Unger. The Adaptive Warehouse Concept for the Resource Management in the WOS . In *Distributed Computing on the Web (DCW)*, pages 167–174, Rostock, Germany, 1999.
15. H. Unger, P. Kropf, G. Babin, and T. Böhme. Simulation of search and distribution methods for jobs in a Operating System (WOS). In SCS A. Tentner, editor, *ASTC High Performance Computing*, pages 253–259, Boston, 1998.
16. B. M. Waxman. Routing of multipoint connections. *IEEE Journal on Selected Areas in Communications*, 6(9):1617–1622, 1988.
17. M. Wulff and H. Unger. Message Chains as a new Form of Active Communication in the WOSNet. In SCS A. Tentner, editor, *ASTC High Performance Computing*, 2000.

Using Corba in the Web Operating System[*]

Oliver Krone[1,3] and Alex Josef[2,3]

[1] Swisscom, Corporate Technology, Switzerland
[2] ETH Zürich, Switzerland
[3] International Computer Science Institute, Berkeley, USA
{krone, arjosef}@icsi.berkeley.edu

Abstract. In this paper we present ongoing work to integrate CORBA into the WOS. We chose CORBA because it is the de-facto standard for distributed object-oriented systems and therefore allows the WOS to be used with real world applications.

1   Introduction

The first generation of the Internet was centered on connectivity, ftp or telnet were the most commonly used tools. With the advent of the WWW, the presentation of information became an important application area and Web browsing based on static HTML pages enriched by interaction based on cgi-scripts and servlets was the state-of the art Web technology. Today, the third generation of the Internet is emerging, centered on service development, deployment and interaction that go far beyond the exchange of static HTML pages.

Given the complexity and development costs for these new Web-based services, it is increasingly important to develop a common service platform to support service provisioning, composition and competition. It is the aim of the WOS Project Group to develop such a service platform, also known as the Web Operating System, or WOS™ for short [1,2]. In order to be successful, the WOS must be able to integrate legacy software in its architectural model. Since CORBA has been widely used in industry to develop distributed object-oriented software, we focus on the integration of CORBA service into the WOS as a first attempt to realize this integration.

The reminder of this paper is organized as follows: in Section 2, we briefly sketch the communication models of the WOS and of CORBA, and in Section 3 we describe how CORBA clients can seamlessly use WOS services and outline how to use CORBA services in a WOS environment. Section 4 gives an overview on related work and Section 5 concludes the paper with an outlook on future work.

We assume that the reader has a basic knowledge of the architecture of the WOS, see [2] for example for an introduction.

---

[*] Research supported in part by the Swiss National Science Foundation and by the August Karolus Fonds of the ETH Zürich.

P. Kropf et al. (Eds.): DCW 2000, LNCS 1830, pp. 133–141, 2000

2   Communication in the WOS and in CORBA

The WOS uses a two-level approach for communication. For service discovery/location, a so-called WOS Service Request Protocol (WOSRP) is used and for service invocation a generic protocol, called WOS Protocol (WOSP), has been proposed (for details see [3, 5, 6]). The protocols are implemented in layers, starting with a basic communication layer that provides message queues for each protocol: request/reply queues for WOSRP messages and connection-oriented and connection-less queues for WOSP messages to invoke (query for) a service. A WOS node participating in a WOSNet is composed of different modules that register queue servers to this basic communication layer in order to handle incoming WOSRP and WOSP messages, respectively. The queue servers implement the different functionality of each module including management of local resource sets, warehouses, and invocation of local services; the overall architecture of a WOS node can be found in [4].

CORBA makes use of the Internet Inter-ORB Protocol (IIOP) to exchange General Inter-ORB Protocol (GIOP) messages over a TCP/IP network. The GIOP in turn uses the Common Data Representation (CDR) to map OMG IDL types into a raw, networked message representation, see [16] for details.

WOS and CORBA achieve interoperability by using a well-defined protocol to offer services in contrast to an architectural approach (used in Java for example), which uses a common platform to achieve interoperability at communication and service level. Therefore we have to develop a (protocol)-bridge to use the two systems simultaneously.

3   Integrating CORBA in the WOS Architecture

Our approach is based on the first available WOS prototype (version 0.4, entirely written in Java) developed jointly by the University of Rostock, Germany and the Laval University, Canada [17]. This system uses different types of warehouses [19] to store information about WOS services. A profile warehouse is used to store service profiles that consist of a name, and an access object representing an executable to be started upon service invocation. The access object is identified by a key and uses a set of input and output parameters to be passed to the executable upon service invocation. A resource warehouse is used to hold different profiles of a WOS node. We therefore map the triplet [CORBA module, interface name, parameters] onto [profile name, access object key, access object parameters] in order to access the service from within the CORBA environment and vice versa.

3.1 CORBA to WOS Service Invocation

Invoking a WOS service from within a CORBA environment shall resemble a "normal" CORBA remote method invocation:

- The CORBA programmer shall not note any differences when using a WOS service from using a standard CORBA service. The WOS services shall be described using OMG's Interface Description Language (IDL);
- A CORBA client accessing a WOS service shall invoke the service in the usual CORBA way, i.e. by calling the generated helper functions that result from the compilation of the IDL file.

```
Module WOSConnector {

interface BankAccount {
    float balance(in string name) raises (NoExecException);
};

interface BankAccountManager {
    boolean open(in string name) raises (NoExecException);
}};
```

Fig. 1. IDL for WOS services open() and balance().

In order to achieve these goals we developed a generic CORBA WOSServant module, which serves as the default servant for different CORBA interfaces that are used to access their corresponding WOS service counterparts. Therefore, each WOS service signature is mapped onto a corresponding CORBA interface. The following example should illustrate the idea.

3.2 An Example

Imagine two WOS services to access a bank account: open() which opens a new bank account and balance() which returns the balance from an existing bank account. As usual for a CORBA environment, an interface description based on OMG's Interface Description Language (IDL) of these two services must be supplied, see Figure 1.

The IDL has to be compiled in order to generate the appropriate stub classes for the client; we don't need the skeleton classes for the server because we are using an application independent server, based on CORBA's Dynamic Skeleton Interface. Given the generic server described below, the services can then be accessed using traditional CORBA client semantics as shown in Figure 2.

Please note the typed BankAccountManager Interface in Figure 2. The client can directly invoke the open() operation on the manager object, just as if the services were standard CORBA services.

3.3 The Generic WOSAdapater

In order to provide a CORBA client with the look and feel of an ordinary CORBA service when accessing WOS based services, the client has to bind to a server that translates all CORBA IIOP requests to corresponding WOSP requests. This could be done in at least two different ways:

- Simulating a "pseudo" server by using OMG's Interceptors or object wrappers (Figure 3, left): CORBA 2.0 defines several Interceptors to be used at different stages of the execution of a CORBA service: during the binding phase, before and after parameters are marshaled and before and after the actual invocation of a service. Using this technique a tailored ORB could be built that simulates a server for the client. This is probably the most general alternative, however this would mean that we would have to deal with the interpretation of the IIOP protocol, a somewhat tedious task;
- Implementing a generic server by using OMG's Interface Repository (IR) (Figure 3, right): the IR provides a very powerful reflection mechanism to determine the signature of a called CORBA operation at runtime. The IR used in combination with the Dynamic Invocation Interface (DII) and the Dynamic Skeleton Interface (DSI) allows a generic object servant to determine at runtime the signature of the called operation and perform the necessary protocol translations (WOSP ✗ IIOP). Based on the generic object servant, a generic server can be implemented very easily.

```
public static void main(String[] args) {

  org.omg.CORBA.ORB orb = org.omg.CORBA.ORB.init(args, null);

  WOSConnector.BankAccountManager manager =
    WOSConnector.BankAccountManagerHelper.bind(orb,
            "/wos/bank_agent_poa");

  // Request the account manager to open a named account.
  try {
    boolean sucess = manager.open("John Taylor");
  } catch (WOSConnector.NoExecException e) {
    System.out.println("Couldn't open an account: " + e.reason);
    System.exit(-1);
  }
  // Get the balance in a similar way …
}}
```

Fig. 2. CORBA client accessing WOS services.

Since the CORBA client has to provide an IDL description of its WOS services, we opted for the second alternative. A server, so called `WOSAdapter`, therefore consists of a server skeleton that invokes a generic servant (`WOSServant`) to be re-used for every WOS ✗ CORBA IDL interface. The servant uses CORBA's Dynamic Skeleton Interface to dynamically handle incoming service requests. All CORBA client invocations executing a WOS service are performed against this server.

The corresponding server for the client in Figure 2 is shown in Figure 4; it implements the `WOSConnector` of Figure 1.

By taking advantage of the different policies for the CORBA Portable Object Adapter (POA) hosting this servant, the `WOSAdapter` can be implemented in a very flexible way. CORBA 2.0 defines policies on how requests are processed by the POA, whether the servant should be activated implicitly or explicitly, whether an additional servant should be used to dynamically invoke the WOSServant, in case it has not been started yet, and much more.

Please note the initialization of the generic WOSServant(orb, interfaceName, IR) in line (*) of Figure 4: a reference to the Interface Repository of the ORB is supplied so that the servant can determine the signature of the service at runtime. Upon startup, the server connects to either a well-known WOSNode, and/or discovers additional WOSNodes using WOSRP. The application independent WOSServant finally does all the complex work including:

- Storing the interface description for the interface it is responsible for;
- Getting the values and types of the supplied input parameters of the operation;
- Marshaling the values into a WOSP message;
- Constructing an appropriate WOSP message to invoke the service, includes mapping of [CORBA module, interface name, parameters] onto WOS's [profile name, access object key, access object parameters];
- Waiting for a result from the WOS;
- Unmarshaling the return result from WOS and marshaling it into CORBA type holders according to the return type of the operation;
- Sending the result back to the CORBA client.

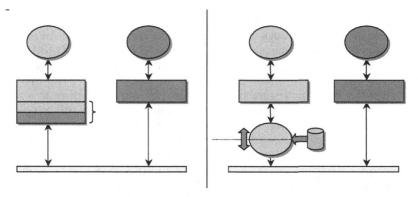

Fig. 3. WOSAdapter in CORBA: pseudo Server and generic Server.

A first version of the WOSservant, which does not handle all possible types, has been realized in less then 300 lines of Java code, an indication of the expressive power of the used CORBA environment Dynamic Skeleton Interface and Interface Repository.

3.4 WOS to CORBA Service Invocation

There are two possibilities to use CORBA services from within the WOS .

```
public static void main(String[] args) {

 try {
  org.omg.CORBA.ORB orb = org.omg.CORBA.ORB.init(args, null);
  POA rootPOA=
   POAHelper.narrow(orb.resolve_initial_references("RootPOA"));

  // Create the manager POA with the right policies (omitted)
  POA wosPOA = rootPOA.create_POA("wos/bank_agent_poa",
                                   rootPOA.the_POAManager(),
                                   managerPolicies);
  // Find WOSNode in WOSNet
  WOSNode myWOSNode = WOSHelper.FindWOSNode();

  // Create generic WOSServant for WOSConnector
(*) WOSServant wosServant = new WOSServant(orb,
                    "::WOSConnector::BankAccountManager",
                    WOSHelper.RepositoryHelper(orb));
  wosPOA.set_servant(wosServant);
  rootPOA.the_POAManager().activate();
  orb.run();
 } catch (Exception e) {
     e.printStackTrace();
 }}}
```

Fig. 4. WOSAdapter based on generic WOSServant.

- The current version 0.4 of the WOS uses a Resource Control Module in which a service can be invoked through an action that is defined in a profile. An action in this context is a shell command, which could be a full-blown CORBA client. Parameter passing is then realized through command line arguments, just like for any other CORBA client that is executed on the command line. However, this means that the WOS framework is used to start up a CORBA client in a rather complicated way and passing of parameters other than basic types will be difficult. Moreover, this approach is far too restrictive for advanced parameter passing and possibly includes performance problems;
- By providing a special version of the Remote Resource Control Unit (RRCU), a WOSNode can be developed which accesses the CORBA services directly through the CORBA API. The invocation of a CORBA service, instead of a WOS resource, would be completely transparent for the client, analogous to the previously described WOSServant approach.

We will describe the second approach in the following.

3.5 The WOS to CORBA RRCU

The WOS warehouse has to provide the functionality to store the necessary CORBA-related information for a particular service. We only face the dynamic service invocation, because a WOSNode with a precompiled stub is not a realistic scenario. In order to invoke the dynamic CORBA service, one or more of the following references are necessary:

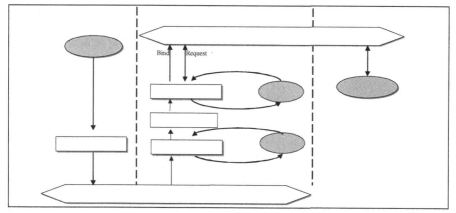

Fig. 5. CORBA service invocation from within the WOS.

- CORBA POA;
- Stringified version of the CORBA object in form of an IOR;
- Reference to a naming service including the name under which the object has been registered;

Therefore, we extended the basic types of the WOS properties with new CORBA-types, which encompass one of the mentioned references to a CORBA object.

Upon service invocation within the RRCU, the WOS-runtime system determines through the type of the properties (i.e. the RRCU checks for an instance of type WOS_CORBA_poa) whether the service refers to a (classical) WOS- or a CORBA-service. In case of a CORBA service, the CORBA-Adapter becomes active. A bind to the servant POA takes place in a way that depends on the available references. So far, we realized two possibilities:

- the POA of the service is provided;
- the repository ID is provided.

After the environment for a CORBA service invocation is set, the method invoke() of the CORBA-Adapter does the main part:

- First, it obtains a reference to the Interface Repository (IR);
- Using the IR, the interface of our service will be described;
- While building the request for a dynamic service invocation, invoke() checks with the interface description whether the provided parameters are valid or not;
- The return type is looked up in the repository and set accordingly in the NV-list for the request;
- The request is sent off via the ORB using the send_deferred() method, which is a non-blocking call to the remote service invocation;
- Upon reception of the return value in form of an any-variable, the type of the any is determined and translated into a string which will be the return value to the RRCU.

While the WOS further develops, a string as a return type is probably the most practical solution. It can contain basic types as well as stringified object references. Transmission of a string over the WOS-Communication Layer will always be supported.

4   Related Work

Sharing services, the main objective of the WOS effort, is currently being developed at several research centers as well as in industry, among them:

- SUN with **Jini** [11]. SUN's Jini is aimed at facilitating the use of networked devices in a "plug-and-participate" way. The idea is to develop Jini compliant devices that can be plugged into a Jini compliant network to share information and to perform tasks. Jini is the ideal platform for rapid prototyping of the next generation WOS, especially the JavaSpace [15] approach with its transaction mechanism and distributed events seems to be the platform of choice for further developments of the WOS;
- Berkeley's **Ninja** project [8]. Ninja uses XML [10] for service description and a Linda [14] like XML Tuple Space for service matching;
- IBM's **T-Spaces** [7]. Like SUN's JavaSpace, IBM's T-Spaces is based on a variant of LINDA's tuple space programming model [14]. It provides group communication services, database services, URL-based file transfer services, and event notification. Jini and T-Spaces underline the importance of integrating coordination technologies into wide-area distributed computing;
- Bell Labs' **Inferno** [12]. Inferno shares with Java the virtual-machine environment for applications, hence providing a high degree of portability. In addition it includes network protocols and services for distributed computing and a stand-alone implementation to be used for minimal hardware requirements.

Both Jini and Ninja handle service lookup and discovery; in addition, the Service Location Protocol (SLP) defined in IETF RFC 2608 [9] proposes a service lookup mechanism based on multicast. A lookup service based on LDAP for CORBA object references has been proposed in RFC 2714 [13].

5   Conclusion and Outlook

In this paper, we presented ongoing work to integrate legacy software into the WOS. Our approach is based on CORBA, the de-facto standard for distributed object-oriented systems. We developed a first prototype to access WOS services from within CORBA, and sketched the possibility to use CORBA services from within the WOS. Since the use of WOS services in a CORBA environment could be achieved relatively easily, we do not expect any major obstacles to fully realize the inverse operation; both worlds seem to cooperate nicely, in fact both systems seamlessly support inter-system protocol exchange.

Future work includes a full implementation of the sketched approaches, a thorough investigation of the SLP and the LDAP object references approach, as well as the development of a statement to position the WOSP and WOSRP protocols in state-of-the-art middleware research. This includes a comparison of WOSRP with other lookup and discovery protocols, and an investigation of how other Naming schemes like the Java Naming and Directory Interface (JNDI) [18] technology, or CORBA's Naming schemes could be used within the WOS framework.

Acknowledgements

We are grateful to Hauke "Django" Coltzau and the whole WOS team at the University of Rostock and Laval University for their outstanding support in introducing us to the internals of the current WOS prototype.

References

[1]   WOS Project Group: http://www.wos-community.org/.

[2]   P. Kropf, "Overview of the Web Operating System (WOS) project", 1999 Advanced Simulation Technologies Conference (ASTC1999), San Diego, California, USA, April 1999.

[3]   G. Babin, P. Kropf, and H. Unger, "A Two-Level Communication Protocol for a Web Operating System (WOS)", 24th Euromico, Sweden, 1998.

[4]   P. Kropf, "An Approach for the Resource Scheduling in the WOS", Distributed Computing on the Web, (DCW'98). Rostock, Germany, June 1998.

[5]   M. Wulff, G. Babin, P. Kropf, and Q. Zhong, "Communication in the Wos", Technical Report, Laval University, Quebec, Canada, 1997.

[6]   G. Babin, H. Coltzau, M. Wulff, S. Ruel, "Application programming Interface for WOSRP/WOSP", Paradis Laboratory, Laval University, 1999.

[7]   T. J. Lehman, S. McLaughry, P. Wyckoff, IBM Almaden Research Center, 650 Harry Rd San Jose, CA 95120, "T Spaces: The Next Wave", http://www.almaden.ibm.com/.

[8]   "Ninja, a scalable Internet Services Architecture", http://ninja.cs.berkeley.edu/overview.html, 2000.

[9]   Guttman, E., Perkins, C., Veizades, J., Day, M., "Service Location Protocol, Version 2", RFC 2608, June 1999.

[10]   XML, http://www.w3.org/TR/1998/REC-xml-19980210.html, 1998.

[11]   Jini, Sun Microsystems, Inc., http://java.sun.com/products/jini, 1999.

[12]   Lucent Technologies, "Inferno: la Commedia Interattiva", http://www.lucent-inferno.com.

[13]   V. Ryan, S. Seligman, R. Lee , "Schema for Representing CORBA Object References in an LDAP Directory", RFC 2714, October 1999.

[14]   N. Carriero, and D. Gelernter. "Coordination Languages and their Significance", *Communications of the ACM*, 35(2), 1992.

[15]   J. Waldo et al. "JavaSpace Specification - 1.0", Technical Report, Sun Microsystems, 1998.

[16]   "The Common Object-Request Broker Architecture: Architecture and Specification", http://www.omg.org.

Clusters, Servers, Thin Clients, and On-line Communities

Peter H. Beckman

Director of TurboLabs
TurboLinux Inc.
beckman@turbolabs.com

During the age of centralized processing and mainframes, terminals were dumb and networking was slow. A few simple networked applications emerged, such as simple games, email, and 'talk' programs. During the mid and late 80s, when I was beginning my Ph. D. in computer science at Indiana University, Unix desktop workstations and windowing interfaces became popular, and the dumb terminal was phased out. Naturally, networked games, email, and 'talk' programs became standard tools, and programmers started creating distributed client/server applications. In the business world, a similar push toward desktop (PC) computing created a new paradigm for computing, with word processing, accounting, and database management migrating to the desktop, and away from the main server.

Shortly thereafter, pundits were declaring the age of 'mainframes' over; the networked desktop and ever faster CPUs would provide enough computational power to address most business applications. Companies rushed to provide desktop applications that could be networked to departmental file servers. The era of the enormous machine room was over; everyone would have plenty of computing resources right on their desktop. Of course, computing paradigms rarely remain constant for long. Shift happens. The Internet, commodity-based cluster computing, and distributed computing services have all pushed computing in new directions.

For years, client/server applications such as email using the POP protocol pushed information management to the desktop. Recently, the Internet has started to reverse that trend. Hotmail.com and others have pushed email services back to the centralized server. Users actually prefer to have all their email in a central location where it can be accessed from any Web portal, be it at a coffee shop, or a friend's house. The popularity of WebTV and inexpensive Internet appliances has shown that with a ubiquitous Internet infrastructure, the average home may need less computational power and storage than once thought. The Internet has facilitated the return of centralized servers. Companies are offering complete financial services, including management of your checking account and paying your bills, all via server-side applications and thin web clients.

The machine room has once again become a mission critical component for companies of all sizes. They are installing racks and racks of servers with commercial and locally-grown high availability software. Scalability, manageability, and automatic failover are hot topics as some services migrate back to the centralized server. Companies such as Exodus.com are providing "commodity" machine

P. Kropf et al. (Eds.): DCW 2000, LNCS 1830, pp. 142–143, 2000.

room services and Internet access, including 7x24 support and a "rebooting service." Clustering commodity Linux boxes has become a common way to provide scalable services to this exploding industry. It has been made possible by the boom in single processor performance. The 'mainframe' has been transformed into distributed clusters.

Concurrently with this shift back to centralized servers, interactive, on-line communities have become stronger than ever. Primitive IRC clients have evolved into sophisticated chat rooms and instant messaging. Industry rags have explained how instant messaging can help businesses communicate it has become legitimate. Sharing information while being 'wired' has lead to the success of applications that foster digital communities such as Napster. However, this explosion of instant communication and communal sharing of data has not been without pitfalls. Copyright issues, information integrity, pornography, and privacy have caused some forms of on-line communities to be banned from campuses.

Where is all this going? What will the future hold? My presentation will focus on the issues and trends transforming computers and the Internet. The new computational engine for the Internet is a centralized cluster of nearly commodity components. Distributed applications will link the centralized servers. Thin clients will be everywhere, from your web-capable cell phone, to your car's navigation system, to web surfing TVs and VCRs. Interactive, on-line subcultures will become even more popular. These on-line interactions will become even more international. The world is changing fast. What will computing look like in 2004? Come and find out.

The GIPSY Architecture

Joey Paquet[1] and Peter Kropf[2]

[1] Concordia University, Montreal, Canada H3G 1M8.
paquet@cs.concordia.ca.
[2] Université de Montréal, Montréal, Canada H3C 3J7.
kropf@iro.umontreal.ca

Abstract. Intensional Programming involves the programming of expressions placed in an inherent multidimensional context space. It is an emerging and highly dynamic domain of general application. The fast growing computer connectivity allows for more and more efficient implementation of distributed applications. The paradigm of intensionality inherently includes notions of parallelism at different levels. However, the currently available intensional programming software tools are becoming obsolete and do not enable us to further push forward practical investigations on the subject. Experience shows that the theoretical advancement of the field has come to acceptable maturity. Consequently, new powerful tools for intensional programming are required. In this paper, we present the design of a General Intensional Programming System (GIPSY). The design and implementation of the GIPSY reflect three main goals: generality, adaptability and efficiency.

1 Introduction

Intensional programming is a generalization of unidimensional contextual (a.k.a. modal logic) programming such as temporal programming, but where the context is multidimensional and implicit rather than unidimensional and explicit. Intensional programming is also called *multidimensional programming* because the expressions involved are allowed to vary in an arbitrary number of dimensions, the context of evaluation is thus a *multidimensional context*. For example, in intensional programming, one can very naturally represent complex physical phenomena such as plasma physics, which are in fact a set of charged particles placed in a space-time continuum that behaves according to a limited set of laws of intensional nature. This space-time continuum becomes the different dimensions of the context of evaluation, and the laws are expressed naturally using intensional definitions [7].

Lucid is a multidimensional intensional programming language whose semantics is based on the possible world semantics of intensional logic [1,10]. It is a functional language in which expressions and their valuations are allowed to vary in an arbitrary number of dimensions. Intensional programming (in the sense of Lucid) has been successfully applied to resolve problems with a new perspective that enables a more natural understanding of problems of intensional nature.

P. Kropf et al. (Eds.): DCW 2000, LNCS 1830, pp. 144–153, 2000.

Such problems include topics as diverse as reactive programming, software configuration [8], tensor programming [7] and distributed operating systems [6]. However, these projects have all been developed in isolation. GLU is the most general intensional programming tool presently available [4]. However, experience has shown that, while being very efficient, the GLU system suffers from a lack of flexibility and adaptability [7]. Given that Lucid is evolving continually, there is an important need for the successor to GLU to be able to stand the heat of evolution.

We propose the design of a general intensional programming system (GIPSY). To cope with the fast evolution and generality of the intensional programming field, the design and implementation of all its subsystems is done towards *generality*, *flexibility* and *efficiency*.

2   Approach

The General Intensional Programming System (GIPSY) consists in three modular sub-systems: The General Intensional Programming Language Compiler (GIPC) ; the General Eduction Engine (GEE), and the Intensional Run-time Programming Environment (RIPE). Although the theoretical basis of the language has been settled, the implementation of an efficient, general and adaptable programming system for this language raises many interrogations. The following sections outline the theoretical basis and architecture of the different components of the system. All these components are designed in a modular manner to permit the eventual replacement of each of its components—at compile-time or even at run-time—to improve the overall efficiency of the system.

2.1   General Intensional Programming Language Compiler (GIPC)

Like all functional programming languages, there are many variants of Lucid, depending on the basic set of types, constants and data operations, i.e. the basic algebra. Nevertheless, all variants of Lucid include function application, conditional expressions, intensional navigation and intensional query.

Language Syntax and Semantics

The language whose syntax and semantics is given in Figure 1 and explained below is capable of expressing all extensions to Lucid, proposed to this day.

This syntax assumes that identifiers (*id*) can refer to constants, data operations, variables, functions or dimensions. This approach comes from the fact that function and dimension identifiers can be first-class values in our version of Lucid. The operational semantics of Lucid is given in a structural operational semantics style. Normally this would mean that semantic judgments would be of the general form $\mathcal{D} \vdash E : v$ i.e. under the definition environment $\mathcal{D}$, expression E would evaluate to value v. However, in Lucid, we must take into account

$$E ::= id$$
$$| \ E(E_1, \ldots, E_n)$$
$$| \ \text{if } E \text{ then } E' \text{ else } E''$$
$$| \ \#E$$
$$| \ E \ @E' \ E''$$
$$| \ E \text{ where } Q$$
$$Q ::= \text{dimension } id$$
$$| \ id = E$$
$$| \ id(id_1, \ldots, id_n) = E$$
$$| \ Q \ Q$$

Fig. 1. Syntax of the Lucid language

the *context of evaluation* of expressions, so we need an additional entry to the left, hence

$$\mathcal{D}, \mathcal{P} \vdash E : v$$

which means that in the definition environment $\mathcal{D}$, and in the evaluation context $\mathcal{P}$ (sometimes also referred to as *point*), expression E evaluates to v. The definition environment $\mathcal{D}$ retains the definitions of all of the identifiers that appear in a Lucid program. It is therefore a partial function

$$\mathcal{D} : \mathbf{Id} \rightarrow \mathbf{IdEntry}$$

where **Id** is the set of all possible identifiers and **IdEntry** has five possible kinds of value, one for each of the kinds of identifier:

- *Dimensions* define the coordinates in which one can navigate. The **IdEntry** is simply (dim).
- *Constants* are entities that provide the same value in any context. The **IdEntry** is (const, c), where c is the value of the constant.
- *Data operators* are entities that provide memoryless functions, e.g. arithmetic operations. The constants and data operators define the *basic algebra* of the language. The **IdEntry** is (op, f), where f is the function itself.
- *Variables* are the multidimensional streams. The **IdEntry** is (var, E), where E is the expression defining it. Uniqueness of names is achieved by performing compile-time renaming or using a nesting level environment [7].
- *Functions* are user-defined functions. The **IdEntry** is (func, id_i, E), where the id_i are the formal parameters to the function and E is the body of the function. The semantics for recursive functions could be easily added, but is discouraged by the nature of intensional programming.

The evaluation context $\mathcal{P}$, which is changed when the @ operator or a **where** clause is encountered, associates a tag to each relevant dimension. It is therefore a partial function

$$\mathcal{P} : \mathbf{Id} \rightarrow \mathbf{N}$$

The operational semantics of Lucid programs is defined in Appendix A. Each type of identifier can only be used in the appropriate situations. Identifiers of type, op, func and dim evaluate to themselves. Constant identifiers (const) evaluate to the corresponding constant. Function calls, resolved by the $\mathbf{E_{fct}}$ rule, require the renaming of the formal parameters into the actual parameters (as represented by $E'[id_i \leftarrow E_i]$).

For example, the rule for the navigation operator, $\mathbf{E_{at}}$, which corresponds to the syntactic expression $E @E' E''$, evaluates E in context $[E' : E'']$, where E' evaluates to a dimension and E'' to a value corresponding to a tag in E'. The rule for the where clause, $\mathbf{E_w}$, which corresponds to the syntactic expression E where Q, evaluates E using the definitions (Q) therein.

The additions to the definition environment and context of evaluation made by the $\mathbf{Q}$ rules are local to the current where clause. This is represented by the fact that the $\mathbf{E_w}$ rule returns neither $\mathcal{D}$ nor $\mathcal{P}$. The $\mathbf{Q_{dim}}$ rule adds a dimension to the definition environment and, as a convention, adds this dimension to the context of evaluation with tag 0. The $\mathbf{Q_{id}}$ and $\mathbf{Q_{fid}}$ simply add variable and function identifiers along with their definition to the definition environment.

The initial definition $\mathcal{D}_0$ includes the predefined intensional operators, the constants and the data operators. Hence

$$\mathcal{D}_0, \mathcal{P}_0 \vdash E : v$$

where $\mathcal{P}_0$ defines a particular context of interest, represents the computation of any Lucid expression, where v is the result.

The GIPSY Architecture and Program Compilation

GYPSY programs are compiled in a two-stage process (see Figure 2). First, the intensional part of the GYPSY program is translated into C, then the resulting C program is compiled in the standard way.

The source code consists of two parts: the Lucid part that defines the intensional data dependencies between variables and the sequential part that defines the granular sequential computation units (usually written in C). The Lucid part is compiled into an intensional data dependency structure (IDS) describing the dependencies between each variable involved in the Lucid part. This structure is interpreted at run-time by the GEE (see Section 2.2) following the demand propagation mechanism. Data communication procedures used in a distributed evaluation of the program are also generated by the GIPC according to the data structures definitions written in the Lucid part, yielding a set of intensional communication procedures (ICP). These are generated following a given communication layer definition such as provided by IPC, CORBA or the WOS [2]. The sequential functions defined in the second part of the GIPSY program are translated into C code using the second stage C compiler syntax, yielding C sequential threads (CST).

Intensional function definitions, including higher order functions, will be flattened using a well-know efficient technique [9]. Because of the interactive nature

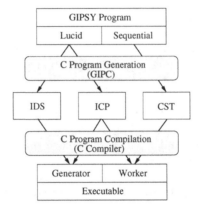

Fig. 2. GIPSY Program Compilation Process

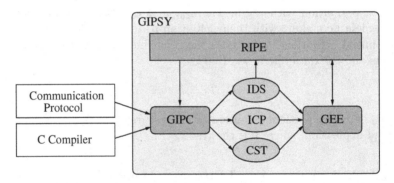

Fig. 3. GIPSY Software Architecture

of the RIPE (see Section 2.3), the GIPC is modularly designed to allow the individual on-the-fly compilation of either the IDS (by changing the Lucid code) ICP (by changing the communication protocol) or CST (by changing the sequential code). Such a modular design even allows sequential threads to be programs written in different languages.

2.2   General Eduction Engine (GEE)

The GIPSY uses a demand-driven model of computation, whose principle is that a computation takes effect only if there is an explicit demand for it. The GIPSY uses eduction, which is demand-driven computation in conjunction with an intelligent value cache called a warehouse. Every demand generates a procedure call, which is either computed locally or remotely, thus eventually in parallel with other procedure calls. Every computed value is placed in the warehouse, and every demand for an already-computed value is extracted from the warehouse rather than computed anew. Eduction thus reduces the overhead induced by the procedure calls needed for the computation of demands.

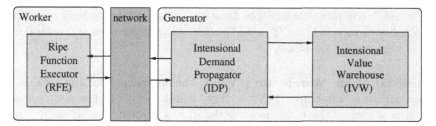

Fig. 4. Generator-Worker Execution Architecture

The GIPSY uses a generator-worker execution architecture. The IDS generated by the GIPC is interpreted by the generator following the eductive model of computation. The low-charge ripe sequential threads are evaluated locally by the generator. The higher-charge ripe sequential threads are evaluated on a remote worker. As shown in Figure 4, the generator consists of two systems: the Intensional Demand Propagator (IDP) and the Intensional Value Warehouse (IVW). The IDP implements the demand generation and propagation mechanisms, and the IVW implements the warehouse. A set of semantic rules that outlines the theoretical aspects of the distributed demand propagation mechanism has been defined in [7]. The worker simply consists of a "Ripe Function Executor" (RFE), responsible for the computation of the ripe sequential threads as demanded by the generator. The sequential threads are compiled and can be either dowloaded/uploaded dynamically by/to the remote workers. Better efficiency can be achieved by using a shared network file system.

Intensional Demand Propagator (IDP) The IDP generates and propagates demands according to the data dependence structure (IDS) generated by the GIPC. If a demand requires some computation, the result can be calculated either locally or on a remote computing unit. In the latter case, the communication procedures (ICP) generated by the GIPC are used by the GEE to send the demand to the worker. When a demand is made, it is placed in a demand queue, to be removed only when the demand has been successfully computed. This way of doing provides a highly fault-tolerant system. One of the weaknesses of GLU is its inability to optimize the overhead induced by demand-propagation. The IDP will remedy to this weakness by implementing various optimization techniques:

- Data blocking techniques used to aggregate similar demands at run time, which will also be used at compile-time in the GIPC for automatic granularization of data and functions for data-parallel applications.
- The performance-critical parts (IDP and IVW) are designed as replaceable modules to enable run-time replacements by more efficient versions adapted to specific computation-intensive applications.
- Certain demand paths identified (at compile-time or run-time) as critical will be compiled to reduce their demand propagation overhead.

– Extensive compile-time and run-time rank analysis (analysis of the dimensionality of variables) [3]. This will be one of the major research topics during the implementation phase.

Intensional Value Warehouse (IVW) The second part of the GEE is the intensional value warehouse (IVW or "ivy" warehouse), which is simply implemented as a cache. The GEE uses the dataflow's context tags to build a store of values that already have been computed (the IVW). One of the key concerns when using caches is the use of a garbage collecting algorithm adapted to the current situation. The use of a garbage collector configured or adapted to the current situation is of prime importance to obtain high performance. The garbage collector has to be implemented as a highly adaptable component, enabling the use of various criteria to identify garbage in the warehouse.

Eduction has many guises. For example, eduction can be a simple one-time process, as in computing in Lucid, or a two-stage show, as in spreadsheet calculations. Also, in software versioning, some kinds of version selection correspond more to an aggregation process than to a selection process: All versions that correspond to the version description are chosen, and these are all coalesced into a single version. This has been implemented in the Lemur system using an intensional versioning technique [8].

A highly modular design and complete specification of generic software interfaces enables the GEE to accept other garbage collecting algorithms with minimal programming cost and replacement overhead. A thorough analysis of the different requirements of each intended application of intensional programming will enable us to identify a minimal set of garbage collecting techniques to be implemented and tested. We will also investigate the possibility of using multi-level warehouses enabling faster access to values accessed regularly and allowing out-of-date computed results to be stored on the file system. Rank analysis also greatly reduces the number of values stored in the warehouse by preventing the storage of values outside the dimensionality of the variables.

2.3 Run-Time Interactive Programming Environment (RIPE)

The RIPE is a visual run-time programming environment enabling the visualization of a dataflow diagram corresponding to the Lucid part of the GIPSY program. The user can interact with the RIPE at run-time in the following ways:

– dynamically inspect the IVW;
– change the input/output channels of the program;
– recompile sequential threads;
– change the communication protocol;
– change parts of the GIPSY itself (e.g. garbage collector).

A graphical formalism to visually represent Lucid programs as multidimensional dataflow graphs had been devised in [7]. For example, consider the Hamming problem that consists of generating the stream of all numbers of the form

$2^i 3^j 5^k$ in increasing order and without repetition. The following Lucid program solving this problem can be translated into a dataflow diagram, as shown in Figure 5:

```
H
where
  H = 1 fby merge(merge(2*H,3*H),5*H);
  merge(x,y)= if (xx<=yy) then xx else yy
  where
    xx = x upon (xx<=yy);
    yy = y upon (yy<=xx);
  end;
end;
```

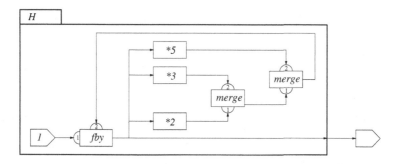

Fig. 5. Dataflow graph for the Hamming problem

Figure 6 represents the dataflow diagram defining the merge function. Such nested definitions will be implemented in the RIPE by allowing the user to expand or reduce sub-graphs, thus allowing the visualization of large scale Lucid definitions.

Using this visual technique, the RIPE will even enable the graphic development of Lucid programs, translating the graphic version of the program into a textual version that can then be compiled into an operational version. However, the development of this facility for graphical programming poses many problems whose solution is not yet settled. An extensive and general requirements analysis will be undertaken, as this interface will have to be suited to many different types of applications. There is also the possibility to have a kernel run-time interface on top of which we can plug-in different types of interfaces adapted to different applications.

3   Summary

It already has been proven that intensional programming can be used to solve critical problems such as tensor programming (TensorLucid [7]), distributed

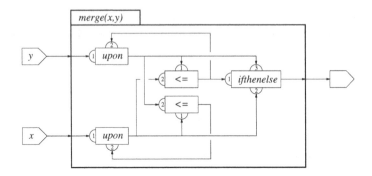

Fig. 6. Dataflow graph for the merge function

operating systems (the Web Operating System [6]) and software versioning (Lemur [8]). The solutions proposed by these three systems use intensional programming implemented in a demand-driven computation framework. This intensional programming framework has proven to provide a superior solution (in terms of expressiveness and inherent distributed computation possibilities) compared to all other techniques currently used to solve these problems. A plethora of other problems of intensional nature can be solved within this framework. Although it has already theoretically proved its usefulness, Intensional programming is still in its infancy, mainly due to a lack of visibility.

The implementation of the GIPSY will enable us to realize the afore mentioned solutions in a unified framework and show the usefulness of the approach. A first prototype implementation of the GIPC and GEE is under way, whereas the implementation of the RIPE will be started after the experimental evaluation of the other two subsystems.

References

1. E. A. Ashcroft, A. A. Faustini, R. Jagannathan, and W. W. Wadge. *Multidimensional, Declarative Programming*. Oxford University Press, London, 1995.
2. G. Babin, P.G. Kropf and H. Unger. A Two-Level Communication Protocol for a Web Operating System (WOS). In *Proceedings of IEEE Euromicro Workshop on Network Computing*, pp. 934–944, Västerås, Sweden, 1998.
3. C. Dodd. *Intensional Programming I*, chapter Rank analysis in the GLU compiler, pages 76–82. World Scientific, Singapore, 1996.
4. R. Jagannathan and C. Dodd. GLU programmer's guide. Technical report, SRI International, Menlo Park, California, 1996.
5. R. Jagannathan, C. Dodd, and I. Agi. GLU: A high-level system for granular data-parallel programming. *Concurrency: Practice and Experience*, (1):63–83, 1997.
6. P.G. Kropf. Overview of the Web Operating System (WOS) project. In *Proceedings of the 1999 Advanced Simulation Technologies Conference (ASTC 1999)*, pages 350–356, San Diego, California, april 1999.
7. J. Paquet. *Scientific Intensional Programming*. Ph.D thesis, Department of Computer Science, Laval University, Sainte-Foy, Canada, 1999.

8. J. Plaice and W. W. Wadge. A new approach to version control. *IEEE Transactions on Software Engineering*, 3(19):268–276, 1993.
9. P. Rondogiannis. *Higher-Order Functional Languages and Intensional Logic*. PhD thesis, Department of Computer Science, University of Victoria, Victoria, Canada, 1994.
10. W. W. Wadge and E. A. Ashcroft. *Lucid, the Dataflow Programming Language*. Academic Press, London, 1985.

A   Semantic Definition of Lucid Programs

$$\mathbf{E_{cid}} : \frac{\mathcal{D}(id) = (\mathtt{const}, c)}{\mathcal{D}, \mathcal{P} \vdash id : c} \qquad\qquad \mathbf{E_{did}} : \frac{\mathcal{D}(id) = (\mathtt{dim})}{\mathcal{D}, \mathcal{P} \vdash id : id}$$

$$\mathbf{E_{opid}} : \frac{\mathcal{D}(id) = (\mathtt{op}, f)}{\mathcal{D}, \mathcal{P} \vdash id : id} \qquad\qquad \mathbf{E_{fid}} : \frac{\mathcal{D}(id) = (\mathtt{func}, id_i, E)}{\mathcal{D}, \mathcal{P} \vdash id : id}$$

$$\mathbf{E_{vid}} : \frac{\mathcal{D}(id) = (\mathtt{var}, E) \qquad \mathcal{D}, \mathcal{P} \vdash E : v}{\mathcal{D}, \mathcal{P} \vdash id : v}$$

$$\mathbf{E_{op}} : \frac{\mathcal{D}, \mathcal{P} \vdash E : id \qquad \mathcal{D}(id) = (\mathtt{op}, f) \qquad \mathcal{D}, \mathcal{P} \vdash E_i : v_i}{\mathcal{D}, \mathcal{P} \vdash E(E_1, \ldots, E_n) : f(v_1, \ldots, v_n)}$$

$$\mathbf{E_{fct}} : \frac{\mathcal{D}, \mathcal{P} \vdash E : id \qquad \mathcal{D}(id) = (\mathtt{func}, id_i, E') \qquad \mathcal{D}, \mathcal{P} \vdash E'[id_i \leftarrow E_i] : v}{\mathcal{D}, \mathcal{P} \vdash E(E_1, \ldots, E_n) : v}$$

$$\mathbf{E_{c_T}} : \frac{\mathcal{D}, \mathcal{P} \vdash E : \mathit{true} \qquad \mathcal{D}, \mathcal{P} \vdash E' : v'}{\mathcal{D}, \mathcal{P} \vdash \mathtt{if}\ E\ \mathtt{then}\ E'\ \mathtt{else}\ E'' : v'}$$

$$\mathbf{E_{c_F}} : \frac{\mathcal{D}, \mathcal{P} \vdash E : \mathit{false} \qquad \mathcal{D}, \mathcal{P} \vdash E'' : v''}{\mathcal{D}, \mathcal{P} \vdash \mathtt{if}\ E\ \mathtt{then}\ E'\ \mathtt{else}\ E'' : v''}$$

$$\mathbf{E_{tag}} : \frac{\mathcal{D}, \mathcal{P} \vdash E : id \qquad \mathcal{D}(id) = (\mathtt{dim})}{\mathcal{D}, \mathcal{P} \vdash \#E : \mathcal{P}(id)}$$

$$\mathbf{E_{at}} : \frac{\mathcal{D}, \mathcal{P} \vdash E' : id \qquad \mathcal{D}(id) = (\mathtt{dim}) \qquad \mathcal{D}, \mathcal{P} \vdash E'' : v'' \qquad \mathcal{D}, \mathcal{P}\dagger[id \mapsto v''] \vdash E : v}{\mathcal{D}, \mathcal{P} \vdash E\ @E'\ E'' : v}$$

$$\mathbf{E_w} : \frac{\mathcal{D}, \mathcal{P} \vdash Q : \mathcal{D}', \mathcal{P}' \qquad \mathcal{D}', \mathcal{P}' \vdash E : v}{\mathcal{D}, \mathcal{P} \vdash E\ \mathtt{where}\ Q : v}$$

$$\mathbf{Q_{dim}} : \frac{}{\mathcal{D}, \mathcal{P} \vdash \mathtt{dimension}\ id : \mathcal{D}\dagger[id \mapsto (\mathtt{dim})], \mathcal{P}\dagger[id \mapsto 0]}$$

$$\mathbf{Q_{id}} : \frac{}{\mathcal{D}, \mathcal{P} \vdash id = E : \mathcal{D}\dagger[id \mapsto (\mathtt{var}, E)], \mathcal{P}}$$

$$\mathbf{Q_{fid}} : \frac{}{\mathcal{D}, \mathcal{P} \vdash id(id_1, \ldots, id_n) = E : \mathcal{D}\dagger[id \mapsto (\mathtt{func}, id_i, E)], \mathcal{P}}$$

$$\mathbf{QQ} : \frac{\mathcal{D}, \mathcal{P} \vdash Q : \mathcal{D}', \mathcal{P}' \qquad \mathcal{D}', \mathcal{P}' \vdash Q' : \mathcal{D}'', \mathcal{P}''}{\mathcal{D}, \mathcal{P} \vdash Q\ Q' : \mathcal{D}'', \mathcal{P}''}$$

Multidimensional Lucid:
Design, Semantics and Implementation

John Plaice

School of Computer Science and Engineering
University of New South Wales
UNSW SYDNEY NSW 2052, Australia
plaice@cse.unsw.edu.au

Abstract. We develop an eductive algorithm for the efficient implementation of Multidimensional Lucid, which includes dimensions as first-class values. By focusing on simple multi-dimensional expressions, we develop a series of operational semantics, ultimately leading to an algorithm that should lead to efficient implementations of Lucid for a variety of physical architectures.

1 Introduction

An *intensional program* is a program that runs in an implicit multidimensional context and that can explicitly manipulate the coordinates of that context, using a (lazy) demand-driven execution model called *eduction*. The term *intensional programming* was first coined by Faustini and Wadge [4], in the context of research in the Lucid programming language, and corresponds to the fact that the semantics of intensional programs use the possible-worlds semantics of intensional logic [9].

Developments in intensional programming have always been reflected by continued developments in the Lucid programming language. The latest incarnation of Lucid [8], which we will call Multidimensional Lucid, allows any ground value to be used as a dimension. However, implementation of the language is non-trivial: traditional eduction techniques, using a static list of dimensions, cannot be applied. since the set of possible dimensions can only be known at run-time.

In this paper, we derive an eductive process that will be usable as the basis for reasonable performance on a number of architectures. We do not focus on the entire language; in particular, we do not examine the implementation of functions.

We begin with a brief history of intensional programming and of the successive stages of Lucid (Section 2). We then present the syntax and semantics of Multidimensional Lucid (Section 3). Sections 4 and 5 give more precise operational semantics, defining how eduction can be used for the language. Section 6 focuses on how to improve the efficiency of this semantics.

P. Kropf et al. (Eds.): DCW 2000, LNCS 1830, pp. 154–160, 2000.

2   Background

The Lucid language was first defined [2,3] in order to succinctly express loop invariants in `while` programs. Using equations such as

```
X = 0 fby X + 1
```

one could define infinite streams, here $(0, 1, 2, \ldots, n, \ldots)$.

The primitive (*intensional*) operators of Lucid allowed for more than just pipeline dataflows. They could also be used for out-of-order execution: the term *eduction* is used to refer to the demand-driven strategy that is used to this day [12]. The primitive operators became *indexical query* (#) and *indexical navigation* (@). Hence the above equation becomes

```
X = if #=0 then 0 else (X @ (#-1)) + 1
```

Successive versions of Lucid have developed through the increased use of dimensions. The original Lucid had only one dimension, corresponding to "time". The version in the first Lucid book [12] had an extra construct, `iscurrent`, that allowed for the implicit creation of a new dimension for the purposes of local computations.

Indexical Lucid,[1] used in the GLU system,[6] introduced the notion of dimensionally abstract functions. Lucid "streams" were no longer restricted to a fixed set of dimensions but, rather, could introduce dimensions at will and have them passed as arguments to functions. Furthermore, all of the intensional operators could take dimensions as parameters. For example, Ackermann's function, given below:

```
A 0 n = n+1
A m 0 = A (m-1) 1
A m n = A (m-1) (A m (n-1))
```

can be redefined as a stream varying in the two dimensions a and b:

```
A = (#.a+1) fby.b (A @.a (1 fby.a (next.b A)))
```

In [8], the semantics of dimensions as values were defined. Basically, any constant can be used as a dimension. This approach greatly simplifies the semantics.

3   Syntax and Semantics

As is standard, we consider Lucid to be a variant of ISWIM.[7] In addition to the typed λ-calculus with operators and syntactic sugar (`where` clauses), there are two operators to manipulate dimensions: intensional query (@) and intensional navigation (#).

The syntax is given in Figure 1. It supposes that there is a basic algebra of constants (`const` c) and data operators (`op` f).

$$E ::= id$$
$$| \;\; \text{const } c$$
$$| \;\; \text{op } f$$
$$| \;\; \text{fn } id_1, \ldots, id_n \; \Rightarrow \; E$$
$$| \;\; E(E_1, \ldots, E_n)$$
$$| \;\; \text{if } E_0 \text{ then } E_1 \text{ else } E_2$$
$$| \;\; \#E$$
$$| \;\; E \text{ @} E_1 \; E_2$$
$$| \;\; E \text{ where } Q$$

$$Q ::= id = E$$
$$| \;\; Q \; Q$$

Fig. 1. Syntax for Lucid

The semantic rules for Lucid are given in Figure 2. In it, the judgments are of the form $\mathcal{D}, \mathcal{P} \vdash E : v$, which means that in definition environment $\mathcal{D}$ and in context $\mathcal{P}$, expression E evaluates to value v. The definition environment is of type $\mathcal{D} : \mathbf{Id} \rightarrow \mathbf{Expr}$ and the context of type $\mathcal{P} : \mathbf{Val} \rightarrow \mathbf{Val}$. When a value v is of the form c, it means that it is known to be a constant value.

$$\mathbf{S_{const}} : \frac{}{\mathcal{D}, \mathcal{P} \vdash \text{const } c : c}$$

$$\mathbf{S_{id}} : \frac{\mathcal{D}, \mathcal{P} \vdash \mathcal{D}(id) : v}{\mathcal{D}, \mathcal{P} \vdash id : v}$$

$$\mathbf{S_{op}} : \frac{\mathcal{D}, \mathcal{P} \vdash E_0 : \text{op } f \qquad \mathcal{D}, \mathcal{P} \vdash E_i : c_i}{\mathcal{D}, \mathcal{P} \vdash E_0(E_1, \ldots, E_n) : f(c_1, \ldots, c_n)}$$

$$\mathbf{S_{cT}} : \frac{\mathcal{D}, \mathcal{P} \vdash E_0 : true \qquad \mathcal{D}, \mathcal{P} \vdash E_1 : v_1}{\mathcal{D}, \mathcal{P} \vdash \text{if } E_0 \text{ then } E_1 \text{ else } E_2 : v_1}$$

$$\mathbf{S_{cF}} : \frac{\mathcal{D}, \mathcal{P} \vdash E_0 : false \qquad \mathcal{D}, \mathcal{P} \vdash E_2 : v_2}{\mathcal{D}, \mathcal{P} \vdash \text{if } E_0 \text{ then } E_1 \text{ else } E_2 : v_2}$$

$$\mathbf{S_{index}} : \frac{\mathcal{D}, \mathcal{P} \vdash E : c}{\mathcal{D}, \mathcal{P} \vdash \#E : \mathcal{P}(c)}$$

$$\mathbf{S_{rel}} : \frac{\mathcal{D}, \mathcal{P} \vdash E_1 : c_1 \qquad \mathcal{D}, \mathcal{P} \vdash E_2 : c_2 \qquad \mathcal{D}, \mathcal{P}\dagger[c_1 \mapsto c_2] \vdash E_0 : v_0}{\mathcal{D}, \mathcal{P} \vdash E_0 \text{ @} E_1 \; E_2 : v_0}$$

Fig. 2. Semantic rules for Lucid

We do not give the semantics for functions, as it does not pertain directly to the subject at hand. It has already been shown [10,11,5] that many Lucid programs with functions can be compiled into multidimensional Lucid programs without functions.

4   Keeping Track of the Context

It should be clear that the semantics as presented in Figure 2 is too inefficient, since no caching of values is taking place. However, we cannot directly build an eductive interpreter since we must keep track of the part of the current context that was necessary to compute the value of an expression at the current context.

The revised semantics is given in Figure 3. In it, the judgments are of the form $\mathcal{D}, \mathcal{P} \vdash E : v, \mathcal{P}'$, which means that in definition environment $\mathcal{D}$ and in context $\mathcal{P}$, expression E evaluates to value v and needs context $\mathcal{P}'$. The definition environment is of type $\mathcal{D} : \mathbf{Id} \to \mathbf{Expr}$ and the context of type $\mathcal{P} : \mathbf{Val} \to \mathbf{Val}$. When a value v is of the form c, it means that it is known to be a constant value.

$$\mathrm{C_{const}} : \overline{\mathcal{D}, \mathcal{P} \vdash \mathtt{const}\ c : c, \emptyset}$$

$$\mathrm{C_{id}} : \frac{\mathcal{D}, \mathcal{P} \vdash \mathcal{D}(id) : v, \mathcal{P}'}{\mathcal{D}, \mathcal{P} \vdash id : v, \mathcal{P}'}$$

$$\mathrm{C_{op}} : \frac{\mathcal{D}, \mathcal{P} \vdash E_0 : \mathtt{op}\ f, \mathcal{P}_0 \qquad \mathcal{D}, \mathcal{P} \vdash E_i : c_i, \mathcal{P}_i}{\mathcal{D}, \mathcal{P} \vdash E_0(E_1, \ldots, E_n) : f(c_1, \ldots, c_n), \cup_{i=0..n} \mathcal{P}_i}$$

$$\mathrm{C_{c_T}} : \frac{\mathcal{D}, \mathcal{P} \vdash E_0 : true, \mathcal{P}_0 \qquad \mathcal{D}, \mathcal{P} \vdash E_1 : v_1, \mathcal{P}_1}{\mathcal{D}, \mathcal{P} \vdash \mathtt{if}\ E_0\ \mathtt{then}\ E_1\ \mathtt{else}\ E_2 : v_1, \mathcal{P}_0 \cup \mathcal{P}_1}$$

$$\mathrm{C_{c_F}} : \frac{\mathcal{D}, \mathcal{P} \vdash E_0 : false, \mathcal{P}_0 \qquad \mathcal{D}, \mathcal{P} \vdash E_2 : v_2, \mathcal{P}_2}{\mathcal{D}, \mathcal{P} \vdash \mathtt{if}\ E_0\ \mathtt{then}\ E_1\ \mathtt{else}\ E_2 : v_2, \mathcal{P}_0 \cup \mathcal{P}_2}$$

$$\mathrm{C_{index}} : \frac{\mathcal{D}, \mathcal{P} \vdash E : c, \mathcal{P}' \qquad \mathcal{P}(c) = c'}{\mathcal{D}, \mathcal{P} \vdash \#E : c', \mathcal{P}' \dagger [c \mapsto c']}$$

$$\mathrm{C_{rel}} : \frac{\mathcal{D}, \mathcal{P} \vdash E_1 : c_1, \mathcal{P}_1 \qquad \mathcal{D}, \mathcal{P} \vdash E_2 : c_2, \mathcal{P}_2 \qquad \mathcal{D}, \mathcal{P}\dagger[c_1 \mapsto c_2] \vdash E_0 : v_0, \mathcal{P}_0}{\mathcal{D}, \mathcal{P} \vdash E_0\ @E_1\ E_2 : v_0, (\mathcal{P}_0 \backslash c_1) \cup \mathcal{P}_1 \cup \mathcal{P}_2}$$

Fig. 3. Semantic rules, keeping track of context information

Of course, if we are going to have two semantics, then we need to relate them.

Proposition 1. *Let E be a Lucid program, $\mathcal{D}$ be a definition environment and $\mathcal{P}$ be a context. Then we have that $\mathcal{D}, \mathcal{P} \vdash E : v$ iff there exists $\mathcal{P}_0 \sqsubseteq \mathcal{P}$ such that $\mathcal{D}, \mathcal{P}_0 \vdash E : v, \mathcal{P}_0$, and for all $\mathcal{P}' \sqsupseteq \mathcal{P}_0$, we have $\mathcal{D}, \mathcal{P}' \vdash E : v, \mathcal{P}_0$.*

Proof. Suppose $\mathcal{D}, \mathcal{P} \vdash E : v$. Since the **S** and **C** rules concur exactly on the value parts, by structural induction, there exists a context $\mathcal{P}_0$ for which $\mathcal{D}, \mathcal{P} \vdash E : v, \mathcal{P}_0$. Since only the $\mathbf{C_{index}}$ rule adds to the context $\mathcal{P}_0$, by induction $\mathcal{P}_0 \sqsubseteq \mathcal{P}$ and $\mathcal{D}, \mathcal{P}_0 \vdash E : v, \mathcal{P}_0$.

5 Eduction

It is now possible to define the eductive process, using a warehouse, a form of cache. Once again, we use the structural operational semantics style. In it, the judgments are of the form $\mathcal{D}, \mathcal{P}, \mathcal{W} \vdash E : v, \mathcal{P}', \mathcal{W}'$, which means that in definition environment $\mathcal{D}$ and in context $\mathcal{P}$, using warehouse $\mathcal{W}$, expression E evaluates to value v, needing context $\mathcal{P}'$ and changing the warehouse to $\mathcal{W}'$. The definition environment is of type $\mathcal{D} : \mathbf{Id} \rightarrow \mathbf{Expr}$, the context of type $\mathcal{P} : \mathbf{Val} \rightarrow \mathbf{Val}$, and the warehouse of type $\mathcal{W} : \mathbf{Id} \times \mathbf{Context} \rightarrow \mathbf{Val}$. When a value v is of the form c, it means that it is known to be a constant value.

$$\mathbf{E_{const}} : \frac{}{\mathcal{D}, \mathcal{P}, \mathcal{W} \vdash \mathtt{const}\ c : c, \emptyset, \mathcal{W}}$$

$$\mathbf{E_{id_W}} : \frac{\mathcal{W}(id, \mathcal{P}') = v \qquad \mathcal{P}' \sqsubseteq \mathcal{P}}{\mathcal{D}, \mathcal{P}, \mathcal{W} \vdash id : v, \mathcal{P}', \mathcal{W}}$$

$$\mathbf{E_{id_N}} : \frac{\mathcal{D}, \mathcal{P}, \mathcal{W} \vdash \mathcal{D}(id) : v, \mathcal{P}', \mathcal{W}'}{\mathcal{D}, \mathcal{P}, \mathcal{W} \vdash id : v, \mathcal{P}', \mathcal{W}' \dagger [(id, \mathcal{P}') \mapsto v]}$$

$$\mathbf{E_{op}} : \frac{\mathcal{D}, \mathcal{P}, \mathcal{W} \vdash E_0 : \mathtt{op}\ f, \mathcal{P}_0, \mathcal{W}_0 \qquad \mathcal{D}, \mathcal{P}, \mathcal{W} \vdash E_i : c_i, \mathcal{P}_i, \mathcal{W}_i}{\mathcal{D}, \mathcal{P}, \mathcal{W} \vdash E_0(E_1, \ldots, E_n) : f(c_1, \ldots, c_n), \cup_{i=0..n} \mathcal{P}_i, \cup_{i=0..n} \mathcal{W}_i}$$

$$\mathbf{E_{c_T}} : \frac{\mathcal{D}, \mathcal{P}, \mathcal{W} \vdash E_0 : \mathit{true}, \mathcal{P}_0, \mathcal{W}_0 \qquad \mathcal{D}, \mathcal{P}, \mathcal{W} \vdash E_1 : v_1, \mathcal{P}_1, \mathcal{W}_1}{\mathcal{D}, \mathcal{P}, \mathcal{W} \vdash \mathtt{if}\ E_0\ \mathtt{then}\ E_1\ \mathtt{else}\ E_2 : v_1, \mathcal{P}_0 \cup \mathcal{P}_1, \mathcal{W}_0 \cup \mathcal{W}_1}$$

$$\mathbf{E_{c_F}} : \frac{\mathcal{D}, \mathcal{P}, \mathcal{W} \vdash E_0 : \mathit{false}, \mathcal{P}_0, \mathcal{W}_0 \qquad \mathcal{D}, \mathcal{P}, \mathcal{W} \vdash E_2 : v_2, \mathcal{P}_2, \mathcal{W}_2}{\mathcal{D}, \mathcal{P}, \mathcal{W} \vdash \mathtt{if}\ E_0\ \mathtt{then}\ E_1\ \mathtt{else}\ E_2 : v_2, \mathcal{P}_0 \cup \mathcal{P}_2, \mathcal{W}_0 \cup \mathcal{W}_2}$$

$$\mathbf{E_{index}} : \frac{\mathcal{D}, \mathcal{P}, \mathcal{W} \vdash E : c, \mathcal{P}', \mathcal{W}' \qquad \mathcal{P}(c) = c'}{\mathcal{D}, \mathcal{P}, \mathcal{W} \vdash \#E : c', \mathcal{P}' \dagger [c \mapsto c'], \mathcal{W}'}$$

$$\mathbf{E_{rel}} : \frac{\begin{array}{c} \mathcal{D}, \mathcal{P}, \mathcal{W} \vdash E_1 : c_1, \mathcal{P}_1, \mathcal{W}_1 \\ \mathcal{D}, \mathcal{P}, \mathcal{W} \vdash E_2 : c_2, \mathcal{P}_2, \mathcal{W}_2 \\ \mathcal{D}, \mathcal{P} \dagger [c_1 \mapsto c_2] \vdash E_0 : v_0, \mathcal{P}_0, \mathcal{W}_0 \end{array}}{\mathcal{D}, \mathcal{P}, \mathcal{W} \vdash E_0\ @E_1\ E_2 : v_0, (\mathcal{P}_0 \backslash c_1) \cup \mathcal{P}_1 \cup \mathcal{P}_2, \mathcal{W}_0 \cup \mathcal{W}_1 \cup \mathcal{W}_2}$$

Fig. 4. Semantic rules with warehouse for Lucid

Once again, we need a proposition.

Proposition 2. *Let E be a Lucid program, $\mathcal{D}$ be a definition environment and $\mathcal{P}$ be a context. Suppose $\mathcal{D}, \mathcal{P} \vdash E : v, \mathcal{P}_0$. Suppose further that $\forall id, \mathcal{P} . \mathcal{W}(id, \mathcal{P}) =$*

$v \Rightarrow \mathcal{D}, \mathcal{P} \vdash \mathcal{D}(id) : v, \mathcal{P}$. Then $\mathcal{D}, \mathcal{P} \vdash E : v, \mathcal{P}_0$ iff there exists $\mathcal{W}' \sqsupseteq \mathcal{W}$ such that $\mathcal{D}, \mathcal{P}, \mathcal{W} \vdash E : v, \mathcal{P}_0, \mathcal{W}'$ and that $\forall id, \mathcal{P} . \mathcal{W}'(id, \mathcal{P}) = v \Rightarrow \mathcal{D}, \mathcal{P} \vdash \mathcal{D}(id) : v, \mathcal{P}$.

Proof. Suppose $\mathcal{D}, \mathcal{P} \vdash E : v, \mathcal{P}_0$. Since the **C** and **E** rules concur exactly on the value and context parts, by structural induction, there exists a warehouse $\mathcal{W}'$ for which $\mathcal{D}, \mathcal{P}, \mathcal{W} \vdash E : v, \mathcal{P}_0, \mathcal{W}'$. Since only $\mathbf{E_{id_N}}$ rule adds to the warehouse, and no rule takes away from it, by induction $\mathcal{W} \sqsubseteq \mathcal{W}'$. That same rule ensures that $\forall id, \mathcal{P} . \mathcal{W}'(id, \mathcal{P}) = v \Rightarrow \mathcal{D}, \mathcal{P} \vdash \mathcal{D}(id) : v, \mathcal{P}$.

6   Optimization and Compilation

The warehouse semantics, although correct, can lead to a lot of unnecessary overhead, since the computed context $\mathcal{P}'$ is dragged along all the time, and prevents ordinary data operations from being undertaken transparently. As a result, any sort of fine-grain computation would just bog down in the overhead.

To remedy this situation, when a variable's defining expression is to be evaluated, it would be best to ensure that all of its dependencies have been calculated beforehand, along with the computed contexts. As a result, then the ordinary computations can easily take place.

Because of the recursive nature of Lucid equations, as well as the uncertainty provoked by the presence of conditional expressions, all programs will have to be transformed so that they conform to the syntax found in Figure 5. Because of Lucid's side-effect-free semantics, this transformation can be undertaken automatically.

$$
\begin{aligned}
E ::= \ & id \\
 | \ & \texttt{const } c \\
 | \ & \texttt{op } f \\
 | \ & E_0(E_1, \ldots, E_n) \\
 | \ & \texttt{if } id \texttt{ then } E_1 \texttt{ else } E_2 \\
 | \ & \#id \\
 | \ & id_0 \ @id_1 \ id_2
\end{aligned}
$$

Fig. 5. Syntax for optimizing Lucid implementations

Using this syntax, it is easy to split the rules for $\mathcal{D}, \mathcal{P}, \mathcal{W} \vdash E : v, \mathcal{P}', \mathcal{W}'$ into two sets of interacting rules, $\mathcal{D}, \mathcal{P}, \mathcal{W} \vdash E : \mathcal{P}', \mathcal{W}'$ and $\mathcal{D}, \mathcal{P}, \mathcal{W} \vdash E : v$. The key rule of interest is given in Figure 6.

$$O_{id_N} : \frac{\mathcal{D}, \mathcal{P}, \mathcal{W} \vdash \mathcal{D}(id) : \mathcal{P}', \mathcal{W}' \quad \mathcal{D}, \mathcal{P}', \mathcal{W}' \vdash \mathcal{D}(id) : v}{\mathcal{D}, \mathcal{P}, \mathcal{W} \vdash id : \mathcal{P}', \mathcal{W}' \dagger [(id, \mathcal{P}') \mapsto v]}$$

Fig. 6. Identifier rule for optimized performance

7   Conclusion

Dimensions as values simplify the semantics of Lucid and implement a variety of features. We have shown that it is still possible to use the eductive process to implement Lucid, and that efficient implementations can be produced automatically. Research still needs to be undertaken to ensure that on-the-fly compilation of expressions can be effected.

References

1. E. A. Ashcroft, A. A. Faustini, R. Jagannathan, and W. W. Wadge. *Multidimensional, Declarative Programming.* Oxford University Press, London, 1995.
2. E. A. Ashcroft and W. W Wadge. Lucid—A formal system for writing and proving programs. *SIAM Journal on Computing*, pages 336–354, September 1976.
3. E. A. Ashcroft and W. W Wadge. Lucid, a nonprocedural language with iteration. *Communications of the ACM*, pages 519–526, July 1977.
4. A. A. Faustini and W. W. Wadge. Intensional programming. In J.C. Bourdeaux, B.W. Hamill, and R. Jernigan, editors, *The Role of Languages in Problem Solving 2.* Elsevier Science Publishers, North-Holland, 1987.
5. J.-R. Gagné and J. Plaice. Demand-driven real-time computing. In *Intensional Programming II*. World-Scientific, Singapore, 2000.
6. R. Jagannathan, C. Dodd, and I. Agi. GLU: A high-level system for granular data-parallel programming. *Concurrency: Practice and Experience*, (1):63–83, 1997.
7. P. J. Landin. The next 700 programming languages. *Communications of the ACM*, 9(3):157–166, 1966.
8. J. Paquet and J. Plaice. The semantics of dimensions as values. In *Intensional Programming II*. World-Scientific, Singapore, 2000.
9. J. Plaice and J. Paquet. Introduction to intensional programming. In *Intensional Programming I*, pages 1–14. World Scientific, Singapore, 1995.
10. P. Rondogiannis and W. W. Wadge. First-order functional languages and intensional logic. *Journal of Functional Programming*, 7(1):73–101, 1997.
11. P. Rondogiannis and W. W. Wadge. Higher-order functional languages and intensional logic. *Journal of Functional Programming*, 1999. In press.
12. W. W. Wadge and E. A. Ashcroft. *Lucid, the Dataflow Programming Language.* Academic Press, London, 1985.

Intensional High Performance Computing

Pierre Kuonen[1], Gilbert Babin[2], Nabil Abdennadher[1], and Paul-Jean Cagnard[1]

[1] GRIP Research Group, Département d'informatique
Swiss Federal Institute of Technology (EPFL), CH-1015 Lausanne, Switzerland
{Pierre.Kuonen, Nabil.Abdennadher, Paul-Jean.Cagnard}@epfl.ch
[2] PARADIS Laboratory, Département d'informatique
Université Laval, Québec, Canada G1K 7P4
babin@ift.ulaval.ca

Abstract. In this paper, we describe how a metacomputing environment called *Web Operating System* (WOS™) together with a new programming paradigm called ParCeL 2 may be used to exploit available computing resources on a parallel/distributed environment. The main feature of the WOS™ is to manage contexts of execution (hardware, software, time, etc). The WOS™ fulfills users' requests while considering all possible execution contexts in order to provide the application with the best resources available. In the model presented, we assume that parallel/distributed HPC applications are written using ParCeL-2. The well defined computing model as well as the hierarchical syntactic structure of ParCeL-2 allow for an automatic adaptation, at execution time, of the size of the different parallel processes, depending on the context of execution. We have called this approach, derived from intensional logic : *intensional High Performance Computing (iHPC)*.

1 Introduction

Until recently, the world of High Performance Computing (HPC) was mainly involved in solving huge numeric problems using matrix calculation (number-crunching). This fact may be attributed to two factors. First, traditional vector and parallel supercomputers were very expensive and especially well designed for the resolution of large numerical problems. Second, most potential users, having large enough budget for buying such machines, were people dealing with linear algebra problems as found in aeronautics, spatial and military industry, chemistry and fluid dynamics. As a consequence, the state-of-the-art in HPC has mainly relied on FORTRAN, inducing poor data structures and imposing poor software engineering approaches in the design of long programs. Application programmers were working in close relation with users of these applications and the main execution paradigm was the batch mode.

Since the beginning of the nineties, distributed computing is emerging and prototypes of parallel applications running on less costly local networks of workstations appeared. These applications were first realized using locally developed communication software and more recently using *de facto* standards such as the Parallel Virtual Machine (PVM) standard, thus popularising the message

P. Kropf et al. (Eds.): DCW 2000, LNCS 1830, pp. 161–170, 2000.
© Springer-Verlag Berlin Heidelberg 2000

passing parallel programming paradigm. This led to the now well established Message Passing Interface (MPI) standard. Following the development of Local Area Networks (LAN) during the eighties, Internet technology has popularized Wide Area Networks (WAN). Message passing programming, first localized on LAN and on massively parallel computers, is now moving to WAN. Habits of users are rapidly changing from a *program centric* vision to a *service centric* vision. Future users will require the realization of a given service in the most efficient environment presently available to them through a WAN.

This evolution in the user's needs has led to the creation of a new high performance computing paradigm called *metacomputing* [Buyya 99]. A major consequence of the emergence of this new paradigm in the world of HPC is the urgent need for new software environments to develop and execute HPC applications. Such environments should give access to existing and new parallel programming tools and allow for an efficient transparent remote execution of wide-area distributed HPC applications. Unfortunately, most of current tools available for High Performance Parallel/Distributed computing require that all the computing nodes be known in advance; each computer involved in the execution must be properly configured and the execution environment must usually know where the different processes of the parallel program will be executed. In this paper, we will show how a new parallel programming paradigm, called ParCeL-2 (Section 2), together with the WOS™ metacomputing environment (Section 3) leads to the concept of *intensional HPC* (Sections 4 and 5). We will show that intensional HPC (iHPC) is an elegant and powerful concept for the realization of HPC applications which are able, at execution time, to automatically adapt themselves to the context of the execution. This capability is of the highest importance for allowing HPC applications to benefit from the computing capacity offered by metacomputing environments since these environments are usually very dynamic and unstable.

2 ParCeL-2: A New Parallel and Distributed Programming Paradigm

More than a new parallel programming language, ParCeL-2 is a new parallel and distributed programming paradigm. Its objective is to provide a minimal set of new concepts to be added to a classical imperative programming language in order to allow an "intuitive" expression as well as an efficient execution of parallel and distributed applications. ParCeL-2 basically provides two main concepts:

- a well defined parallel computing model;
- a hierarchical syntactic structure.

These two new concepts can be integrated in any existing sequential imperative language.

2.1   The **ParCeL-2** Computing Model

The computing model of ParCeL-2 is inspired from the Bulk Synchronous Parallel (BSP) model [Valiant 90]. In BSP, a parallel program consists of a set of parallel processes each executing a sequence of *supersteps*. A superstep is composed of two phases: a computation phase and a communication phase. Supersteps are separated by synchronization barriers. The execution of a program using the BSP model can be represented as in Fig. 1.

During the computation phase of a superstep, a process executes computations which only manipulate data local to this process. These data can be local variables or data that have been received from another process. A process can send data to other processes in the course of a computation phase but the actual transmission of data happens at the end of each superstep. No data are exchanged during computation phases; this means that data sent from a given process P_1 to another process P_2 during superstep s, will only be available to process P_2 at the beginning of the next superstep, that is superstep $s + 1$. It can be observed that this computing model is intrinsically a distributed memory Multiple Instruction Multiple Data model (MIMD-DM).

ParCeL-2 extends the BSP model with several new features. The most important ones are:

- The specification of the communications allowed between processes (links). These allowed communications are typed and directed links;
- A more complex synchronisation mechanism between processes. As opposed, to the BSP definition, ParCeL-2 allows processes to have synchronisation periods that are an integer multiple of the execution environment's global clock period.

A more complete presentation of the computing model of ParCeL-2 can be found in [Cagnard 00].

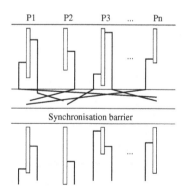
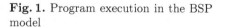

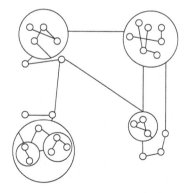

Fig. 1. Program execution in the BSP model

Fig. 2. Program execution on four processors.

2.2   The Hierarchical Syntactic Structure of ParCeL-2

A ParCeL-2 program can be represented as a directed graph where nodes symbolize processes and directed links, the communications allowed. A major difficulty when designing a parallel application is to determine the size of the nodes, i.e., the *grain of parallelism*. This problem is discussed in [Foster 94], where the author presents a design methodology for parallel programs. This method, called PCAM, is based on four steps:

- Partitionning;
- Communication;
- Agglomeration;
- Mapping.

The first two steps focus on parallelism and seek to discover algorithms that exhibit maximum parallelism. The third and fourth steps focus on performance issues. In particular, the agglomeration phase aims to determine the suitable size for the grain of parallelism.

Up to this point, we have seen a ParCeL-2 program as a flat structure where each process is at the same level. The main objective of the hierarchical syntactic structure of ParCeL-2 is to allow for aggregate processes. The ParCeL-2 paradigm is based on the assumption that, in most cases, the design of parallel applications can lead to programs composed of a large number of fine grained processes, that is, processes which execute only a small number of instructions. We call these small processes *cells*, by analogy to cellular automata. In ParCeL-2, aggregates of cells can be constructed in order to build abstract cells whose behavior is the result of the parallel execution of the cells they contain. In other words, a cell can be:

- a sequential process, called an *elementary cell*;
- an aggregate of cells, called a *complex cell*.

An illustration of such a program is given in Fig. 2

The concept of agglomeration of cells has two advantages. First, it provides means for information hiding because the rest of the program does not see if a cell is an elementary or a complex cell. Second, it allows creating cells of size greater than the elementary cells and consequently, adjusting the grain of parallelism.

We can deduce, from the description above, that ParCeL-2 is not an object oriented model in the strict sense, since it does not provide any inheritance between cell types, for example. However, it provides several features from object oriented models that are useful in software engineering for high performance computing. These features are information hiding and aggregation, achieved through the hierarchical syntactic structure, and the fact that only local data can be modified by a given cell, access to data from other cells happens only through well determined interfaces, the communication channels.

2.3 Compiling and Executing **ParCeL-2** Applications

From what has been said above about ParCeL-2 computing model, we note that one of the main characteristics of ParCeL-2 is that processes can either be elementary cells, thus very similar to traditional processes in parallel programs, or complex cells, themselves composed of elementary or complex cells. Hence, a ParCeL-2 program can be represented by a structure like a multilevel-oriented graph where each node corresponds to a cell (elementary or complex) and each edge corresponds to a link. As a consequence, the main program is also a cell. Thus, the global structure of a ParCeL-2 program is intrinsically a recursive structure; a program may be viewed at any level of abstraction desired: from the extremely low level where one sees only elementary cells, up to the extremely high level where there is a single complex cell, the main program. Moreover, due to the well-defined parallel computing model of ParCeL-2, a compiler can easily compile any cell in a very efficient sequential process. Consequently, a ParCeL-2 program can be compiled and executed in a number of different ways. The first extreme case consists of compiling the main program (the outermost cell) into a single large sequential program which can be efficiently executed on a single processor. The other extreme case is to compile all elementary cells of the program in a different sequential process. All the intermediate solutions are also possible. In other words, we are now able to choose the grain of parallelism at compilation-time instead of design-time. This feature is central for the realization of intensional HPC.

3 Metacomputing

A metacomputer is a set of computers sharing resources and acting together to solve a common problem given by the user [Buyya 99]. A metacomputer comprises many computers and terabytes of memory in a loose confederation, tied together by a network. The user has the illusion of a single powerful computer; he manipulates objects representing data resources, applications or physical devices. A metacomputer is a dynamic environment that has some informal pool of independant nodes, each relying on its own complete operating system, and which can join or leave the environment whenever it desires. In other words, a metacomputer is an extremely moving environment where the real target architecture for an application is only known at execution-time.

3.1 The Web Operating System

The Web Operating System (WOS™) [Kropf 99] was developed to provide a user with the possibility to submit a service request without any prior knowledge about the service (where it is available, at what cost, under which constraints) and to have the service request fulfilled within the user's desired parameters (time, cost, quality of service, etc.). Three features make the WOS™ a very attractive environment for metacomputing:

1. *Open Access.* Most of the metacomputing projects, such as Globus [Foster and Kesselman 97; The Globus Project], Legion [Grimshaw *et al.* 97; Lindahl *et al.* 98], and NetSolve [Casanova and Dongarra 97], require login privileges and a global catalog of resources. This may be interesting for small networks but could be impractical for large ones. Contrary to this, the WOS™ uses distributed databases, called warehouses, that allow open access and search procedures. The search engine takes into account the dynamic nature of the Web. The WOS™ is based on a demand-driven computation model: users' queries are only processed when needed and prior results are stored in the warehouses, where they can be accessed later on.

2. *Universality.* The WOS™ aims to supply users with adequate tools that allow the implementation of specific services not initially foreseen. In order to achieve this goal, a generic service protocol (WOSP), provided by the WOS™, allows the WOS™ node administrators to implement a set of services, called a *service class*, dedicated to specific users' needs. WOSP is in fact a generic protocol defined through a generic grammar [Babin *et al.* 98]. A specific instance of this generic grammar provides the communication support for a service class of WOS™. This specific instance is also referred to as a *version of WOSP*; its semantics depends directly on the service class it supports. In other words, knowing a specific version of WOSP is equivalent to understanding the semantics of the service class supported by that version. Several versions of WOSP can cohabit on the same WOS™ node.

3. *Intensionality.* The WOS™ manages contexts: hardware, software, time, place, etc. The basic nature of the WOS™ is to answer users' requests while considering all these contexts; the WOS™ node will provide the best resources available, as a function of the current context, which always changes.

3.2   The Web Operating System and High Performance Computing

A version of WOSP, HP-WOSP [Abdennadher *et al.* 00], has been defined specifically to configure and execute HPC applications in the WOS™ environment. Specifically, it supports the communication requirements for HPC applications, which are:

- To locate potential computation nodes with the appropriate set of resources (hardware and software) and to reserve these resources. This is called the configuration stage;
- To launch the execution of the parallel program. This is called the execution stage.

4   Intensional HPC

The Intensional HPC (iHPC) approach is the integration of intensional logic, HPC, and metacomputing. Let us look at these three perspectives of iHPC in more details.

Intensional logic is based on the notion that an expression is always evaluated within a certain context [Paquet 99]. For instance, the expression "how is the weather?" will yield very different answers, depending on where and when it is evaluated. In most natural languages, such ambiguities are easily processed because most conversations are done within a specific context. It is not that easily handled in computer science, however. Intensional logic, and its specialized versions modal logic and temporal logic, provide the tools to manage such context-dependant expressions. In intensional logic, this context is represented as a multidimentional space, where many, possibly decomposable dimensions constrain the evaluation of an expression. This means that the expression might have an arbitrary large number of values, each one depending on a set of dimension values. Clearly, one cannot compute all the values of an expression, based on all its dimensions. Some computing "trick" must therefore be used. This "trick" is called *eduction* [Swoboda and Wadge 00]. Simply put, the eduction model of computation states that a value should only be computed when required. That value should be stored, so it can be reused instead of recomputed. For us, iHPC can only exist if all the concepts of intensional logic and eduction are applied.

From an HPC perspective, iHPC involves many changes in the way of developing HPC applications, which are usually parallel applications. For iHPC to be achieved, a parallel application should be described in such a way that all implementations could be extracted from the same design. An implementation is in fact a specialization of a design where all decisions about the specific (implementation and execution) constraints are made. The design description method selected should allow for multiple dimensions of constraints to be represented within the same design. Furthermore, an implementation should be automatically produced by setting all the constraints. Therefore, we need a compiler that can take as input a multidimensional design and all the values for the different constraints. We call such a compiler an *intensional compiler*.

However, to truly be intensional, and therefore to fully take advantage of eduction, an iHPC environment must wait until the last minute to compile the necessary pieces of code. This should occur during the configuration stage of the parallel execution. This is where metacomputing comes into play. Metacomputing tools can be used to evaluate the user's constraints for the execution of a parallel application and to identify a set of computation nodes that can run the parallel application within the user's constraints. The selection of nodes is done in parallel with the selection of the compilation parameters (design and execution contraints) to suit the user's needs. This selection is dynamic and should also use eduction. Once all suitable nodes have been identified and that a proper implementation was constructed, the application can be executed.

To summarize, an environment can only be called an iHPC environment when all the following requirements are met:

– The environment supports the execution of HPC applications;
– Intensional logic transcends all components of the environment:
  • Eduction is used as an execution model (dynamic selection of computation nodes);
  • Eduction is used as a compilation model (intensional compiler).

Other researchers have thought of using intensional logic to perform high performance computing. The GLU (Granular LUCID) parallel programming environment was developed for parallel computing [Jagannathan and Dodd 96; Jagannathan et al. 97]. The GLU environment provides a "collage" of C functions using LUCID. Yet, it does not provide an intensional HPC environment, since the grains are fixed (they correspond to the C functions) and the environment does not use an intensional compiler.

5   Towards an Intensional HPC Environment

We argue that the combination of ParCeL-2 and the WOS™, in particular the HP-WOSP service class, constitutes an iHPC environment. To demonstrate this, we will focus on the problem of choosing the grain of parallelism. The correct size of the grain depends on the characteristics of the parallel architecture which will execute the program. In other words, it depends on the context of the execution. If that context is a metacomputing environment, the exact characteristics of the target architecture are only known at execution-time. As a consequence, the size of the grain should be fixed only at execution-time if we want to adopt the iHPC philosophy.

Let us suppose that we have developed a service (an application) using the ParCeL-2 programming language. This service is represented by its resource needs: CPU and network performance, particular software resources, etc. Let us also suppose that we make this service available in the WOS™ environment. When a WOS™ node receives a request for the execution of this service, it can act in two different ways. First it can decide that it has enough resources to execute the service locally. In such a case, it would like to execute a fully sequential version of this service. Otherwise (i.e., no WOS™ node can provide the resources needed by the service), the WOS™ node can decide to split the program (the main cell) into its components in order to execute the service in parallel. Therefore, it will transform the received request into several requests, that is, one for each cell (elementary or complex) which composes the main program. In so doing, the WOS™ node becomes a client which requests for the execution of several services. Since "children" cells are less complex than the father cell, there is a higher probability to find a WOS™ node providing the requested resources. The same reasoning can be recursively applied for each service request sent by the current WOS™ node, until all the requests are eventually applied to elementary cells. In other words, a ParCeL-2 application does not represent only one service, but rather all the services corresponding to all the possible decompositions of the ParCeL-2 application (Section 2.3). In general, it is not reasonable to generate all these services when making a ParCeL-2 application available on the WOS™. A more efficient solution consists in using an intensional compiler. When a node receives a request and decides to run the service locally, it will look whether or not it possesses the sequential version of the service. If not, it will compile it and keep this sequential version for future use.

At the end of this configuration phase, the main service is seen by the system as a set of sub-services, each of them is assigned to a WOS™ node and represents an elementary or complex ParCeL-2 cell. At this stage of our research we assume that this assignement is static and therefore no process migration or fault tolerancy policy are considered. The above description shows that, at least for the problem of choosing the grain of parallelism, the association of the WOS™ and ParCeL-2 creates a iHPC environment. This follows from the requirements elicited in Section 4:

1. This combination supports the execution of HPC applications:
   - ParCeL-2 is a design and programming tool for HPC applications using a BSP model of computation and an MIMD parallel programming model;
   - The WOS™ provides a specialized service class, materialized through HP-WOSP, to configure and run HPC applications.
2. This association uses an eduction approach to configure and execute an HPC application:
   - The WOS™ provides the mechanisms to dynamically select and configure the nodes that will be used for the execution;
   - This dynamic selection also involves the dynamic identification of the grains of parallelisms, which can be identified in the ParCeL-2 model of the application.
3. The combination of the WOS™ and ParCeL-2 can support an intensional compilation approach:
   - A parallel application made with ParCeL-2 yields multiple possible implementations, which vary based on the grain of parallelism, the links established, and the actual resources available;
   - The WOS™ is used to supply the parameters required by an intensional compiler to only build the required executables.

6   Conclusion

In this paper, we have shown that the WOS™, together with the ParCeL-2 programming language, leads to the creation of an environment which exhibits the characteristics of an intensional High Performance Computing (iHPC) environment. Specifically, we showed that the approach is intensional for the determination of the grain of parallelism and the selection of the nodes that will execute these grains. Further investigations are required to validate the concepts presented in this paper. We are currently implementing an HPC version of the WOS™ (HP-WOS) that will allow us to compare the performances of our approach with other the performance of already available tools such GLOBUS or NetSolve.

Although we only consider a single dimension in this paper, namely the grain of parallelism, we are investigating the possibility to extend our approach to the selection of the memory model (distributed or shared). This will add an extra selection criteria for the nodes, i.e, another dimension in our iHPC environment.

We also ignored other run-time issues, usually associated with high performance computing, namely, load distribution (static and dynamic), inter-process communications, and synchronization. The GLU environment might provide us with interesting approaches which could be integrated into our vision of intensional HPC.

References

Abdennadher et al. 00. Abdennadher, N., G. Babin, P. Kropf and P. Kuonen, "A dynamically configurable environment for high performance computing," in *High performance computing 2000 (hpc 2000)*, Washinton, DC, USA, April 2000.

Babin et al. 98. Babin, G., P. Kropf and H. Unger, "A two-level communication protocol for a Web Operating System (WOS™)," in *IEEE Euromicro Workshop on Network Computing*, pp. 939–944, Västerås, Sweden, August 1998.

Buyya 99. Buyya, R., *High performance cluster computing : Architectures and systems*, vol. 1, Prentice Hall PTR, Upper Saddle River, N.J., USA, 1999.

Cagnard 00. Cagnard, P.-J., "The parallel cellular programming model," in 8th euromicro workshop on parallel and distributed processing (euro-pdp 2000), pp. 283–289, Rhodes, Greece, IEEE Computer Society, January 2000.

Casanova and Dongarra 97. Casanova, H. and J. Dongarra, "NetSolve: A network server for solving computational science problems," *International Journal of Supercomputer Applications and High Performance Computing*, 3(11), pp. 212–223, 1997.

Foster 94. Foster, I., *Designing and building parallel programs, concepts and tools for parallel software engineering*, Addison Wesley, 1994.

Foster and Kesselman 97. Foster, I. and C. Kesselman, "Globus: A metacomputing infrastructure toolkit," *International Journal of Supercomputer Applications*, 1997.

Grimshaw et al. 97. Grimshaw, A., W. Wulf, J. French, A. Weaver and P. Reynolds, "The Legion vision of a Worldwide Virtual Computer," *CACM*, 40(1), January 1997.

Jagannathan and Dodd 96. Jagannathan, R. and C. Dodd, *GLU programmer's guide*, Technical report, SRI International, Menlo Park, CA, USA, 1996.

Jagannathan et al. 97. Jagannathan, R., C. Dodd and I. Agi, "GLU: A high-level system for granular data-parallel programming," *Concurrency: Pratice and Experience*, (1), pp. 63–83, 1997.

Kropf 99. Kropf, P., "Overview of the WOS project," in *1999 Advanced Simulation Technologies Conferences (ASTC 1999)*, San Diego, CA, USA, April 1999.

Lindahl et al. 98. Lindahl, G., A. Grimshaw, A. Ferrari and K. Holcomb, *Metacomputing — what's in it for me ?*, http://legion.virginia.edu/papers/why.pdf, last visited on Jan. 20, 2000.

Paquet 99. Paquet, J., *Intensional scientific programming*, Phd Thesis, Faculté des études supérieures, Université Laval, Québec, Canada, 1999.

Swoboda and Wadge 00. Swoboda, P. and W.W. Wadge, "Vmake, ISE and IRCS: General tools for the intensionalization of software systems," in *Intensional Programming II*, World-Scientific, Singapore, 2000.

The Globus Project. The Globus Project, *The Globus project*, http://www.globus.org, last visited on Jan. 20, 2000.

Valiant 90. Valiant, L. G., "A bridging model for parallel computation," *Communications of the ACM*, 33(8), pp. 103–111, August 1990.

Java Mobile Agents Implementing On-line Algorithms to Improve the QoS of a 3D Distributed Virtual Environment

Marc Bui[1] and Victor Larios-Rosillo[2]

[1] Laboratoire de la Recherche en Informatique Avancée, Université Paris 8,
15, rue Catulienne, 93526 Saint-Denis France
Phone, Fax: +33.(0)1.48.09.23.86,
mbui@univ-paris8.fr
[2] HEUDIASYC U.M.R. C.N.R.S. 6599, Université de Technologie de Compiègne,
B.P. 20529, 60205 Compiègne Cedex France,
Phone: +33.(0)3.44.23.44.23 ext.4269, Fax: +33.(0)3.44.23.44.77
vlarios@utc.fr

Abstract. With the explosion in Global Networks such as the Web, communities take advantage sharing and working with the big amount of information and services available.

Within this context a promising area for the communities when dealing with the information on the man-machine interface is Distributed Virtual Reality. However, distributed applications must deal with issues such as robustness, scalability, heterogeneity, uncertain online inputs and good Quality of Service (QoS). The work presented in this paper describes our enterprise improving the QoS of DVRMedia, a Multi-User Virtual Reality system for the Web [9]. This tentative brings us to deal with an abstract model so called the *k-server problem*. We propose a solution with the integration of two paradigms: online algorithms and mobile agents. Both paradigms allow us to design a scheme for improving the QoS and to drive an implementation in Java. The solution is validated with experiments and its implementation on DVRMedia.

1 Introduction

In recent years, there has been an important growth of global networks such as the Internet and the Web. The improvements on the communication infrastructure and personal computers can explain in part this growth but it could also take credit from the offered services and their use. Such services may manage efficiently and securely the big amount of information available. In addition, the users take advantage of such networks working in communities where they exchange and share the information. Areas such as electronic commerce, multimedia services and collaborative applications are some examples of interest.

An application offering a service for the Web communities working on global networks is expected to be implemented in a distributed architecture with components that can be running on heterogeneous platforms. The application may

P. Kropf et al. (Eds.): DCW 2000, LNCS 1830, pp. 171–181, 2000.
© Springer-Verlag Berlin Heidelberg 2000

be adaptive to the rapid changes on the underlying structure of the network. It is desirable to guarantee a certain degree of scalability, robustness, data coherence (when concurrency), security and a good QoS [12]. Such distributed applications have often to compute online without complete knowledge of the future.

In this context, Virtual Reality is an area of research that takes advantage of global networks because it promises a solution for the man-machine interface problem when dealing with the big amount of information and services generated on the Web [3].

3D networked Virtual Environments (net-VEs) offer a richer representation and interaction with the information. VR today is possible because special purpose graphics hardware technology has improved steadily and graphics software tended to a suite of standards. However, there still exist a gap on implementing 3D net-VEs on the Web global networks because they demand a considerable amount of processing capacity. The challenge in developing such applications involves also multiple computer science domains such as distributed systems, graphical applications, and interactive applications [13]. On distributed systems they must contend with all the challenges of managing network resources and all the aspects enounced before for an application on global networks. On graphical applications, they must maintain smooth, real-time display frame rates and carefully allocate the CPU among rendering and other tasks. Finally on interactive applications they must process online data input from users, users should see the virtual environment as it exist locally, even though its participants are distributed at multiple remote hosts. To conclude, 3D net-VEs on global networks have many challenges because they need to keep a good QoS to be functional [11].

QoS on 3D net-VEs refers to the performance guarantees on the throughput (bandwidth), network latency and jitter. Network latency is the time it takes to get information from one site to others trough the network. For example, when a net-VE user performs an action, remote users will receive the result of the action after a delay. The jitter is because networks can offer variability in delays resulting in a jerky representation of remote participant actions. With a large network latency and jitter there is a lack of consistency between users with an impact in their coordination. Latency and jitter are present when the network and processing power reach their maximal capacity as limited resources. So, a better QoS can be expected if such resources are allocated efficiently.

In this paper we focus our attention on improving the QoS of a 3D net-VE system. We develop an approach using two computer paradigms: online algorithms and mobile code. The online algorithms are implemented on mobile code that improves the QoS by dealing with an online abstract model so called the k-server problem. This k-server approach is tightly integrated within the net-VEs but it could be applied for similar systems in the Web where the QoS is an essential factor in maintaining a distributed consistency. Such Web applications can concern distributed database services for the e-commerce, or it can be extended to other Web collaborative applications. Finally, this approach is tested in DVRMedia, a 3D distributed net-VE system [9] that we have developed.

The paper is organized as follows: section one describes the problem, section two discusses the state of the art and the approaches in online algorithms in relation with our problem, section three discuss the implementation of the solution using mobile code and the results. Finally we drive some conclusions and the perspectives on further works.

2   3D Net-VEs: The Problem Context

A 3D net-VE allows communities of users located at different geographical sites to interact in real time. Each user accesses his or her computer workstation, using it to provide a user-interface to the content of a VE. These environments aim to provide users with the sense of realism incorporating realistic 3D graphics and stereo sound, to create an immersive experience. In such environments, multiple users have the ability to interact with each other, share information, and manipulate objects in the environment. 3D net-VEs are appropriated for applications that demand the creation of telepresence. DVRMedia is a 3D net-VE system that we developed to support and access VEs within a distributed architecture [9].

On the behalf of a distributed application, a VE in DVRMedia is partitioned in clusters of servers that processes the changes in the environment due to the participant's interaction. Because a VE is composed mainly of 3D objects, each cluster can be compared as a database manager controlling concurrently changes in objects where the main operations are: insert, delete, and modify (read/write). Any change in the database must be updated to all the participants. Clusters are interconnected altogether with links called "portals" [5] providing a behavior to scale the VE, see figure 1. Changing from cluster to cluster must be fast and transparent for each participant.

A cluster supports simultaneously multiple user connections that can demand a considerable amount of processing capacity. As the number of the net-VE participants increases, the cluster must scale to handle them if it reach the limit of his resources. To scale, the cluster can have replicas with fast connections on different machines. On each cluster replica, there are two parameters to take care in terms of QoS: the available processor resources and the communication bandwidth.

Many efforts were taken to improve the QoS on net-VEs, most of them aims to reduce the communication overhead. Hagsand, Lea et Stenious [7] proposed the use of *Auras* and an *Aura Manager (AM)*. Each dynamic object defines an aura that represents a portion of the virtual space that is monitored by the *AM*. When two auras intersect, this is seen as an indication of mutual interest and thus a potential for exchange of information. Each AM monitors a region of the VE and they are organized in a hierarchy that could be extended. However, this approach has been focused on reducing message passing for the DIVE system [6]. DIVE is based on a peer to peer distributed architecture where all the processing power rests on the clients.

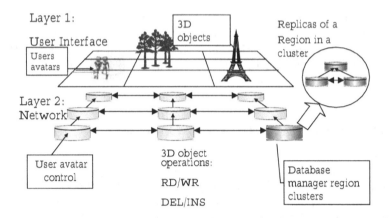

Fig. 1. The VE is partitioned in regions managed by a cluster. Each cluster is composed by a set of replicas where users are connected. Replicas keep coherence updating changes due to users interactions as in a distributed database.

Sung, Yang and Wohn [14] propose the use of a multicast based optimistic concurrency control mechanism to increase the responsiveness. A hierarchy is implemented to enable concurrent manipulation of objects on the tree. A tree is composed of object sub-trees leaving to scale the system. A user manipulates an object without validation sending a request to get the token for such object that takes the time traveling on the tree and that is usually quickly. However, on this approach (as in DIVE) the use of multicast specialized networks is considered but there are no previsions for a network like the Internet. In such networks, using optimal protocols is not enough; sensing the network state and the server's load to be adaptive is important for the QoS.

Besides, Awerbuch and Singh proposes an abstract online strategy [1] that maximizes the total number of users connected, subject to the network capacity constraints. This strategy gives theoretical abstract results that could promise some improvements for the QoS in VEs.

The users geographical network location and the their required processor resources have an impact in the overall performance of the cluster. When a user access a cluster, the better replica must be matched. It is difficult to predict when a participant will request a service. The problem is related about how to provide the best QoS with the available resources (cluster replicas) and this problem is intrinsically online because it requires immediate decisions to be made in real time.

3   Improving the QoS on Distributed VEs: The Problem Specification

In this section, we present some elements to formalize the problem. An abstraction has to be introduced in order to define a policy for the QoS. We found in the literature a close analogy in online computation and with an extensively studied problem of *k-server* systems.

The online nature of the problem presents a complication to estimate the net-VE participants requests and to serve them optimally. In online computation, an algorithm must produce a sequence of decisions that will have an impact on the final quality of its overall performance. These decisions must be made based on past events without information about the future.

Online algorithms base concepts. The performance of an online algorithm [2] is measured by comparing its performance to the one of an optimal off-line algorithm. An off-line algorithm is an ideal algorithm that has full knowledge of the future. The quality is represented by a competitive factor that falls into the framework of worst case complexity. In order to test the performance of an algorithm the worst inputs are furnished. The performance of an algorithm is related to a final cost for such set of inputs. So each decision taken by the algorithm for a given input involves a cost depending in the problem to solve and it could be represented in term of resources like time complexity, amount of processing power to use, amount of memory or communication efforts.

Let $A_{on}(r_i)$ be the performance of the online algorithm compared with that of the optimal off-line algorithm $A_{off}(r_i)$ and is defined as:

$$A_{on}(r_i) \leq (\alpha) \cdot A_{off}(r_i) \tag{1}$$

This relation gives the competitive α *constant ratio* for an online algorithm and we will say that an online algorithm is $\alpha - competitive$.

For any request sequence σ, the optimal off-line cost and the optimal off-line schedule to serve the requests is achieved by reduction to a minimum cost / maximum flow problem. Because we are interested in a particular problem so called the k-server system that we will explain in more detail on next paragraphs, we advance that the time needed to calculate the optimal off-line cost and schedule is $O(k \cdot n^2)$, where n is the number of requests in σ, and k is the number of servers.

The k-server problem. The *k-server* problem [10] is an abstraction of the problem of satisfying a list of requests. Moreover, the model and the k-server conjecture has been catalyst for the development of competitive analysis. One of the goals on this problem has been to find "fast" server algorithms: those that can compute each answer in constant time (real time). This model provides an interesting abstraction for a number of problems that could be found in the Web distributed applications maintaining consistent services.

Let $G = (V, E, w)$ be any weighted undirected graph of N nodes. G introduces a k-server problem by letting $d(x,y)$ be $w(x,y)$ if w is a weighted edge in $E(x,y)$; otherwise is the distance induced by the transitive closure of the relation w. So, the cost/distance incurred to service r_j from s_i would be the weight $d(s_i, r_j)$ on the edge (s_i, r_j) in G.

The k-server problem is better explained with a fire car example. Suppose that there is a k number of fire cars in a city. When a fire alarm r occurs, a

fire car must be dispatched to the emergency site to stop the fire. We ignore
the length of time needed to travel to the site and the length of time needed to
stop the fire for a given car and count only the distance that the fire car must
travel. The fire alarms arrive in a sequential order and the dispatcher does not
know how many and where they will occur. Each fire alarm must be attended
in order. We know only the distance from the car to the emergency site and the
objective is to minimize the cost of traveling for all the available fire cars.

They are some results when working with the k-server problem that bounds
the maximal performance that we can expect for a given k-server online algorithm. It lies on parameters like the number of servers, the kind of the request
distribution, the network architecture and if the used algorithm is randomized or
sequential. From the k-server conjecture by Manasse, McGeoch and Sleator [10]
any metric space allows for a deterministic k-competitive, k-server algorithm.
It has been shown that a deterministic lower bound for the competitive ratio
of a k-server online algorithm, given in a graph G with at least $k+1$ nodes is
$\frac{k}{(k-h+1)}$ for any $1 \leq h \leq k$ where h is the number of simultaneous requests.

The k-server as a solution for the DVRMedia QoS. In our net-VE
system we have an l number of replicas grouped in a cluster, with a c number
of interconnected clusters composing the VE where the total number of nodes
n is done by $n = \sum_{i=0}^{c} l_i$. The nodes are arranged composing a logical network
and they are implemented in k-machines. Users may place a set of r requests to
access a new cluster or to demand a service that should be provided by one of
the k-machines. Because on each cluster there is a limited amount of resources,
the aim is to provide the best service to requests that can be interpreted as
minimize the resource cost to match and serve a request . Because replicas and
clusters are fixed, we need a behavior to match the requests and then route them
to the optimal k-server machine. However, this is only an abstraction of the real
problem.

There are two network topologies that can be used within the replica-cluster
architecture oriented to net-VEs [5]: Multiple replica servers can be arranged
in a ring or in a hierarchy. Figure 2 shows both network topologies. When a
user place a request matching the best suited replica depends on the topology
and the algorithm. For the k-server, there is one work with given results that
can be adapted: the k-server tree algorithm by Chrobak and Larmore [4]. In
addition, the line and the ring are a particular case of the tree and thus, the
same algorithm can be applied. The *competitively ratio* α that we can expect for
this algorithm is k.

The algorithm description is as follows: Consider any configuration of k
servers and a request r on the tree. A server s_i is a *neighbor* of the request
if there is no other server on the simple path from s_i to r. Let $\|s_i, r\|$ represent
the unique arc-length in the tree of the unique simple path from s_i to r and
$(s, r]$ is the interval with s_i excluded. All the servers neighboring the request
start moving towards r at constant speed. When two servers are located at the
same interval, they are neighbors of the request. We consider arbitrarily only
one of them to be a neighbor and we stop the other. Notice that the number of

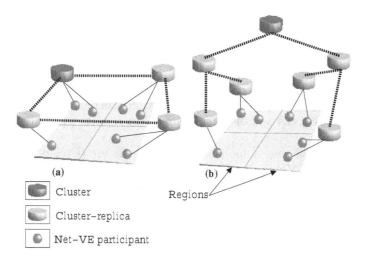

Fig. 2. The users are located in different regions managed by the replicas where the network topologies are: (a)Multiple servers into a Ring and (b) Multiple servers arranged into a hierarchy.

servers that move in a particular request may decrease during the service process since a moving server may become blocked by other servers (it may stop being a neighbor) while traveling toward the request. More precisely, the algorithm can be formulated as follows:

while none of our servers is in r **do begin**
    let $d = min_i \|s_i, y_i\|$ where $y_i \in (s_i, r]$ is either a vertex or r
    move each neighbor server s_i by d towards r
end.

4   The k-Server Implementation as a QoS Solution

In this section, we show how this abstract problem is implemented and adapted using mobile agents programmed in Java.

Implementation choices. Most of the actual Web technology is founded on static components within the model of Object Oriented components. However, to pass from the k-server abstract model to a practical implementation we need to adopt a uniform and democratic paradigm. We consider the servers fixed and thus we need one behavior to match and route the requests. So, one module must integrate the processor services (a cluster) and a sort of a mobile component may represent the k-servers managing the resources, respecting the Web dynamics.

The emergent paradigm of mobile agents offers modularity and more flexibility than the traditional static solutions. Those issues agree with the implementation of a politic to improve the QoS because mobile agents do not need to know the global state of the system or the network. Therefore, mobile agents have a natural correspondence with the online paradigm.

The k servers can be implemented with mobile agents but they can not process heavy tasks because for technical reasons, a mobile agent need to be light and fast. On the contrary, the migration process of an agent can take many resources resulting on a bad degree of QoS. Therefore, the mobile agents can match the requests and dispatch them to the clusters that will provide the services.

Because most of the components of DVRMedia are developed in the Java language, we adopt Mobile Agents technology known as *Aglets* [15] [8]. An Aglet is a mobile Java object visiting aglet-enabled hosts in a network. Some of the reasons that decided the use of mobile agents in our application are:

- They execute asynchronously and autonomously offering the ability to sense their execution environment and react autonomously to changes, even if a network failure arrives. These properties make easier to build robust and fault tolerant distributed systems.
- They reduce network load and encapsulates protocols needed to keep working the distributed system. Against the static solutions where multiple interactions are needed to accomplish a given task, mobile agents can solve the problem locally.
- They are naturally heterogeneous and tightly integrated with the Web. Java applets may launch mobile agents from Web browsers and may receive the agents they have launched after they completed their remote execution.

The experimental framework. The application is implemented as follows: k *mobile agents* are created by a *root agent* on an initial site. Each agent represents the cluster available resources and they have an online algorithm implemented. To start the system, the *root* spreads randomly the k agents on the network. When a user places a request, a request message is sent in broadcast to the network. When a k-server agent catches a request, each agent compute the itinerary to match it and moves using the rules of the *k-server algorithm for the tree*. At each move, the agent senses if it is still a neighbor and if the request is still active. On the contrary, it stops and waits for a new request. At the same time, an isolated enabled host has an agent with the task of monitoring the movements of the aglets and evaluates the algorithm performance. Figure 3 shows the application monitor.

At each move, the k-agents measure the state of the cluster in terms of communication bandwidth and free resources and when an important change is detected the clusters root is notified. So, the k-agents can have a global image of the system to optimize their routing decision. An important change means that in some points of the network the bandwidth is under the requirements of the application or that a current server attends the maximal load. Notifying the root can be seen as a centralized computation but the hierarchy can be partitioned to scale if necessary. When a request is matched, the agent consults the root and decides which replica server may process the request.

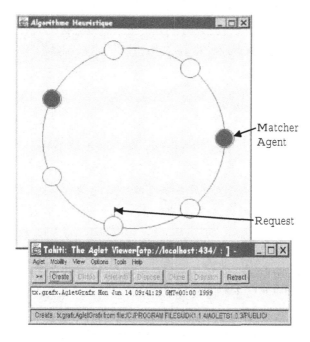

Fig. 3. Screen shot of the monitor graphics interface to evaluate the QoS on the system and the *Thaiti* aglets server.

Strategies for serving requests. The main issue of the experiment of this study is to see how the QoS is improved on the system by using online algorithms. We are interested to see that the k-server *minimizes* their number of *moves* to serve the requests. Also, we know that any move of the k-server aglets have a cost in communication and in processor resources.

Two algorithms have been implemented: The k-server tree algorithm and the greedy algorithm [2]. The strategy of greedy is as follows: when a request arrives each agent computes their path and sends it to the root. Once the root has all the paths he decides to *move only the nearest server*(an arbitrary choice if there are more than one) to the request.

Experimental results. Experimental results are currently undergoing but we compared both algorithms with a random set of requests where we focused our attention in the final number of moves needed to serve. For the comparison we ran the test with 5, 11 and 15 nodes and two matching agents. Each test has been performed on a PC linux server. The results are shown in figure 4.

It can be seen that as the number of nodes on the network is increased, the greedy algorithm is linear. In contrast, the online algorithm appears more efficient in terms of moves needed to serve the indeed requests as the sequence advances.

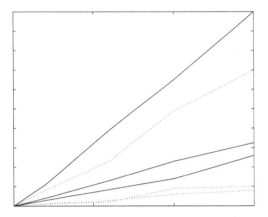

Fig. 4. Performance results for both greedy (continuous line) and k-server tree (doted line) algorithms with n at 5, 11 and 15 nodes.

5   Concluding Remarks and Perspectives

Implementing distributed net-VEs on global networks offers a challenge on keeping a good QoS on the overall system. This is due to the considerable amount of processing capacity required in real time and because the system must scale to the number of participants.

Our results shown that the QoS is improved in DVRMedia using two paradigms: *online algorithms* and *mobile agents*. A better QoS is claimed because the use of resources is optimized helping to prevent latency and jitter on the framework. In the case of the k-server algorithms, mobile agents fits well because the online algorithms implementation do not demand a heavy code or a big amount of memory. These issues help the agents to keep a good mobility avoiding an extra load in the system needed to keep working the mobile agents. In traditional approaches, the tasks of the k-server algorithms may be done by a distributed scheduler and replacing the mobile code by heavy protocols to ensure the system optimal resource management. A such static solution may be difficult to scale and to adapt to furthers architectures on the Web. In contrast, mobile agents give more flexibility and in the case of net-VEs, they help to reduce the network overload. However, there exist a lack of maturity on this technology where is preferable to use it for light tasks like the online algorithms than for complex computations.

Online algorithms yield a good approximate solution for our problem in net-VEs but often many of them are difficult to implement because they propose solutions for abstract models. However, the k-server system can be adapted for other systems on the Web maintaining consistent states in distributed services and improving the QoS like in Web multimedia applications for communities. It is interesting to observe that as the system grows in size, a competitive QoS can be expected by using online algorithms because the requests are served with an optimal use of resources.

We plan to stage major experimental events with a more important number of nodes and k-servers to find the optimal framework for our system where other online algorithms must be also tested and evaluated. It seems that the initial configuration of the k-server agents is important and in some cases, online algorithms with a random factor in decisions can be better for some distributions of system inputs. The number of k-server agents in the system and the nodes bounds also the competitive α factor.

References

1. Awerbuch, B., Singh, T.: Online Algorithms for Selective Multicast and Maximal Dense Trees Proceedings of the ACM STOC 97, El Paso Texas USA, February (1997) 354–352
2. Borodin, A., El-Yaniv, R.: Online Computation and Competitive Analysis. Cambridge University Press (1998)
3. Brooks, F.P.: What's Real About Virtual Reality?. IEEE Computer Graphics and Applications, Vol. 19, Num. 6 (1999) 16–27
4. Chrobak,M., Larmore, L.L.: An Optimal Online Algorithm for K-Servers on Trees. SIAM Journal of Computing, Vol. 20, Num. 1 (1991) 144–148
5. Funkhouser, T. A.: Network Topologies for Scalable Multi-User Virtual Environments. Proceedings of the IEEE Virtual Reality Annual International Symposium (1996) 222–228
6. Hagsand, O.: DIVE - A Platform for Multi-User Virtual Environments. IEEE Multimedia, Vol. 3, Num. 1, (1996) 30–39
7. Hagsand, O., Lea, R., Stenius, M.: Using Spatial Techniques to Decrease Message Passing in a Distributed VE System. Proceedings of the VRML 97 Symposium, Monterey CA USA (1997) 7–15
8. Lange, D.B., Oshima, M.: Programming and Developing Java Mobile Agents with Aglets. Addison Wesley (1998)
9. Larios-Rosillo, V.M.: DVRMEDIA: a 3D Multi-User Distributed Virtual Environment. Proceedings of the DCW99 Rostock, Germany (1999) 51–62
10. Manasse, M. S., McGeoch, L.A., Sleator, D.D.: Competitive Algorithms for On-Line Problems. Proceedings of the 20th Annual ACM Symposium On Theory of Computing (1988) 322–333
11. Park, K.S., Kenyon, R.V.: Effects of Network Characteristics on Human Performance in a Collaborative Virtual Environment. Proceedings of the IEEE VRAIS 99 Houston Texas, USA, March (1999) 104–110
12. Reynolds, F.D.: Evolving an Operating System for the Web. IEEE Computer, Vol. 29, No. 9 (1996) 90–92
13. Singhal, S., Zyda, M.: Networked Virtual Environments: Design and Implementation. ACM Press SIGGRAPH Series - Addison Wesley, New York (1999)
14. Sung, U., Yang, J., Wohn, K.: Concurrency Control in CIAO. Proceedings of the IEEE VRAIS 99 Houston Texas, USA, March (1999) 22–28
15. Wong, D., Paciorek, N., Moore, D.: Java-based Mobile Agents Communications of the ACM, Vol. 42, Num. 3, March(1999) 92–102

IDEAL: An Integrated Distributed Environment for Asynchronous Learning *

Yi Shang and Hongchi Shi

Deptartment of Computer Engineering & Computer Science
University of Missouri-Columbia
Columbia, MO 65211, USA
{ShangY, ShiH}@missouri.edu

Abstract. In this paper, we present the design and implementation of IDEAL, an Integrated Distributed Environment for Asynchronous Learning. The learning environment supports a Web-based distributed community for student-centered, self-paced, and highly interactive learning. IDEAL enables the students in the community to learn from each other and enhances their learning experience. Implemented using the prevalent Internet, Web, intelligent agent, and digital library technologies, IDEAL adopts an open architecture design and targets at large-scale, distributed operations. In the initial implementation, a number of prototypes using different Java-based software development environments have been developed.

1 Introduction

Information technology has been increasingly used in education to implement automatic and asynchronous teaching methods and support student-centered, self-paced, highly interactive learning. There has been significant research on technology for education, such as work on stand-alone learning systems [12,13,20], Web-based tools and learning systems [6,19], multimedia interaction [7,9], learning models [4,8], and asynchronous learning [6,11,18,1]. However, most of them fall into the category of traditional intelligent tutoring systems that focus on one-to-one interaction. They do not support learning community where students and instructors can interact and learn from each other. IDEAL (Integrated Distributed Environment for Asynchronous Learning) is a distributed environment designed to provide the basic communication and interaction mechanism for a learning community. It is a multi-agent system with an open, scalable system architecture. It is (a) Internet and Web based, (b) customized to individual students, (c) designed to support the interaction among students in the learning community, and (d) operated on a distributed, heterogeneously networked environment. It consists of the following elements:

---

* Research partially supported by the National Science Foundation under grants DUE-9851485 and DUE-9980375 and by the Research Board of the University of Missouri System.

P. Kropf et al. (Eds.): DCW 2000, LNCS 1830, pp. 182–191, 2000.
© Springer-Verlag Berlin Heidelberg 2000

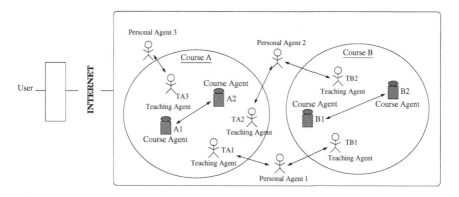

Fig. 1. The framework of IDEAL, a multi-agent system supporting distributed learning community.

- intelligent agents for modeling pedagogy and students, managing and coordinating interaction among users in a distributed community; and
- a Web-based interface for course delivery, assignment submission, and course-related communications;
- a digital library of student profiles and course materials including examples and exercises.

This paper is organized into four sections. Section 2 discusses the design of IDEAL. Section 3 presents preliminary implementations. Finally, Section 4 concludes the paper.

2   A Multi-agent System for Asynchronous Learning

IDEAL is a Web-based interactive learning environment that supports distributed learning community. Its framework is shown in Figure 1.

2.1   Multi-agent Software System

Several characteristics specific to asynchronous learning make multi-agent systems attractive. First, the students of a virtual class on the Internet are widely distributed, and the number of potential participants is large. This renders static and centralized systems inadequate. A distributed multi-agent system with personalized agents for each student is very attractive. Secondly, the classes are dynamic in nature. The background, knowledge, and skill of active students will change over time. The learning materials and teaching methodologies of the courses will change too. Thirdly, students have different background and personality. Teaching methodology should be tailored toward each student's interest and knowledge to make teaching and learning more effective. Furthermore, students often enroll in several courses at the same time. Coordination of learning on different topics for each student will enrich the learning experience. Finally, students tend to get together to discuss study topics and share common interests. Smooth communications, including visualizing and sharing common contexts, need to be supported. Multi-agent systems have become a promising paradigm in education [3,24].

IDEAL consists of a number of specialized agents with different expertise. In IDEAL, each student is assigned a unique personal agent that manages the student's personal profile including knowledge background, preferences, interests, courses enrolled in, etc. The personal agent talks to other agents in the system through various communication channels. An online course is supported by a collection of teaching and course agents. The course agents manage course materials and course-specific teaching techniques for a course. Multiple course agents exist on distributed sites to provide better efficiency, flexibility, and availability. The teaching agents can talk to any course agent of a course and often choose one nearby for better performance. The course agents also act as mediators for communication among students.

A teaching agent interacts with a student and serves as an intelligent tutor of a course. Each teaching agent obtains course materials and course-specific teaching techniques from a course agent and then tries to teach the materials in the most appropriate form and pace based on the background and learning capability of the student. The teaching agents may adopt various cognitive skills such as natural language understanding, conversation, natural language generation, learning, and social aspects. These skills make it easier for students to interact with the teaching agents through natural forms of conversation and expression. By using multimedia presentations including graphics and animation, the teaching agents help make clear difficult concepts and operations.

The basic components of a teaching agent are a domain expert module, a pedagogical module, and a student modeler. The domain expert module creates exercises and questions according to the student's background and learning status, provides solutions, and explains the concepts and solutions to remedy student's misconceptions. It contains a problem generator, a problem solver, an explanation generator, and a domain knowledge base. The pedagogical module determines the timing, style, and content of the teaching agent's interventions. It is a rule-based production system that uses the student model and pedagogical knowledge to determine the appropriate actions. The student modeler provides a model of a student based on his characteristics, knowledge background, preferred learning strategies, and interests. It may also incorporate the information gathered through dialogues with the student and the student's learning profile such as the actions the student performed and the explanations he asked for.

2.2   Community Interaction

In a learning community, instructors and students work together systematically toward shared significant academic goals. Collaboration is stressed, competition is deemphasized. The instructor's primary role shifts from delivering content to setting up learning environments and serving as coach, expert guide, and role model for learners. The student's role changes as well, from relatively passive observer of teaching and consumer of information to active co-constructor of knowledge and understanding [2,10,22].

There are three major issues in the online support of a learning community: how to support various communication channels including one-to-one, one-to-many, and many-to-many, how to find other people that share similar interests, and how to visualize and share common contexts. Active support using agent technology based on interaction between software agents and between humans and software agents is necessary in addressing these issues [14].

The learning community enabled by IDEAL contains a collection of personal units and course agents. A personal unit consists of a user and his or her personal agents. Each personal agent can acquire the user's profile and help the user by gathering, exchanging, and viewing information. The course agents provide shared information, knowledge, or contexts within the course community and act as mediators for informal communication between people. They can collect the user profiles and maintain information on the course community.

When a user wants to find the other users with similar interests, the course agent computes relevance scores of the students in the course based on the degrees of common interest using the users' profile data. The user may set the weightings of the factors in computing the relevances. When people with similar interests are found, the user can multicast a message to them.

The course agent also provides a common discussion area for the students in the course. It classifies the messages posted by the users according to several criteria, such as topic, time, and importance. A user can decide whether to join a discussion or can guess to whom a question relating to a topic should be asked. Users can also grasp the relations between topics, what topics have been discussed, and what topics are currently important.

2.3   Security Mechanisms

IDEAL requires implementation of security mechanisms due to the sharing of a large amount of data among distributed agents and the presence of mobile code. The required security services range from authentication to integrity and also include non-repudiation and access control. Two common elements in these services are cryptographic techniques and intrusion detection [5].

Public key cryptography has been used for checking the integrity of software obtained through insecure channels. When a piece of electronically signed software is submitted for execution on another node of an insecure network, there are two implications:

- Software that migrates over the network may not be changed by active attackers without being noticed at the receiving end.
- The entity that has prepared and sent the code over the network will not later be able to deny this fact.

In anomaly detection that aims at avoiding illegal access or operations, the current behavior is observed and compared to see if it corresponds to some past behavior. The rules used in the identification and detection can either be generated by experts or automatically.

To address the security issues in IDEAL, we have two security agents at each host: a message security agent (MSA) and a controller security agent (CSA). The MSA deals with services related to the exchange of messages, such as electronic signature and cryptography, and the CSA provides services to check adequate use of resources by detecting anomalies [5]. The security agents perform the following actions:

- Digital signature of the message. The MSA-send uses the sender's private key to sign the message, and then sends to the receiver the certified public key.
- Signature check. The MSA-receive uses the sender's public key to check the electronic signature.
- Sender reliability check. The MSA-receive accesses a list of all the nodes considered to be unreliable (supplied by a separate authority) and if the sender is on the list, it refuses to execute the code received.
- Control and execution of code. The CSA execute the code received after having checked for any anomalies.

The received code might be unreliable due to two reasons: (1) the sender may have changed its policies and may have planned attacks; (2) the software may contain bugs that endanger local security. The CSA adopts rule-based anomaly detection and intrusion identification mechanisms to provide access control and protect the system's integrity.

2.4   Student Modeling

Student modeling is crucial for an intelligent learning environment to be able to adapt to the needs and knowledge of individual students [4,16]. In the system, a student is modeled based on his personal information, learning style, and performance data. How well a topic is learned is judged by the student's performance on and his access patterns to the course materials. The access patterns include how much time he has spent studying a topic, whether he used corresponding multimedia materials such as audio and video, and if the topics were reviewed multiple times. Specifically, the performance on a topic is determined based on the following three factors:

1. Quiz performance. Quizzes give the learning environment the most direct information about the student's knowledge.
2. Study performance. The main interaction that students have with the learning environment is through viewing or listening to the course materials in multimedia forms. The study score is used to judge how much comprehension the student has gained through these activities.
3. Reviewed topics. The review score on a topic records how much the student has returned to review the topic again. It is based on how many times the topic is reviewed and how much of the materials is viewed each time. If a student is reviewing frequently, then he has not learned the material.

These three scores, quiz performance, study performance, and reviewed topics, are then combined into a single value, *learned score*, indicating how well the topic is learned.

2.5   Pedagogical Modeling

Adopting the asynchronous learning approach requires a pedagogical shift from preparation to assessment and a methodological shift from lecturing to mentoring. Traditional instructional methods require the instructor to spend a great deal of time preparing prior to a course. When using the asynchronous learning environment, the teaching agents select exercises and problems that best suit the course objectives and the individual students.

Curriculum sequencing is a key component of pedagogical modeling [21,23]. In IDEAL, the topics are represented in a dependency graph, with links representing the relationship between topics. Each topic is divided into subtopics corresponding to smaller grained units that allow the intelligent tutor to reason at a finer level. When a subtopic is displayed to the student, the actual content is dynamically generated based on the student model.

Curriculum sequencing can be seen as a two-step process: finding relevant topics and selecting the best one. A student is ready to learn a topic only if he has performed sufficiently well on its prerequisites.

A *ready score* of a topic indicates whether the student is ready to learn the topic or not. It is calculated based on the topic's learned score and its pretopics' learned scores. If a given topic's learned score is too low, it should be presented again, perhaps being taught differently than it was the first time. In order to start a new topic, a student should show sufficient scores in its pretopics. One formula of the ready score is the weighted-sum of the topic's learned score and its pretopics' learned scores with predetermined weights.

In our system, the student has the option of letting the teaching agent choose the next topic or choosing it himself. In both cases, the student must achieve sufficiently high ready score for the topic. If the teaching agent is asked to choose the next topic, it will choose one with the highest ready score. If the student decides to choose the next topic, he is presented the topic dependency graph annotated with suggestions on which topics to repeat and/or which new topics to study.

3   Preliminary Implementations

Implemented using the prevalent Internet, Web, intelligent agent, and digital library technologies, currently IDEAL consists of interface agents, personal agents, teaching agents, and course agents. The personal agents maintain user preferences such as preferred fonts, color, and layout. The teaching agents filter contents based on a student's personal characteristics (e.g., a bright student might be allowed to skip some contents) and track such things as dependencies among the content pieces (e.g., one may need to teach some background before covering a more advanced topic).

IDEAL runs on top of a scalable, reliable, and high-performance distributed environment. The environment consists of high-performance workstations and storage devices connected via high-bandwidth, low-latency networks. The agents run concurrently on the servers and workstations in the distributed environment with operating system level support for software agents. The courseware and student profile database are stored in RAIDs and accessed through the system area network (SAN) consisting of RAIDs and servers connected via a Fibre Channel switch. The multimedia courseware is in the form of XML documents and organized as a flexible, extensible, and scalable digital library [8,9]. The Web-based interface acts as a bridge between the student and IDEAL. This interface interacts with the HTTP Web server for adaptive delivery of electronic courses over the WWW, assignment submissions, and student learning assessment. The Web-based interface with a rigorous authentication process is implemented using new technologies, Java Servlets and JSP (JavaServer Pages).

The multi-agent system is implemented in Java so that the software agents can run on heterogeneous platforms and the lightweight applets can be connected to the Internet. Prototypes of the multi-agent system are being developed on top of distributed object-oriented software environments including Java Remote Method Invocation (RMI), JATLite [17], and JavaSpace [15].

Java RMI provides an intermediate network layer that allows Java objects residing at distributed sites to communicate using normal method calls. It is reliable, has good performance, and works on many computing platforms. JATLite allows users to quickly create software agents that communicate robustly over the Internet and supports mobile agents. JATLite provides a variety of agent functionalities including registering with an Agent Message Router (AMR) using a name and password, connecting/disconnecting from the Internet, sending/receiving message asynchronously, and transferring files with FTP. A problem with the current implementation is that the software is not very stable and sometimes hangs completely. JavaSpace supports robust distributed communication and data interchange and provides a simple, expressive, and powerful tool that eases the traditional burden of building distributed applications. JavaSpace is very new, has not been fully developed, and is slow.

IDEAL has been implemented using both Java RMI and JATLite. Agents communicate with each other in XML messages. The following features are implemented in both JATLite-based and Java RMI-based IDEAL prototypes:

- User to personal agent interaction. Besides a GUI interface implemented using Java Swing package, intelligent interface agents, such as Microsoft Agents, are used to enhance the user interface. Microsoft Agents are animated characters that can talk. They support speech to text and text to speech conversion.
- Personal agent to teaching agent interaction. The personal agent connects to a server which creates a teaching agent for the user. The teaching agent then formats and presents the lessons to the user through the personal agent.

Real-time streaming media such as streaming audio and video are supported in the system based on Java media framework (JMF) 1.2.

- Personal agent to personal agent interaction. A chat system is developed for real-time communication between users through their personal agents. A central chat server contains the information of active personal agents and keeps track of their chat connections.
- Teaching agent to course agent interaction. The course agent maintains multimedia course materials in XML. The course materials are stored either as XML files or in a database such as a MySQL database. Using XML makes it easy to create course materials in virtually any form of multimedia and also allows a user to customize display through different style sheets.
- Course agent to course agent interaction. Multiple course agents for the same course may exist on distributed sites to provide better efficiency and availability. They communicate to each other periodically to update their course materials.
- Agent list. The router in JATLite or the mediator in RMI provides a list of all registered agents on the network and their current state of connection. An agent can request the address of other agents by giving their names.
- Email and FTP. An agent can send an email message to another agent. Agents can upload and download files from the FTP servers.
- Multithreading. Agents have multithreaded capabilities so as to serve multiple users and other agents at the same time.

The advantage of JATLite over RMI is that the Agent Message Router (AMR) is already written, whereas in RMI a similar facility has to be written from scratch. The functions of AMR are as follows:

- Message queuing. AMR provides a message depository where the messages received from the sending agent are stored and forwarded to the receiving agent when it connects. Since the router queues the messages, the messages do not get lost if the receiving agent goes down, which adds robustness.
- Applet agent communication. Due to security limitation of applet in Java 1.1, the applet agent can only communicate with the server that spawned it. The router running on the server as a Java application facilities the communication between applet agents on hosts outside the server domain.
- Agent Naming Service (ANS). The router maintains the dynamically changing agent addresses so that the agents do not have to remember and maintain all the possible receiver addresses that may change frequently.
- Scalability. When the number of agents in the system increases, the number of router can be increased to handle the additional communication load.
- Security. The router provides security check using the agent's name and password.

In our limited experimental tests, both prototypes are quite efficient in communication between the personal and course agents. However, in chatting between the peers, the JATLite system is much faster than the RMI system. The message latency of the JATLite system is very small, while in the RMI system it takes long time to make the connection, and the communication is slow after the connection.

4   Conclusion

IDEAL enables the distributed learning communities to scale over the Internet. The system is designed to be flexible, adaptive, and open so that it can deal with the dynamic nature of a distributed learning community where the course materials, pedagogy, students and their skills, and community groups change over time. Personalized teaching agents make the learning process more interesting and effective. Student modeling is applied to provide adaptive guidance, adaptive navigation support, and adaptive help. The community interaction mechanisms are developed to support smooth communication among the users and enhance their learning experience through collaboration in a community environment. Prototypes of IDEAL have been implemented using several Java-based development environments.

References

1. Agent Resources. http://www.cs.umbc.edu/agents/.
2. T. A. Angelo. The campus as learning community: Seven promising shifts and seven powerful levers. *AAHE Bulletin*, 49(9):3–6, 1997.
3. L. Barnett, J. Kent, J. Casp, and D. Green. Design and implementation of an interactive tutorial framework. *SIGCSE Bulletin*, 30(1):87–91, March 1998.
4. J. E. Beck and B. P. Woolf. Using a learning agent with a student model. In B. P. Goettl, H. M. Halff, C. L. Redfield, and V. J. Shute, editors, *Intelligence Tutoring System (Proc. 4th Int'l Conf. ITS'98)*, pages 6–15. Springer, 1998.
5. F. Bergadano, A. Puliafito, S. Riccobene, G. Ruffo, and L. Vita. Java-based secure learning agents for information retrieval in distributed systems. *Information Sciences*, 113:55–84, 1999.
6. P. Brusilovsky, J. Eklund, and E. Schwarz. Web-based education for all: A tool for developing adaptive courseware. *Computer Networks and ISDN Systems*, 30:291–300, 1998.
7. C. Buron, M. Grinder, and R. Ross. Tying it all together: Creating self-contained, animated, interactive, web-based resources for computer science education. *SIGCSE Bulletin*, 31(1):7–11, March 1999.
8. C.A. Carver, R.A. Howard, and W.D. Lane. Enhancing student learning through hypermedia courseware and incorporation of student learning styles. *IEEE Trans. on Education*, 42(1):33–38, February 1999.
9. C. Chou. Developing hypertext-based learning courseware for computer networks: The macro and micro stages. *IEEE Trans. on Education*, 42(1):39–44, February 1999.
10. K. P. Cross. Why learning communities? why now? *About Campus*, 3(3):4–11, 1998.
11. A. Davidovic and E. Trichina. Open learning environment and instruction system (oleis). *SIGCSE Bulletin*, 30(3):69–72, September 1998.

12. J. Gray, T. Boyle, and C. Smith. A constructivist learning environment implemented in java. *SIGCSE Bulletin*, 30(3):94–97, September 1998.
13. H. Hamburger and G. Tecuci. Toward a unification of human-computer learning and tutoring. In B. P. Goettl, H. M. Halff, C. L. Redfield, and V. J. Shute, editors, *Intelligence Tutoring System (Proc. 4th Int'l Conf. ITS'98)*. Springer, 1998.
14. F. Hattori, T. Ohguro, M. Yokoo, S. Matsubara, and S. Yoshida. Socialware: Multiagent systems for supporting network communities. *Communications of the ACM*, 42(3):55–61, March 1999.
15. E. Freeman S. Hupfer and K. Arnold. *JavaSpaces Principles, Patterns, and Practice*. Addison-Wesley, 1999.
16. A. Jameson. Numerical uncertainty management in user and student modeling: an overview of systems and issues. *User Modelling and User-Adapted Interaction*, 5:193–251, 1996.
17. JATLite. http://java.stanford.edu/java_agent/html.
18. H.A. Latchman, C. Salzmann, D. Giblet, and H. Bouzekri. Information technology enhanced learning in distance and conventional education. *IEEE Trans. on Education*, 42(4):247–254, November 1999.
19. G.S. Owen. Integrating World Wide Web technology into undergraduate eduation. *SIGCSE Bulletin*, 28(1):101–103, 1996.
20. S. Ritter. Communication, cooperation and competition among multiple tutor agents. In B. D. Boulay and R. Mizoguchi, editors, *Artificial Intelligence in Education: Knowledge and Media in Learning Systems. (Proc. of AI-ED'97, 8th World Conf. on AI in Education)*. 1997.
21. M. K. Stern and B. P. Woolf. Curriculum sequencing in a web-based tutor. In B. P. Goettl, H. M. Halff, C. L. Redfield, and V. J. Shute, editors, *Intelligence Tutoring System (Proc. 4th Int'l Conf. ITS'98)*, pages 584–593. Springer, 1998.
22. V. Tinto. Universities as learning organizations. *About Campus*, 1(6):2–4, 1997.
23. G. Weber. Individual selection of examples in an intelligent learning environment. *Journal of Artificial Intelligence in Education*, 7(1):3–31, 1996.
24. G. Weiss, editor. *Multiagent Systems: A Modern Approach to Distributed Artificial Intelligence*. The MIT Press, Cambridge, MA, 1999.

Design and Implementation
of a Distributed Agent Delivery System

Stephen A. Hopper, Armin R. Mikler, and John T. Mayes

Computer Science Department
University of North Texas
Denton, TX
{shopper,mikler,mayes}@cs.unt.edu

Abstract. Among the most significant changes that have affected the domain of computer networking is the proliferation of distributed applications and services, particularly within wide-area networks such as corporate intranets and most notably within the Internet. As the demand for such applications and services continues to expand, the need for a generic, open solution facilitating the distribution of data and services becomes increasingly apparent. Researchers have recently begun to investigate the feasibility of using the Mobile Agents Paradigm as an integral part of distributed computing infrastructures. In addition to facilitating the exchange of data and the access to services, agents serve as abstractions that separate the communication of data from the location and format of data that is transferred among the nodes of the distributed environment. This paper discusses the goals, design and implementation of a particular multilingual mobile agent development kit, the Distributed Agent Delivery System (DADS). DADS supports multiple agent languages types, and is deemed sufficiently lightweight to be deployed in performance-sensitive environments. DADS thus provides the fundamental mechanisms for the development of distributed applications that would scale well with the ever-increasing size and complexity of modern distributed infrastructures.

1 Introduction

Mobile agents have begun to radically alter the way that we view the exchange of information across distributed environments [1]. Modern communication infrastructures, such as Internet2 and the Next Generation Internet, give rise to very large distributed systems that may consist of hundreds or even thousands of computing nodes. The spatial and temporal nature of the distributed infrastructure requires the underlying mechanisms to scale easily with the size and dynamics of the computational environment. Mobile agent systems are deemed to provide the necessary scalability to solve many problems related to managing

P. Kropf et al. (Eds.): DCW 2000, LNCS 1830, pp. 192–201, 2000.
© Springer-Verlag Berlin Heidelberg 2000

and controlling large distributed computational infrastructures: agents facilitate autonomous administration, resource monitoring and resource management. Additionally, it is possible for multiple agents which are spread across multiple hosts to collaborate to provide a requested service and/or optimize response and computation time for a requested service. That is to say, we need to account for the fact that there does not exist a fixed structure of how data and services are allocated within a distributed environment.

In order to illustrate the advantages that agents can present, it is first necessary to examine contemporary network design paradigms. Currently, at least two widely used network application methodologies prevail in the field of network system design: *Client/Server*, and *Peer-to-Peer*. The Client/Server paradigm maps well to an environment in which nodes fall into the roles of *data/service owner* and *data/service user*, whereas the Peer-to-Peer methodology applies to networks composed of nodes that are both owners and users of data and services. These approaches suggest the roles that nodes play within a distributed system. Not only do these methodologies define the roles of nodes, but also affect the design of those nodes. For instance, nodes that are "servers" (in the case of Client/Server) will be designed such that a main loop waits for connections and spins off threads of control to service requests [6]; nodes that act as Peer-to-Peer clients are likely to implement a link resumption scheme to resume lost connections. Most importantly, however, these methodologies encourage developers to couple the format and location of data with the processing of these data.

For instance, a web server would likely be tightly coupled with the fact that data is being transferred via TCP/IP. Such a server would naturally associate the source address that originated a particular connection with the destination machine that initially requested the data. One might rightly suggest that a web server should neither be concerned with the location of a host that requests data, nor with the format in which the host initiates the request. This not only yields a tight coupling of the web client with the web server, but also implies that if data is transferred over a different underlying communication channel, HTTP and TCP/IP must rest atop the new protocol stack. Even if the web server and clients are re-written to support a new environment, they generally would need to be re-installed on every node throughout a network. Mobile agents offer a solution to this coupling of systems by introducing a mobile sub-layer that renders the static coupling unnecessesary. In fact, the agent paradigm enables developers to de-couple the communication from the processing of data. If the channels over which data is communicated should change, systems that utilize mobile agents simply introduce new agents into the network, which reflect these changes [8].

In section 2 we discuss the goals, design and implementation of a particular multi-lingual mobile agent development kit, the Distributed Agent Delivery System (DADS). Section 3 describes the Agent Delivery Protocol specification. Section 4 concludes the paper with a summary of the project and directions for future work.

2 Distributed Agent Delivery System (DADS)

DADS can be viewed as a collection of lightweight daemon processes, which by means of the Agent Delivery Protocol (ADP), exchange agents that will perform domain specific tasks. The ADP represents a multi-lingual solution as it is oblivious to the implementation language of the agent being transported. The support for multiple agent languages solely depends on the availability of the corresponding interpreters or runtime systems at the nodes where the agents are to execute. ADP is a simple, lightweight protocol that does not use any cumbersome encoding scheme, thereby allowing the DADS to perform equally well in performance-sensitive environments as well as in distributed environments such as the Internet.

2.1 DADS Components

The DADS manifests a *service* that resides on the set of participating nodes. Henceforth, these nodes will be referred to as patrons, as they provide the necessary support for the agents to execute a domain specific task and at the same time, act as customers that may utilize the agents on behalf of the system. In general, the DADS is not formally coupled with applications that interact with the agents that are transferred. Hence, the DADS provides an ideal solution for the development of heterogeneous distributed applications. The canonical DADS architecture consists of five components, namely Mobile Agents, an Agent-Based ADP, a Patron-Based ADP, an Agent Interpreter, and Domain-Specific Protocols.

- *Mobile Agents* : The agents are a crucial element towards the development of an agent-based system. Without exhibiting a specific behavior, the infrastructure supporting the mobilization of agents is useless. Hence, each agent is the realization of the domain-specific task that is to be performed.
- *Agent-Based ADP* : Agents and nodes must support a common protocol to support the migration of agents. In order for an agent to move itself, this protocol must be supported from the perspective of the agent. Hence, associated with each agent is an Application Program Interface (API) that provides the agent with specific functions for using the ADP.
- *Patron-Based ADP* : The patron refers to a node which utilizes agent services. For an agent to migrate to a patron, the patron must support the Agent Delivery Protocol. Hence, a patron-specific API for using ADP functionality is imperative.
- *Agent Interpreter (on every participating node)* : Because agents move to and from patrons that execute on a variety of different architectures, a platform-independent, interpreted language must be selected and supported on every patron.
- *Domain-Specific Protocols (to be used between agents and patrons)* : Because most (but not all) agents will need to communicate with the patrons, an extensible protocol should be developed.

Of these items, only the agent code fragment and the domain-specific protocols are specific to a particular agent-based system. That is to say that the *Agent Interpreter* and the implementations of the *Agent-based ADP* and the *Patron-Based ADP* can be reused in any system that utilizes similar underlying communication protocols. For instance, every agent *will* be transferred from one location (patron) to the next via a well-understood protocol over a well-known network port, and every agent can be interpreted by at least one interpreter (see Figure 1). The DADS thus encapsulates the agent-based ADP implementation, the patron-based ADP implementation, as well as the integration of one or more interpreters.

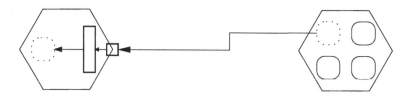

Fig. 1. Agent Transfer from Node 2 to Node 1

2.2   Domain-Specific Protocol

In developing an agent system that *forces* the separation between the details of a communication system and the data that it communicates, designers must develop an abstract protocol for the transfer of the data from the agent to the rest of a system. Because the agent can manipulate the data presentation, this data protocol can take the most convenient and/or most intuitive form [7].

For instance, an agent that communicates to patrons that are running embedded telephony software with an underlying signaling system interface such as Signaling System #7 (SS7) [2] could present a Remote Procedure Call (RPC) [10] interface to the patron. Requests could be forwarded and serviced as SS7 transactions, but from the patron's perspective the interface to the embedded system is RPC, not SS7. Likewise, an agent could relay Web data across a series of firewalls or gateways, and present HTTP data directly to the requesting patron. In these examples, however, the agent must have a method to communicate with the patron. One approach is to designate an internal port (such as a TCP socket, named pipe, etc.) that allows a generic agent to communicate with a patron. However, specific agent types, such as Java-based agents, have built-in inter-process communication mechanisms that would allow an agent to interface directly to the patron (without a secondary protocol).

Agents allow designers to disregard the location and format that data takes on its path across the network, but one must nevertheless consider the ultimate format that data should take when the agent presents it. In developing a protocol to communicate with mobile agents, it should be flexible and extensible. The advantage of agents could be undermined by a poor protocol that limits its communication with the rest of a system [13]. It should be noted that some agent systems will not require the creation of such a protocol. For instance, an agent which simply travels across a series of workstations and executes a command on each might only return an exit status to the initiating patron.

3   The Agent Delivery Protocol (ADP)

The ADP is actually the composition of two distinct protocols: one supports connection-oriented, reliable transport, while the other supports connectionless, unreliable connectivity. The current implementation of ADP depends upon the availability of a reliable connection-oriented transport mechanism such as TCP. However, the ADP specification also supports a connectionless communication scheme that is designed such that any connectionless transport medium could be used as well. ADP is intended to rest atop the transport-layer of a protocol stack (i.e., it uses transport-layer functionality) and not at the network-layer as *Active IP* [12]. An ADP-based agent is thus expected to provide its own *pseudo-application* layer to applications that make use of its services.

Both the connection-oriented and connectionless ADP protocols are similar in content such that they communicate mobile agent code and data in a segment that is referred to as an Agent Data Unit (ADU). The structure of the ADU for both, connection-oriented and connectionless ADP is depicted in Figure 3. The ADU consists of code and data which is compressed according to the compression specification format specified in RFC1950 [3]. The length of these fields is included in the ADU, along with the uncompressed length which is used in the allocation of buffer space to accommodate the uncompressed size. In addition, the ADU specifies the agent type, i.e., the language used to program the agent.

The use of connection-oriented ADP is recommended when agents (including their data) are expected to be rather large (more than a few hundred kilo-bytes, for instance) and the overhead of transporting them is outweighed by the need for a reliable connection. Because the transport layer ensures the ordering and integrity of data, there is no need to support reverse acknowledgements. An example Message Sequence Chart of a successful ADU transfer is depicted in Figure 2. Only two possible outcomes exist in the transfer of an ADU across a reliable connection: (1) the ADU will be transferred successfully and the initiating agent will close the connection, or (2) the connection will be lost and the receiver will be left with an empty or truncated ADU. Since the partial delivery is supported under connection-oriented ADU transfer, the ADU format only contains the fields necessary for the delivery of agent code and data (see Figure 2).

In the support of an unreliable, connectionless transport medium (such as UDP), the associated message exchange would contain additional messages (see Figure 2). Because the transport layer is unreliable, reverse acknowledgements are needed. Many connectionless transport-layer protocols set bounds on the maximum size of a packet, or the Maximum Transport Unit (MTU). For this

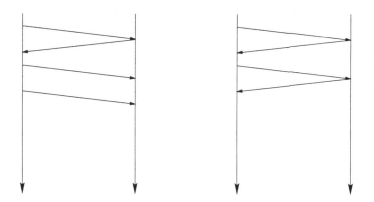

Fig. 2. Connection-oriented (left) and connection-less (right) ADP

reason, a provision must be made for the division of the ADP ADU into multiple fragments or "capsules." Since the order of delivery cannot be guaranteed, a two-byte agent identifier plus a one-byte Message Sequence Number (MSN) must be added to every fragment that is sent (see Figure 3). The sequence number indicates the last successfully received capsule starting with 1. The sequence number zero is reserved to indicate packet transfer failure.

From the perspective of the agent that is migrating to a patron, fragments should be sent in "bursts" consisting of a collection of capsules (the exact number is left as an implementation detail). Simultaneously, the agent should allocate another thread of control that waits for acknowledgements. The MSN of each acknowledgement should be stored, replacing the last. After each burst, the sender should validate the stored MSN. If the MSN was contained within the range of at least the last two bursts, the sender should resume the bursts normally. If the stored MSN is not within the range of the last two bursts, the sender should wait for the stored MSN to be updated for two times the average round-trip time (RTT) between the time that a capsule was sent and its acknowledgement was received, at which point the entire burst is retransmitted. If an acknowledgement with a MSN of zero is received, the transfer is halted.

The receiver will simply wait for the reception of capsules of a particular *Agent ID*. Following every new successfully received, consecutively delivered capsule, a MSN counter should be incremented and a new acknowledgement containing the MSN should be sent. All capsules should be ordered according to their MSN and duplicate capsules should be discarded. If no packet has been received within the timeout period, or if the transfer must be stopped due to a catastrophic software failure on the Patron, an acknowledgement with a MSN of zero should be returned. The exact value of this timeout period can be configured and should be long enough to ensure that an error has occurred, but short enough that the timeout delay does not significantly impact performance (from the perspective of the user).

The initial phase of the DADS (supporting connection-oriented ADP with no support for key-based security) has been completed. Although this comprises the bulk of the work toward the completion of the DADS development project, the completion of the connectionless portion of the ADP protocol suite will enable DADS to represent a viable solution for generic, multi-lingual agent development.

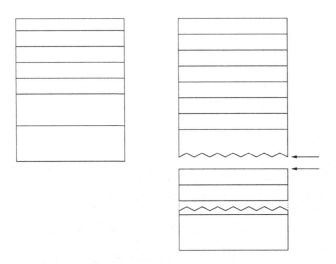

Fig. 3. Connection-oriented (left) and connection-less (right) ADP Packet

3.1   Patron-Based ADP

In the creation of a network service that receives, executes, and manages agents for an entire node, the first assumption is that there *can* be a large number of agents that will be in motion. For this reason, the first requirement dictates that the patron, implemented as a daemon process, be as efficient as possible and support multiple streams (or threads) of control in order to optimize the processing of multiple concurrent agents. In addition, such a daemon is expected to be written only once, so it must be largely platform independent such that the portability of the daemon can be maintained. This implies a loose coupling between platform-unspecific modules and the rest of the system. Finally, since the ideal agent implementation language has not yet been determined, DADS must be extensible. The daemon must support multiple agent language types and allow for the support of future types in a generic fashion.

The implementation of the Patron-Based ADP can perhaps be best represented at a high level as a protocol stack (see Figure 4). As is typical of most protocol stacks, arriving data (agents) can be understood as moving *up* the stack, whereas outgoing data move *down* the stack. Since the patron *accepts* agents, the data flow will be described as moving *up* the stack.

The Transport/Socket Layer can be understood as the level of the application which interfaces with the BSD Socket layer (or any transport interface).

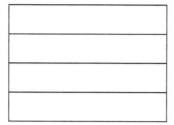

Fig. 4. Patron's Protocol Stack

This layer merely writes (acknowledgements) and reads data (transport units), passing read data to the packet layer, which assembles transport units into an ADP ADU. The Translation Layer reads the fields in the packet into a ADU object, and decompresses agent code and data. Finally, the Agent Execution Layer is responsible for executing the agent according to the type held in the ADU object. This layer represents the core of the agent daemon.

Currently, the Patron only supports Perl agents, which are perhaps one of the more complicated agent languages to support. In the current implementation, all agent types extend the base class *Agent*. Support for Java, [4] Python, etc. could be easily added by creating a new agent class and by inheriting the functionality provided by the *Agent* class.

Because the Perl agents must be executed by a monolithic Perl interpreter (a binary which is typically rather large), execution of large numbers of Perl agents, each of which causes the *fork()* and *exec()* of a new interpreter, could be more costly than the interpretation of the agent itself. For this reason, DADS maintains a process table, or a "pool" of running Perl processes, each of which is merely waiting for input in the form of Perl code. This code and the persistent data that an agent saves prior to its migration is transferred to the Perl processes prior to the agents resumed execution.

3.2   Agent-Based ADP

In comparison to the requirements of a patron, those of the agent are seemingly trivial: an agent must be able to move from one host to another and initialize itself at the point of execution at each new node. However, because the programming interface for the development of new agents will, in effect, be the primary point of contact between users and the Development Environment, the interface must be intuitive and above all, simple.

The design of a particular Agent-Based ADP implementation roughly corresponds to the lower three layers of the ADP implementation of the patron (see Figure 4). However, in the agent, data can be described as moving *down* through the stack. Thus, the translator will compress data/code, and the packet layer will compose transport units rather than assembling them. The agent execution layer is not relevant because the agent sends itself, and it is *already* executing.

Because DADS currently supports Perl, the following discussion focuses on the implementation of the Perl module that will provide an API for the developer of a new agent. The implementation of APIs for other agent types should follow the same model and would likely be nearly as straightforward. The following represents the entirety of the interface:

- *Init()*. Agents that have just migrated need to recover the data that has accompanied them. This method should be called immediately following a migration.
- *Move(LOCATION)*. To migrate to another host, an agent should call this method to move to a new location. The task of packing and compressing the data and agent code is encapsulated within this routine.
- *Event(SEVERITY, EVENT)*. Agents that need to report an event can use this interface. Events will be fed to a logging mechanism on the currently running host.

In addition, the agent is expected to place all data and state information that will be accessed across moves in the global stack *@MyData*. This data will be serialized in network-byte order and compressed prior to a move, and decompressed and de-serialized following a call to *Init()*. In order to preserve their state across migrations, agents must record all persistent data and provide a way to regain that state after a move. An example of a Perl Agent can be found at *http://www.nrl.csci.unt.edu/projects*.

4   Conclusion

The initial phase of the DADS, supporting connection-oriented ADP with no support for key-based security, has been completed. Although this comprises the bulk of the work toward the completion of the DADS development project, more has yet to be done. Nevertheless, DADS represents a viable solution for generic, multi-lingual agent development.

Current work is focusing on the implementation of the connectionless (UDP) ADP protocol. UDP support will be critical for the ultimate support of the Intelligent Agent-Based File System (IAFS) [5], which will depend on reliable high-performance data transfers. Because the connection-oriented ADP implementation has already been completed, the addition of UDP support should be straightforward.

The inclusion of security features will need to be completed in order for the system to be practical in all but the most secure networks. Because an agent-based network solution is clearly susceptible to attack by malicious "hackers," the ADP must be rendered as secure as possible. One approach is to only accept agents that have been authenticated by a trusted agent authenticator. This would work well in a system whose agent population is relatively homogeneous, but would be cumbersome if new kinds of agents were constantly being created. In this case, DADS would provide a "sandbox" for agents to execute within. The creation of such a two-tier security scheme would provide a scalable solution for most network applications requiring built-in security features.

Finally, distributed applications should be developed that utilize the services that DADS provide. Because DADS provides a lightweight, multi-platform service that could be resident on all participants of a distributed network, the use of agents can be effected without coupling applications with the details of agent migration. Currently, the Intelligent Agent-Based File System (IAFS) [5] is nearing completion, and will provide an excellent test-bed for the investigation of the performance characteristics of DADS within a distributed computing environment.

References

1. Bhattacharjee, Samrat, Kenneth L. Calvert, and Ellen W. Zegura. "An Architecture for Active Networking." Submitted to *IEEE Infocom '97*. 1997.
2. CCITT. "Introduction to CCITT Signalling System No. 7: Recommendation Q.700." Fascicle V.17. 1988.
3. Deutsch, P., and J-L Gailly. "ZLIB Compressed Data Format Specification version 3.3." *Network Working Group, Request for Comments: 1950*. 1996.
4. Gosling, James, and Henry McGilton. "The Java Language Environment: A White Paper." *Sun Microsystems, Inc.* 1996.
5. Hopper, S. A., A. R. Mikler, H. Unger, P. Tarau, and F. Chen. "Mobile Agent-Based File System for the WOS: An Overview." *1999 Advanced Simulation Technologies Conference*. 1999.
6. Karimi, Jahangir. "A Software Design Technique for Client-Server Applications." *Concurrency: Practive and Experience*. Vol. 11(1). 1999.
7. Maes, Pattie. "Modeling Adaptive Autonomous Agents." *Artificial Life Journal*. Vol. 1, No. 1 & 2. MIT Press, 1994.
8. Oliveira, Luiz A. G., Paulo C. Oliveira, and Eleri Cardozo. "An Agent-Based Approach for Quality of Service Negotiation and Management in Distributed Multimedia Systems." *Mobile Agents: First International Workshop, MA '97*. Berlin, 1997.
9. O'Reilly, Tim, Cameron Laird, Larry Wall, and Nathan Torkington. "Perl: a technology white paper." *O'Reilly and Associates*.
10. Srinivasan, R. "RPC: Remote Procedure Call Protocol Specification Version 2." *Network Working Group, Request for Comments 1831*. 1995.
11. Tennenhouse, D. L., and D. J. Wetherall. "Towards and Active Network Architecture." *Multimedia Computing and Networking '96*. 1996.
12. Wetherall, David J., and David L. Tennenhouse. "The Active IP Option." *Proceedings of the 7th ACM SIGOPS European Workshop*. Connemara, Ireland, 1996.
13. Wooldridge, M., and N. R. Jennings. "Pitfalls of Agent-Oriented Development." *Proceedings of the Autonomous Agents '98 Conference* Minneapolis, 1998.

Author Index